'Whom God hath joined together'

The work of marriage guidance

Jane Lewis, David Clark and
David H.J. Morgan

Tavistock/Routledge
London and New York

First published in 1992
by Routledge
11 New Fetter Lane, London EC4P 4EE

Simultaneously published in the USA and Canada
by Routledge
a division of Routledge, Chapman and Hall Inc.
29 West 35th Street, New York, NY 10001

© 1992 Jane Lewis, David Clark and David H.J. Morgan
© Postscript 1992 Douglas Hooper

Typeset by Selectmove Ltd, London
Printed and bound in Great Britain by
Mackays of Chatham plc, Chatham, Kent

British Library Cataloguing in Publication Data
Lewis, Jane *1950–*
    'Whom God hath joined together': the work of marriage guidance.
    1. Great Britain. Marriage. Counselling
    I. Title II. Clark, David *1953–* III. Morgan, D. H. J. (David Hopcraft
    John) *1937–*
    362.8286

Library of Congress Cataloging in Publication Data
Lewis, Jane (Jane E.)
    Whom God hath joined together: the work of marriage guidance /
    Jane Lewis, David Clark, and David Morgan.
        p.   cm.
    Includes bibliographical references and index.
    1. Marriage counseling—Great Britain—History. 2. National
    Marriage Guidance Council (Great Britain)—History. 3. Relate
    (Organization)—History. I. Clark, David, 1953–   . II. Morgan,
    David, 1937–   . III. Title.
    HQ10.5.G7L48   1992
    362.82′86–dc20

ISBN 0–415–05553–9
        0–415–05554–7 (pbk)

91–13910
CIP

'Whom God hath joined together'

Today issues of family policy and in particular the high divorce rate are increasingly matters of social and political concern. This timely book presents the first complete analysis of the history and development of marriage guidance in England. Drawing on the insights of both history and sociology, the authors set the subject in the context of changes in marriage itself, as well as changes in the wider society. They examine the relationships between the changing construction of the problem of marriage and divorce and the changing approaches of the marital agencies, and give an in-depth case study of the National Marriage Guidance Council (now renamed Relate) in order to examine the dynamics of survival and change within a voluntary organisation.

In Part One David Morgan explores the theoretical issues raised and identifies a number of important themes, such as the shift from 'movement' to 'agency', and transformations in the institutional and relational aspects of marriage. Part Two, by Jane Lewis, gives a detailed account of the early ideas surrounding marriage guidance and the subsequent organisational history of the NMGC. In Part Three David Clark looks closely at the theoretical debates which accompanied the development of marital work within the organisation, paying special attention to the relationship between 'guidance' and 'counselling'.

The authors have drawn on a wide range of source material, including previously un-researched archives as well as interviews with key figures in marriage guidance. Though they are broadly sympathetic to the work of marriage guidance, they raise important questions about the ways in which services for those experiencing difficulties in marriage have been thought about and organised. They highlight major contradictions that exist within Relate, such as the nature of its views on marriage and family life, and conclude that a lack of clarity on these issues may impede future developments.

Jane Lewis is Reader in Social Administration at the London School of Economics. **David Clark** is Principal Lecturer in Sociology at Sheffield City Polytechnic. **David Morgan** is Senior Lecturer in Sociology at the University of Manchester.

Contents

Preface

This project was conceived from the outset as an encounter between history and sociology and has been developed using the theories and methods of both disciplines. Our book seeks to tackle a large and still under-researched topic, the history and development of marriage guidance, mainly in England. We have tried to set this subject in the context of changes in marriage itself, as well as changes in the wider society, recognising that all are interconnected. In doing this, two aims have been uppermost. Firstly, we have examined the relationships between the changing construction of the problem of marriage and divorce and the changing approaches of the marital agencies. Secondly, we have conducted an in-depth case study of the National Marriage Guidance Council (NMGC, and since 1988, Relate) in order to examine the dynamics of survival and change within a voluntary organisation.

The exploration of these themes has led us through a wide range of source material. The NMGC has considerable archival sources and these have been systematically explored and analysed. We also located other archival sources for the early period (all these are referred to in the notes). A search of secondary published materials on marriage and the family and marital work was carried out for the whole period. We conducted interviews with over forty key informants; some of these were at the time in the employ of Relate, others had been holders of significant positions in the past, as paid officers or volunteers (see Appendix 1). We also attended a number of important meetings in the life of the organisation (see Appendix 1). In the course of all this, which involved numerous visits to Relate's national headquarters in Rugby, we benefited from informal discussions and observations concerning the many changes taking place in the organisation during the main study period (Autumn 1988–Autumn 1989).

Indeed, it was the case that our main fieldwork coincided with a period of rapid change, following an acute financial crisis in the organisation. This certainly had an effect on the organisational climate during the period of our data gathering and, it has been suggested, may also have served to colour some of the accounts which we gathered from Relate employees in our interviews. Although it was not a preplanned element in our research design, to study an organisation at a time of crisis does of course have special consequences. As therapists are well aware, periods of crisis also provide particular opportunities, and some of these we have been able to document, revealing the organisation grappling to clarify its role as it moves into the 1990s. We acknowledge that what we have said about this process rests essentially upon our interpretation of the available evidence; and such is the rate of change within Relate that some further developments of which we are aware are not included, having taken place beyond the period of our study. With both the question of interpretation and the relatively arbitrary cut-off point for our research in mind, we asked the Director of Relate if he wished to take the opportunity to have a view from the agency incorporated into our book. This he agreed to, and Professor Douglas Hooper has written a postscript which provides an interesting agency commentary.

Although we make reference on numerous occasions to various marital agencies, our focus is in the main on the NMGC. Insofar as the activities of others, such as the Catholic Marriage Advisory Council, Jewish Marriage Council and Family Discussion Bureau/Institute of Marital Studies touch on the work of the NMGC, then we have included reference to them. An important aspect of this, for example, has been the influence of psychodynamic approaches to marital work, developed at the Tavistock, upon thinking and practice within marriage guidance. Detailed histories of these other agencies have not yet been undertaken and would cast further light on the arguments developed here. Another area which our study has not been able to examine directly is that of the client perspective. Limitations of time and resources meant from the outset that we could not undertake a detailed study of the clients of marriage guidance and we have therefore only been able to access their experiences through the research efforts of others.

While, as three researchers working together, we take collective responsibility for the whole of what is written here, it is important to emphasise that this is a book in three parts, each separately authored. In Part I, David Morgan explores some of the theoretical issues which are raised in looking at the interconnections between the work of marriage guidance, changes in marriage, and changes in the wider society; he identifies a number of important themes – movement–agency, institution–relationship, public–private, 'medicalisation' – and suggests that a modified life-course perspective may be helpful in making sense of these. In Part II, Jane Lewis offers a detailed account of the early ideas surrounding marriage guidance and the subsequent organisational history of the NMGC; she shows how the organisation gradually loses its 'public' voice on marriage, which is replaced by a growing emphasis on the more 'private' activity of marital counselling and how this sets in train a number of fundamental tensions. In Part III, David Clark examines some of the theoretical debates which accompanied the development of marital work within the organisation, paying special attention to the relationships between 'guidance', 'counselling' and 'therapy'; he goes on to show how these are linked to continuing problems in understanding the extent to which the service provided has been effective or useful. Taken together, the three parts serve not only to problematise our understanding of marriage, marital problems and intervention in marriage, but also to raise important questions about the ways in which services for those experiencing difficulties in marriage have been thought about and organised. The book therefore has a critical tone. Insofar as some of its readers will be those who have had or continue to have an active stake in the development of marriage guidance services, we hope that what we have written will serve as a worthwhile account of past events and a useful stimulus to further development.

Acknowledgements

We are grateful to a number of individuals and institutions for support and encouragement with this project. David French has shown a lively interest in the study throughout and along with his executive committee was good enough to grant us wide-ranging access to NMGC/Relate archives and to Relate staff. Our thanks go to all our interview respondents, for their generosity with time, information and insights. David Barkla has been unstinting in his patient and expert help with Relate's archival material. Sarah Nettleton worked as a research assistant on the project from October 1988 to April 1989. Janet Finch and Alan Sanders both offered helpful comments at different stages. Staff at the British Library of Political and Economic Sciences were of particular assistance. Our thanks go to the Economic and Social Research Council for its financial assistance with grant No. R000231060. Jane Lewis finished her part of the manuscript in Stockholm where, as Kerstin Hesselgren Professor with the Swedish Council for Research in the Humanities and Social Sciences, she was able to enjoy somewhat more time for writing than is habitually the case at the LSE.

Part I
David H.J. Morgan

Introduction

This study deals with the changes in the ideologies and practices of voluntary organisations with a special interest in marriage, in this case focusing largely on the National Marriage Guidance Council/Relate.[1] Yet clearly such changes do not take place in isolation and the reader will soon become aware of other changes, changes in marriage itself and in the wider British society, taking place in the background. The first chapter looks at these changes and how they might be connected. The cat's-cradle of interconnections between these three sets of changes is complicated enough. However, further complications arise when it is considered that we are not simply concerned, in some pure sense, with these changes and interconnections *themselves* (assuming that these changes could be adequately characterised) but with the constructions of, understandings about, and theories concerning such interconnected processes of change.

This observation is based upon the recognition of a number of related and general points about theory and the practice of theorising. In the first place there is the sociological truism that changing practices are interwoven with the beliefs and understandings about these changing processes; beliefs and constructions emerge out of practices and simultaneously constitute these practices. One less heralded consequence of this recognition of the constant and necessary interplay between beliefs and practices is the argument that theory is not simply some specialised activity undertaken by scholars but is itself a practical activity necessarily bound up with the business of everyday living. Individuals have theories about their own marriages, about marriages in general and about other broad processes of social change. These are everyday and routine accomplishments, a necessary part of the process of making sense of the everyday world. These theories will almost certainly be partial, unexplored and inconsistent but this does not make them any less effective in day-to-day living.

However, for professionals or other specialists, theory and theorising is more intimately and explicitly linked to their own routine daily activities. This is especially true for many of the people who occupy the centre stage in this present study. Their routine of work dealing, directly or indirectly, with people who come to them with problems about their marriages, is directly informed by theories about interpersonal relationships, personal and interpersonal growth and, most directly, about the counselling process itself. Such theories themselves are presented as arising out of particular practices of therapy or counselling. Further, such theoretical understandings may be turned upon the organisations within which such counsellors and managers work.

It is important not to see theories as bounded bodies of thought and knowledge, separately attached to equally distinct groups of social actors. While professionals, managers and others have their own theories shaping and arising out of their routine daily practices, they are also influenced, in varying degrees, by theories produced in academic contexts and by lay persons as well. This is clearly seen, for example, in the area of gender where it would often seem to be the case that everyday, widely diffused 'common-sensical' notions of the 'spheres' and behavioural characteristics of women and men were incorporated into the work of marriage guidance (MG), whether that work was to do with counselling, with more public pronouncements or, indeed, with the day-to-day, but changing, processes within the organisation itself.

This sense of interplay between the knowledges and theories of different sets of persons is also true when we come to consider the three main areas that constitute the subject matter of this study. Theories about the changing nature of British society, of marriage and of changes within the MG organisations are all inter-related and shape each other. For example, one theory might see changes in British society bringing about particular strains upon marriage which, in turn, affect the work of marriage guidance. As will be shown, there are more complicated ways of understanding these inter-relationships and these will be explored in the latter part of the following chapter. First, however, we shall consider these three broad divisions separately.

NOTES

1 In Part I 'MG' will refer to marriage guidance in general. The National
Marriage Guidance Council (NMGC) changed its name to 'Relate' in 1988
and these terms will be used when the specific agency is indicated. 'MG'
was the term used by members of the NMGC to refer to the organisation
during the 1970s and its usage persists in some parts of the organisation.
In Part II of this book, the use of this term has been confined to the period
1968–85.

1 Marriage and society: understanding an era of change

ORGANISATIONAL CHANGES

Part II of this book documents and analyses the complex patterns of change that have occurred in the fifty years of NMGC/Relate's history. A common way of describing, and sometimes even of explaining, such changes is in terms of key individuals. Talk about such individuals is, of course, a common feature of life in many organisations and certainly the relatively short history of marriage guidance in Britain has managed to throw up several such dominant and influential persons: David Mace, John Wallis, Nicholas Tyndall, David French and several others.[1]

Sociologists tend to be unhappy about talk of influential individuals, seeing, perhaps, in such talk vestiges of some 'great man theory of history'. Yet many accounts, written and unwritten, at least begin with references to such individuals and we should, therefore, take these accounts seriously as a point of departure. They are not simply products of a 'logic of history' but, equally, it could hardly be argued that the individuals who occupied the top positions in MG at different stages in its history were completely interchangeable. They are not simply 'symbolic leaders' (Klapp 1964) since they have some measure of fixed and formal status and authority within the organisation, but their influence does not derive simply by virtue of their occupation of such offices (Burns and Stalker 1961: 212). We are looking at an interplay between positions at the top of an organisation (positions which themselves do not remain static in terms of formal and informal definition) and individual characteristics and careers.

Two general points seem to be clear. The first is that such individuals are the subjects of gossip and talk by people at all levels of the organisation. They continue to be talked about as key points of anchorage in understanding the history of MG, and the way in which such individuals are described, as much as the substance of such talk, both shapes and is shaped by the culture of the organisation. The second is that influential individuals write and theorise about the organisation of which they are a part and such theories themselves become part of the culture of the organisation and may, indeed, be influential in shaping as well as accounting for change. The bibliography contains many books and articles written by members of the organisation and their theories, and others, were also found with varying degrees of elaboration and sophistication in the interview transcripts. We found accounts in terms of class and background, in terms of individuals or in terms of organisational theory. Analogies and metaphors were frequent: the organisation was like an individual, like a marriage or more generally like a biological organism.

One such influential theory was provided by Robert Chester when he wrote, in 1985, of MG undergoing a shift from 'movement' to 'agency' (Chester 1985). It is perhaps important to note that Chester, while actively involved in MG, was both an insider and an outsider and it was perhaps this dual position that enabled this particular theory to become so influential within the organisation itself. At the time of publishing this model, Chester was both a senior lecturer in sociology and chairman of NMGC's Research Advisory Board.

Chester's contrast between 'social movement' and 'service agency' is fairly straightforward and the main features of the contrast are presented in Figure 1, a more-or-less direct extrapolation from his paper. These elements, although listed separately, are clearly supposed to hang together in some kind of functional package. Certainly, it is relatively simple to find contrasting quotations which would appear to fit this kind of model. Thus, writing of the earlier period, Wallis and Booker (themselves centrally involved in MG) state:

> Looking back through the early minute books it would seem that all the original group shared in common were a conviction that the rapidly increasing divorce rate was a social and personal disaster and, secondly, a determination to find some way to prevent or lessen it.
>
> (Wallis and Booker 1958: 7)

A dramatic contrast is provided by this quotation from a management consultant's report, itself influenced in some measure by Chester's formulation:

It will therefore be important for MG to establish a range of performance criteria which could provide an objective basis on which individual MGCs can evaluate their own performances . . .

(Coopers and Lybrand 1986: 14)

Further more detailed evidence and illustrations are provided in the chapters to come.

Figure 1.1   Social movement to service agency

SOCIAL MOVEMENT	SERVICE AGENCY
Values to promote	Objectives to achieve
Members to affirm values	Personnel to implement objectives
'Donation of a service of care in the furtherance of ideals'	'Paid and routine application of skills'
Amateur	Professional
Unpaid	Paid

(Based on Chester 1985)

One set of questions that might be asked about such a formulation highlights the causal factors which are stated or implied. Roughly speaking, such sources of change may be located within organisational processes themselves and may be seen as a feature of all such organisations or, alternatively, the source of change may be located historically in the wider society in which the particular organisation is located. While this kind of movement/agency contrast has some affinities with a whole range of sociological accounts of organisational processes, it is likely that Chester wants to focus more specifically on voluntary organisations which, he suggests, have a kind of 'natural history' (Chester 1985: 7). Doubtless, however, theories of professionalisation, bureaucratisation, the 'iron law of oligarchy', the movement from sect to church or the routinisation of charisma have some affinities or overlaps with this account and may well have been a kind of diffuse set of influences. Certainly, the story that Chester has to tell is not an unfamiliar one.

Chester's account, however, wishes the reader to consider processes more specific to voluntary bodies:

. . . a group of enthusiasts initiate voluntary action in the service of their values, experience growth in organisation, come to need paid organisers, become aware of deeper training needs, come to feel professionally competent, and shift to a paid basis.

(Chester 1985: 7)

He gives, as other illustrations, the Probation Service and the Family Service Units. Handy notes how members of voluntary organisations like to emphasise the 'voluntary' and play down the 'organisation' (Handy 1985: 2) but also seeks to distinguish between types of such organisations. Thus MG is more concerned with 'service delivery' than with either 'mutual support' or 'campaigning' and hence is mmore likely to be also concerned with questions of organisation (Handy 1988: 112–14).

Such models of organisational change have been subjected to a variety of criticisms. They may be said to be excessively pessimistic, to allow too little part for human agency and to ignore the actor's frame of reference. Another set of criticisms would argue that such models tend to be too formal and to ignore cultural and historical variation. Chester, in fact, does seem to come down in favour of a more historically based and more external explanation. The sources of the changes are not simply to be found *within* the organisation, but in the interaction between that organisation and a changing environment. Here Chester refers to 'the general expansion and professionalisation of helping and care services' (Chester 1985: 7) and to the extension of pecuniary considerations into areas hitherto thought to be immune from such concerns. He also sees as influential changes in attitudes towards marriage in the direction of a 'relativisation' associated with the contrast between 'institution' and 'relationship' (see below, pp. 12–16 for further discussion).

On the borders of the internal and external influence lie 'probable changes in the motivations and aspirations associated with MG's recruitment pool', a shift from 'middle class philanthropy and civic concern' to a stress on 'self-realisation and personal growth' (Chester 1985: 8). Among other things this suggests some generational effects reflected in insider talk of 'sixties style counsellors and eighties style managers' or in Handy's description of the 1968 generation's radical downgrading of terms such as 'success', 'structure', 'professionalism' and 'leadership' (Handy 1985: 9).

There are two further points that may be made about Chester's account. As will be shown further in Chapter 5, it was not simply a detached academic statement of model building; rather it was a piece of applied theorising and one which was intended to make some kind of impact within the organisation under review. Here, as in many similar accounts, there is some blurring of the analytical and the normative and of the descriptive and the prescriptive and the model can be seen as having ideological implications. In a variety of ways, therefore, such theorising becomes part of the organisation being theorised.

In the second place, Chester's account necessarily has to take into consideration the special features of the people employed and deployed within the organisation, and in particular of the counsellors and their careers, backgrounds, expectations and culture. Consideration of changes in the theory and practice of counselling may allow for some complications in the original model such that, for example, it may be seen as a shift from a movement involved chiefly in the promotion of marriage, to a movement defending a particular therapeutic culture and on to a limited shift in the direction of a service agency (see Chapter 6).

Accounts of changes in counselling need to consider two sets of developments: changes informing the actual practice of counselling and those to do with the place of counselling within the organisation as a whole. In the case of the former, the very broad trends would be the growth of a Rogerian, non-directive perspective and its partial replacement by a more eclectic approach. Other associated but distinguishable trends would include the growth of specialised marital sexual therapy and the growing focus on the couple, rather than the individual, as the client. In the case of the overall place of counselling within the work of the organisation, we have the growing definition of counselling and, in particular, marital counselling as the primary task (a focus that reached its peak in the Tyndall years) and the more recent growth of an emphasis on publicity, associated with the competition for funds in a context where public support has declined in real terms and charities and voluntary organisations are competing for funds in the private sector.

What is clear about the various changes, in terms both of the overall orientation and structure and of the various models of counselling available, is that such changes do not exist simply at the level of theory or of practice but of both of these together. We are talking of changes within the culture of an organisation. This was certainly a theme that emerged in many of the sources, both published and verbal.

That particular organisations and occupations can be described as having a culture has long been recognised in sociological writings. The term 'culture' is used here to indicate a whole way of life, a focus on those features which are held to make a particular group distinctive: a network of shared experiences and symbols, ways of seeing and speaking and of being in the world. While all institutional settings develop some degree of cultural specificity, some cultures seem to be more distinct and bounded than others. What brings about this sense of distinctiveness varies from case to case but of significance in marriage guidance would be the processes of recruitment and training (including possible similarities in social background), the tensions and stresses of the 'work', the continuing importance of group or interpersonal relationships within the organisation and the possible 'spill-over' of organisational life into personal or domestic life. Finally, this work of culture creation is a continuous and reflexive process, especially in this case where the perceived or actual culture of the organisation may itself, especially in times of crisis, become both a topic of reflection on the part of the members and a resource to be drawn upon to account for their current situations.

This may be made a little more concrete by considering the phenomenon, referred to in several of the accounts (including Chester 1985) as 'Rugby magic'. The use of this term denotes a perception of a distinctive counselling culture based upon Rugby, at one and the same time the organisational centre and the training centre for counsellors. The term also refers to a particular period, the influence of which, although dwindling, is still felt. It was compounded of an emphasis on individuals rather than problems, the experiential nature of residential training for counsellors, the particular open-ended values of humanistic psychology (which included a scepticism of positivistic methods and scientific measurement) and, finally, an emphasis on the importance of confidentiality in the relationship between counsellor and client, such that the details of their encounters were not available for public scrutiny. The stress was on uniqueness: the uniqueness of individuals, of marriages and of the counselling encounters.

There have been some suggestions that marital counsellors tend to have certain personality characteristics in common. They may be resentful of authority and social rules (Dryden and Hunt 1985: 132–3). An American study suggested that they had very similar personality profiles to those of their clients – with both sets different from the average person and from clients undergoing individual therapy (*ibid.* 132). There are links between these sub-cultural features and the understanding of marriage as a relationship rather than as an institution. Wallis's idea of marriage as 'a living, feeling relationship between unique individuals' (Wallis 1970: 8) could readily be applied to the culture of counselling itself, certainly to the culture identified as 'Rugby magic'.

It is important, however, to recognise that 'Rugby magic' was never the whole story and that the construction and deployment of this term within the organisation reminds us that culture is a complex and often contradictory thing. Within MG's 'mixed economy' of professionalism and volunteerism there have been and continue to be tensions between education and training, between regions and centre and most of all between the technical and the managerial staff. There is disquiet about the desired number of interviews with clients, about the virtues and special nature of marital therapy versus family therapy, and about whether clients should pay or not. This suggests that MG culture is not made up simply of the counsellors and their worlds and world-views, but is a more complex and contradictory unity made up of managers and counsellors, centre and region and so on. These contradictions and tensions enter into the daily talk and experiences of members and again become part of the overall culture.

This discussion of culture, its complexity and compound and contradictory nature, probably serves to blur the simply unilineal and unidirectional models suggested in the movement/agency distinction. These models have some uses – they certainly sensitise the reader to the range of issues to be considered – but are probably ultimately of limited value. However, insofar as such models become part of the culture, they deserve to be taken seriously. Further, this discussion of culture reminds us that we need to look beyond the organisation itself if we are to understand changes within it: to look at changes in marriage itself and in the wider society.

CHANGES IN MARRIAGE

Developments in marriage are ultimately bound up with perceptions of marriage as a changing institution and concerns about and interpretations of such changes. The 'facts' of marital change, like the 'facts' about anything else, exist within a web of interpretations and evaluations. Marriage, as a topic, may not be the same for counsellors as for advertisers or 'lay' persons. Clearly, of central importance for the people and organisations discussed in this book, are rises in the divorce and remarriage rates. Chapter 2 refers to a perceived sense of crisis in marriage in the late 1940s and, with some variations, this sense of crisis has never been far away. The more recent facts of divorce and remarriage that continue to give rise to concern are summarised by Clark and Haldane (1990: 23–4). These include the fivefold increase in the number of divorces between 1960 and 1980; the familiar estimate of one third of marriages now taking place ending in divorce; the involvement of children in six out of ten divorces; and the fact that one in every three marriages is a remarriage for at least one of the partners. Such facts are often quoted and frequently form the basis of publicly expressed concern and speculation. Burgoyne, Ormrod and Richards referred to the development of a kind of 'folk-sociology' of divorce, which found explanations in the changing role and status of women, and rising expectations of marriage as a relationship, together with widely available methods of contraception and the growth of permissiveness (Burgoyne, Ormrod and Richards 1987: 19).

We now have a mass of publications and broadcasts about the experiences of divorce and marriage, how to stay married, how to get divorced or to survive divorce. The annual statistical monitoring of our marital practices has become a source of regular media comment. Yet sociological studies of marriage, although increasing slowly in number, remain relatively few and such studies that we do have cannot readily be put together in order to construct any kind of model of social change. A limited number of small scale studies carried out without any attempt at replication, while containing much that is insightful and useful, can only suggest shifts in practice and beliefs at a more general or societal level.

In the absence of a detailed understanding of married life, one particular account of marital change has assumed a considerable dominance, both in sociological writings and in public statements on behalf of those with an interest in marital problems. This is the argument that such changes may be described in terms of a move from 'institution' to 'relationship'. There are some variations in the accounts and in the terminology used but, generally, they provide an interesting example of the interplay between different professional, and other, understandings of marriage. The statement is made clearly at the beginning of a promotional video on behalf of Relate. Burgess and Locke, who wrote of a move from 'institution' to 'companionship' but who are usually credited with having originated the formulation, refer to the importance of marital counselling and the then recent work of Carl Rogers (Burgess and Locke 1945: 738). This broad sociological understanding appears in Church of England reports as well as in works on marital counselling.

Giddens has recently written of 'our peculiar concern with 'relationships' in these terms: 'Relationships are ties based upon trust, where trust is not pre-given but worked upon, and where the work involved means *a mutual process of self-disclosure*' (Giddens 1990: 121, his emphasis).

What this means in practice becomes clear in numerous publications written by people with an interest in marital counselling and therapy. Dicks referred to his ideal of marriage as 'permanent, satisfying, enhancing the identities of both partners' (Dicks 1967: 230), Wallis to 'a living, feeling relationship between unique individuals' (Wallis

1970: 8) and Hooper to 'an intimate environment in which the critical qualities of security and personal care may develop' (Hooper 1985: 276). Such understandings of marriage would appear to be widely diffused, not simply among marriage counsellors and therapists but in official Church of England publications (the Archbishop of Canterbury's Group on the Divorce Law 1966; Church of England General Synod 1978, for example) and in some more everyday lay perceptions (e.g. Mansfield and Collard 1988; Ambrose *et al.* 1983: 49).

There is some recognition that such an understanding of marriage is specific to Western society. In many of the writings there is, as has already been indicated, an implied or stated contrast with some earlier state when marriage was regarded more as an institution. Such a contrast, in fact, has quite a long sociological pedigree (for further detail see Morgan 1990). Yet closer examination of these and other texts, as well as of the key terms themselves, begins to throw up further complexities and ambiguities which warrant exploration. For one thing, conventional sociological understandings of the term 'institution', referring to persisting and patterned elements of social structure, would certainly allow for and include a 'relational' understanding of marriage. Similarly, social psychological under-standings of 'relationships' would include some elements of regularity and stability of expectations (e.g. Argyle and Henderson 1985: 4). Further, the fact that the term 'relationship' comes to take on a range of connotations, wider and deeper than the simple 'state of being related', is itself a matter of some sociological significance.

Figure 2 indicates some of the elements of this contrast. They are derived from a variety of sources but taken together might seem to constitute some kind of ideal typical polarity. The general understanding seems to be that there has been a progression over time from the left side to the right side, although the period over which these various changes are supposed to take place may vary considerably. Generally speaking, the lower down the table we move, the more recent the changes and, hence, the more relevant for the present discussion.

Nevertheless, even a brief consideration of the elements begins to throw up some ambiguities. Consider, for example, the idea of choice. There may be an increasing freedom of choice in terms of whom one might marry (although the extent to which this is something new in British history is a matter of debate) but the extent to which a person is 'free' not to marry is somewhat more complex (Barker 1978: 240; Gillis 1985). Certainly, there is greater freedom to leave a marriage

Figure 1.2 From 'institution' to 'relationship'

INSTITUTION	RELATIONSHIP
Less freedom of choice of marriage partners	Greater freedom of choice
Marriage linked to wider societal and/or kinship obligations	Marriage relatively separate from wider societal and/or kinship obligations
Emphasis upon economic aspects of marriage, e.g. property and the sexual division of labour	Emphasis upon the emotional and interpersonal aspects of marriage
Public emphasis	Private emphasis
Marriage as one of a set of social relationships	Marriage as *the* central adult relationship
Relative inequality within marriage; patriarchy	Relative equality within marriage; companionship
Little emphasis on mutual sexuality; sexuality linked to procreation	Positive emphasis on sexuality; sexual dysfunction seen as a sign of marital problems

although there is no choice of the number of spouses at any one time and single-sex partnerships may be stigmatised as 'pretended family relationships' (Weeks 1991). Similarly, to take another example, the notion of growing equality has been the subject of considerable critical attention from feminist writings.

Some of the further difficulties with this opposition may be indicated briefly. In the first place there is the ethnocentrism of many of these formulations, the assumption that these trends will come to characterise most of the modern world; to this extent, they are part of a general, and increasingly criticised, 'modernisation' package. Similar complexities arise, as has been noted, when we consider the time scale. Where there are implied contrasts with 'the past', this may be thirty years ago (e.g. Dominian 1985: 37), or located in some construction of 'Victorian' England, or prior to the Industrial Revolution. More recent historical accounts have been critical of this kind of modelling and of the periodisation associated with it and have argued either in favour of an idea of companionate marriage, going back for several centuries (e.g. MacFarlane 1986), or for more complex and varied shifts between institutional and relational aspects over time (Gillis 1985). Within any one period, and certainly in modern times, there seems to be scope for considerable variation according to class, religion and ethnic group. Finally, the increasing development of a feminist critique of family studies has emphasised the need to look at gender divisions within marriage and the possibility that husbands and wives may understand and experience marriage in different ways.

The fact that these understandings of marital change are so widely diffused and understood, while being subjected to relatively little critical examination, suggests that the model may have some ideological implications as well as providing a theoretical abstraction of marital change. Certainly, there seems to be an unspoken assumption that the trends described in this contrast are generally to be applauded as ones which correspond with other values of choice, democracy and personal fulfilment. More narrowly, there are affinities between the constructions of marriage as a relationship and the elaboration of a relational understanding of the counselling interaction.

The contrast between the institutional and the relational is not, therefore, simply a theory about changing marriage but may be seen as part of a wider and more coherent world view. The actual historical, certainly the long-term historical, perspective seems somewhat more complicated. Among the ways in which marriage could be seen as becoming more relational we might include the declining role played by immediate community controls and surveillance and the growing emphasis upon sexuality in marriage. On the other hand, there are ways in which marriage might be seen as becoming more institutional. Here we would include the growing tendency (at least up to the 1960s) for marriage to be defined as the 'normal' adult status, using that word in both its statistical and normative sense. Further, taking a longer view, marriage has become more a matter for state regulation and concern, these concerns being augmented in recent decades by professional concerns.

Hence we should be prepared to see shifting configurations of the institutional and the relational at the societal level and we may also see these different 'mixes' apparent at the individual or the couple level. The themes of identity and stability within marriage discussed by Askham, may each signify different combinations of the institutional and the relational (Askham 1984). Kiely argues for a continuum from companionship marriage to institutional marriage that applies to actually existing marriages rather than to changing marriage over time (Kiely 1984). Further, these mixes may change over the life-course, with some kind of shift towards the more institutional level becoming apparent when children are planned or appear. One way of beginning to reformulate the problem would be in terms of different patterns of control, constraint or regulation in relation to marriage.

There are, then, various paradoxes and tensions thrown up by this more critical examination of the institutional/relational contrast. There is the paradox of 'choice' where almost everyone is 'choosing' marriage or a marriage-type relationship. There is the paradox of a personal fulfilment which is, however, in some sense, mass produced. For the counsellor/therapist there is the dilemma of recognising or arguing for some historical change in the nature of marriage while also implicitly supporting the idea of some deep emotional structure which is relatively unaffected by historical change. There is also a kind of paradox in arguing for the uniqueness and specialness of any one individual marriage while also indicating a basic sameness about marriage, and a sameness that does not simply arise out of institutional underpinnings. Many of the accounts, indeed, recognise the different mixes of the public and the private, and the institutional and the relational, and the possible tensions between them (e.g. Dicks 1967: 8; Clulow and Mattinson 1989: 11). Nevertheless, these tensions between the institutional and the relational do not, as yet, appear to be at the forefront of either theory or practice.

That there have been changes in marriage during the period under examination is not in question. What is significant is the growing professional and public focus upon certain sets of changes rather than others (e.g. divorce rather than, say, patterns of living arrangements and housing). What is also important are the various theories, models and explanations that may be brought forward in order to make sense of these changes. While there is a plurality of such accounts – growing permissiveness, growing affluence, rising expectations and so on – one popular and widespread account is that of transition from institution to relationship. This provides a framework for understanding both divorce and remarriage and for providing a rationale for particular modes of intervention into marriage. It is also clear that it is not simply a model about marriage but a model about marriage in the context of a changing society.

SOCIETAL CHANGES

It would be an impossible task to describe the whole range of economic, demographic, political and social changes that have taken place within British society during the period under consideration. The links between the particular, marriage and marital agencies, and the general processes of social change are mediated through a complex nexus of relevancies and understandings. Put another way, we are only concerned with those features of societal change that have already been put on to the agenda, for whatever reason, by those with a particular interest in marriage and marital problems.

For example, many of the writings and individuals consulted referred to the impact of World War II and its assumed effect on marital, gender and sexual relationships. It is clear that this event was seen as being especially consequential and that these understandings had consequences for the way in which marriage was seen as being 'in crisis'. Historians have, indeed, attempted to provide assessments of the impact of the war on domestic relationships (Summerfield 1984; Costello 1985) and clearly sociological discussions should look more closely at the impact of such specific major historical events. At the very least, the ending of World War II provided a readily identifiable focal point for the articulation of concerns about marriage and sexual relations.

Moving away from specific events to consider equally specific but more long-term social processes, two sets of changes would seem to be worthy of mention. In the first place, there was the post-war construction of the Welfare State, together with subsequent challenges to it. While there is a variety of ways in which the impact of such processes and changes may be characterised, one way of particular relevance to the present discussion may be in terms of the fluid boundaries between the public and the private, about the rights and responsibilities of citizens and, increasingly, about the role of volunteers in the mobilisation of care. Perhaps of greater importance was the growing affluence of many sections of the middle and working classes and the associated growth of consumerism. For one thing, these developments contributed to the commonly stated view that affluence and the growth of leisure gave people time to turn from their more immediate needs to considering the quality of their interpersonal lives. Individuals, so the argument went, expected more out of marriage than simple mutual support and had more time to 'work at' their marriages and other interpersonal relationships. It is likely that these rather rosy assumptions came to be questioned increasingly over our period; certainly, we find the relaunched Relate concerned with the marital and interpersonal problems of the unemployed, the poorer sections of society, members of immigrant communities and so on.

Another set of factors of major concern to people associated with MG has to do with changes in the gender order. These clearly have a direct impact upon marital relationships and would include, centrally, the increasing rates of labour market participation for married women. Less easy to quantify, but at least of equal importance for many of the spokespersons for MG, has been the growth of a broader, more diffuse, 'feminist' consciousness or the development of what has been identified as the 'I'm not a feminist, but' phenomenon. This includes a recognition of, and a challenge to, some of the more clearly outdated expressions of male prejudice, a growing recognition of issues such as domestic violence and sexual harassment as matters to be accorded some degree of serious attention and the widespread understanding and use, sometimes ironically, of terms such as 'sexist' and 'male chauvinist'. Part of these changes has been some kind of challenge, partly implicit but sometimes explicit, to constructions of men and masculinity. Whether or not these changes add up to a wholesale challenge to the gender order is open to question but the development of a continuing public debate about gender relations and constructions is clearly a factor of some importance. It certainly entered the writings of many of those concerned with marital matters from the earliest points of our historical period, and not only influences perceptions of marriage and marital problems but also shapes understandings of the workings of the marital agencies themselves.

There are two themes of social change which deserve attention simply because they are so often seen as being significant by people involved in MG and because they have clear links with marital and domestic relationships. The first is to do with 'permissiveness' and, possibly, the associated but distinct concept of 'secularisation'. If we treat the latter term as signifying a decline in the range and depth of religious influences, its relevance for the present discussion would seem to have several strands. It is clearly significant for the growing perception of marriage as a 'relationship' rather than as an 'institution'. There is also the argument that the growth of counselling and therapy represents some kind of 'functional alternative' to organised or official religion; hence references in the titles of books to 'secular priests' (North 1972) or to 'the faith of the counsellors' (Halmos 1965). However, the picture does not seem to be one of a straightforward substitution of a secular world-view for a religious one. Apart from agencies dealing with particular religious communities it is noticeable how the influence of Christian, especially Nonconformist, backgrounds continues within the practice of marriage guidance.

However, a very popular piece of 'folk ideology' is to provide for a linkage between secularisation and 'permissiveness' (see MacIntyre (1967)). As the historical chapters demonstrate, concern about sexual permissiveness and sexual radicalism was a major part of the backcloth against which MG developed. A sense of a debate about what might be said and what might not be said is, as Chapters 2 and 3 show, an important feature of the early history of the NMGC where, it is argued, the organisation often provided a respectable forum for the discussion of 'non-respectable' topics such as birth control and premarital sex.

However, the connotations of 'permissiveness' were generally wider than issues about what may be discussed openly. The focus in such debates was on sexual relationships, often placed within a framework of discussion about control and authority, sometimes between men and women but most explicitly between parents and children. Included here are issues to do with a move away from a strong normative linkage between legitimate sex and marriage and a recognition of a wider range of forms of sexual expression within and outside marriage. Sexual permissiveness, viewed as both expression and behaviour, may sometimes be seen as a direct cause of marital problems and divorce and sometimes as a consequence of these problems. In its turn it may be linked to other social changes such as the growth of affluence, the development of television, the increase in the number of mothers in paid employment and so on. Even where sexual permissiveness might, at least in some of its manifestations, be approved as 'greater sexual freedom' or 'greater sexual honesty', it still remains a major feature in the understanding of social changes in the post-war period.

The other set of changes is to do with something called 'privatisation'. Here the reference is to an increasing recognition of the private sphere, usually identified with the household and domestic life, as a legitimate central life interest. Such changes may be applauded, when developments are associated with personal choice and freedom, or regretted when they are linked to the decline of public life. These 'privatisation' changes are certainly related to affluence, consumerism and, in some degree, to permissiveness in so far as this may be linked to ideas about expanding personal freedom. The development of the elaborated private world is associated with the growth of leisure, however much in practice this linkage might blur over significant differences in terms of class and gender. The private sphere becomes more than a castle to be defended; it is a garden to be cultivated and enjoyed. Marriage and family relationships are seen as a central aspect in this increasing growth of and sometimes celebration of the private sphere.

Generally, the changes that have been considered may be seen, on the one hand, as developments that encourage or facilitate greater professional or quasi-professional interventions into marriage (leisure, affluence, privatisation and so on) and, on the other, as changes which render marriage increasingly problematic and which create a demand for such interventions. These would include World War II, affluence and, more recently, factors such as unemployment. A word which enters into the accounts of many concerned with marital problems to describe these changes or conditions is 'turbulence'. While this term has its probable origins in some Tavistock-based systems theorising (Emery and Trist 1972), it would seem to be used as a kind of shorthand term to describe and account for the times in which we live, times which create and sustain a need for agencies such as Relate or the NMGC. Constructions of times being out of joint or troublesome are scarcely new but clearly form an important part of the ideology and rhetoric of those who wish to make some kind of intervention into public or private lives. Turbulence would seem to refer not so much to any specific sets of changes, although these might be itemised, but to the fact of change itself and, more important, to the perceptions of the pace of that change. The idea of diffuse social turbulence highlights, at one and the same time, the importance of domestic and interpersonal relationships as refuges from a world of crumbling landmarks and shifting values, while also indicating the very vulnerability of these refuges.

To conclude this section, it should be reiterated that these social changes are not simply a set of 'facts' that unambiguously form the background for the issues that are central to this book. They are cultural and historical themes – undoubtedly based upon real changes – which are of particular salience to people when they come to talk about marriage and marital problems.

MAKING THE CONNECTIONS

Changes in the organisation of MG, of marriage itself and in the wider society have been considered separately. However, at each point in the discussion it becomes clear that these three elements cannot be considered in isolation from each other and that there is a need to develop ways of understanding how they interact. Further, it is important to explore the ways in which these interconnections are understood by the participants themselves and how these understandings enter into everyday practice.

One relatively straightforward way in which these connections are made, especially by people connected in some way with MG, is in terms of a simple 'needs and responses' model. At an individual level people find that they are having difficulties with their marriages and seek help. At a societal level there comes a point where these individual private problems become public issues (Mills 1959) and this is not a matter of simple aggregation. From the earliest days of the history of MG, the rising rates of divorce are seen as both individual tragedies and as something approaching a social disaster. Although the language and the emphases may vary over the decades, the argument has been more or less the same, namely that divorce is not simply a matter of personal unhappiness for the individuals concerned but that it also has wider economic, social and possibly political implications. Whether or not the emphasis is on saving marriages or on easing some of the personal unhappiness involved in separation and divorce, there is a clear statement of an urgent social need and of the role, potential or actual, of MG in meeting these needs.

Further, this model does not simply provide a linkage between marital problems and marital agencies, between immediate problems and institutional responses. Connections are usually made with some features of the wider society. Thus social change itself, the increasing 'turbulence' of society, produces more strains on marriages which produces a greater need for advice, information and guidance. Intervening variables may be the breakdown of traditional networks of support and the decline of the influence of organised religion, providing a greater need for new sources of specialist advice. A more conservative version of this model, and one certainly not absent from our data, would see marital strain and breakdown as contributing to a wider set of social strains and providing a greater need for some kind of professional or quasi-professional intervention, ideally supported by the state, into marriage and the family.

However, this simple need/response model has several fairly obvious limitations, some of which are recognised by the practitioners themselves. As we see in Chapter 6, the ability of MG to identify the needs and to respond to them, or to provide clear indicators of its success in responding to needs has sometimes been open to question. There has always been, perhaps inevitably, some mismatch between the distribution of marital problems in the population as a whole and the deployment of skills and resources of MG towards responding to these problems, a mismatch which may be variously explained as a function of a lack of adequate funding or of problems in training and/or management.

At a more complex level, the need/response model seems to accord too passive a role to agencies such as MG. For one thing, MG has always (although to varying degrees) been involved in publicity and education and this would include interventions in the direction of alerting the public as to the growth of marital problems. Further, as the historical chapters make clear, MG has changed over time and has elaborated particular skills and expertise around the identification and handling of marital problems. Thus the developing responses of MG also go some way to creating, expanding or modifying the needs to which they are, in theory, responding.

This may be illustrated by considering the concept of 'marital problem' itself. Married or cohabiting individuals will inevitably experience a whole range of crises, unhappinesses and stresses. The interesting question here is how they come to recognise these problems as 'marital problems', as opposed, say, to individual psychological problems, economic problems, problems at work or simply normal features of day-to-day living. The identification of marital problems, even at times of divorce, is not a straightforward process. It requires a frame of reference, a language, both to understand these difficulties in this way and to see them as being, in principle, open to help and amelioration.

Marital agencies, therefore, do not simply respond to needs, societal and individual; they also in some way play a part in creating these needs. One formulation of the way in which MG agencies have played a part in the shaping of 'marital problems' has been in terms of 'the medicalisation of marriage' (Morgan 1985: 33–56). This notion has been subjected to some criticism (Woodhouse 1990) and certainly the history of the NMGC would not appear to fit clearly within this model, especially if by 'medicalisation' some kind of sequential process is implied. As other chapters in this book demonstrate, the more overtly medical models seemed to be found in the early history of MG and these tended to fade or to be challenged in the face of the growth of more specific models of marital counselling. Certainly, there is not a straightforward progression from guidance through counselling and on to therapy. Marital problems generally do not appear to have undergone the same processes of medicalisation that some other 'social problems' and practices have (Conrad and Schneider 1980; McWilliams 1985).

Nevertheless, there would seem to be some merit in unpacking the concept of 'medicalisation' a little further to see if it can tell us something about the interplays between organisational change, marital change and social change. At the outset it should be recognised that there would appear to be some implied value judgement in the use of the term 'medicalisation' in contexts such as these. The term suggests or implies some degree of inappropriateness; this is certainly true in the case of talk about 'the medicalisation of childbirth', for example. Even if a value judgement is not being implied, the deployment of the term may be seen as an example of sociological irony, the elaboration of a perspective that would not necessarily be recognised and may well be denied by the persons involved.

Medicalisation may simply imply that a set of practices or understandings is coming under the ambit of medical personnel. In the history of interventions into marriage there is some sign of this as evidenced, for example, by some of the people and bodies that provided evidence for the report, *Marriage Matters* (Home Office and DHSS 1979) or by the location of the Institute of Marital Studies at the Tavistock and of the Marriage Research Centre at the Middlesex Hospital. However, this does not add up to a wholesale 'take-over' of marital research, counselling and therapy by medically trained personnel and, indeed, the idea of the 'medical model' does not necessarily imply this (Conrad and Schneider 1980: 107).

Medicalisation, therefore, does not necessarily mean a literal adoption by medical agencies, although these may play a part. The usage of the term is often more metaphorical, implying that interventions into marriage are in some ways similar to medical interventions or consultations. Here we may consider, firstly, the overall framework of understanding, one which sees a set of symptoms as standing for an underlying condition, a condition which is made available for some kind of treatment. Such treatment, in its turn, will bring about some kind of transition from sickness to health. Thus the idea of 'the presenting problem' has structural affinities with the concept of a 'symptom'; in both cases there is an implied relationship between more obvious or more immediate external signs and some deeper, underlying condition which may be obscure to the person presenting but which may be revealed through counselling or therapy. A successful encounter would be one where the patient/client felt 'better' afterwards or, more to the point, where a couple felt they were 'getting along better'.

To some extent this may be a function of language. In the early history of MG there was talk of the provision of an 'ambulance service' and of marital 'casualties'. Divorce might be seen as taking on 'epidemic' proportions. Dicks, in 1967, referred to 'aetiology' and 'therapeutic techniques' from the perspective of the Tavistock (Dicks 1967: 230). Such terminology is probably more than an 'historical accident' and may reflect quite broad shifts in the way in which human problems were being understood. Nevertheless, it is important to stress that such medical metaphors and language did not have unchallenged dominance within MG. The term 'patient', for example, is generally eschewed, with 'client' as the preferred term.

Closely associated with this framework of understanding were the actual frameworks of interaction, the relationship between the 'client' and the 'counsellor'. By whatever route the client or clients end up in a room with a counsellor, it is clear that the former are to some degree seeking help from the latter. The counsellor is external to the people seeking help; she or he is outside their immediate family or friendship networks, a stranger. The relationship is perceived and constructed as being one where the counsellor has some measure of skill, training, experience or expertise which the others do not have. However, the open, friendly style may seek to minimise this. Implied here, too, is a lack of reciprocity; the counsellor is not expected to exchange marital problems with the clients. All in all, the Parsonian model of the 'sick role' would seem to have certain applicability in some, if not all aspects of client/counsellor encounter (Parsons 1951: 428–79)

Thus it is possible to speak of medicalisation in this context by referring to the general framework of understandings within which the counselling encounter takes place. We may also speak of medicalisation in an even more general sense, seeing the counselling encounter as having features in common with some broad trends in society as a whole in terms of the ways in which 'problems' are understood and treated. It is a banality to say that people have always 'had problems'. What is subject to historical variation is the wider framework of meaning within which 'problems' are identified and explained and the extent to which such problems are perceived as being amenable, at least in principle, to solutions. Thus Conrad and Schneider argue for a process of 'medicalisation', for the most part during the twentieth century, in connection with a whole range of social and personal problems. The broad trajectory is in terms of a move from 'badness' to 'sickness' a process accompanied by the development of a new group of control experts, who in their turn provide further elaborations and sharper definitions of the medical dimensions of the problems concerned (Conrad and Schneider 1980: McWilliams 1985).

Perhaps the major theoretical contribution to this debate is provided by Foucault's discussion of the 'clinical gaze' (Foucault 1973). Indeed, his description of this 'gaze', although elaborated in a more strictly 'medical' context, could be almost a description of marital counselling:

In the clinician's catalogue, the purity of the gaze is bound up with
a certain silence that enables him to listen. The prolix discourses of
system must be interrupted . . .

(Foucault 1973: 107)

In counselling and therapy the cultivation of this gaze is all important.
In the counselling encounter nothing is irrelevant: the silences as well
as the utterances, body posture and general demeanour, matters such
as timekeeping or whether the clients come singly or together. The
development of this gaze, which it may be argued informs a whole
range of activities such as police work, education and selling as
well as therapies, is bound up with particular understandings of
the person, the relationships between mind and body and so on.
Marital counselling, therefore, may be seen as part of this very
general historical process.

Medicalisation may be seen as a theme in the issues under
examination but it is not the whole story. Firstly, there are
various areas for which this term might seem more appropriate
than others. Chief among these would be the development of marital
sexual therapy (MST), with its strong behaviourist influences. Sexual
problems are more easily describable in physiological terms: failure
to reach orgasm, lack of an erection, premature ejaculation and
so on. Further, the description of sexual problems in more or less
physiological terms can have the consequence, perhaps even the
function, of editing out or suppressing other ways of understanding
sexuality in terms of moral or religious values. Further, again, the
treatment of sexual problems may be more readily identified in
terms of success or failure. It may be argued, therefore, that the
medical model has become more to the fore in the treatment of
sexual problems within relationships. Indeed, the very successful
identification of a set of problems as 'sexual' and their treatment
by specialists recognised as being separate from marital counsellors
may be seen as a clear example of the work of the clinical gaze in
the area of interventions into marriage. It is also, of course, part of
the elaboration of sets of discourses around sexuality and regulation
of the body (Foucault 1979).

However, the other side of this coin is that it is recognised that other
aspects of marriage may not be so readily identified and treated and
hence it is increasingly likely that a client (a couple or an individual)
may have a variety of counselling 'careers', including marital sexual
therapy as well as marital counselling. This suggests, perhaps, that
we should write of 'medicalisations' in the plural rather than of a

unitary process of medicalisation. What does seem to be certain is that medicalisation or the clinical gaze do not appear as inevitable, built-in or inexorable features of the counselling encounter. Medicalisation may indeed be seen as a danger or as something to be avoided or at least denied; medicalisation and demedicalisation should be seen as part of the same story (Conrad and Schneider 1980: 271). The move away from an earlier fairly explicit medical model is certainly part of the story of the history of the NMGC. Perhaps Weick's distinction between a 'disease-orientated' model and a 'health-orientated' model is useful here (Weick 1983). Earlier writings concerned with marriage did tend in some of their terminology to talk in terms of disease and cure. Later, the stress was on the relative 'health' of the clients, while assessing that 'health' within a framework that retained some features of medicalisation or the clinical gaze.

If the complex interplay between changes in marriage, in marital agencies and in society as a whole suggests fluctuation and oscillation rather than a clear progression from 'a' to 'b', this is perhaps nowhere clearer than in considering the complex distinctions between 'public' and 'private'. This is a commonly used distinction within sociology, especially as a consequence of a feminist critique, although its complexities have not always been fully recognised. What needs to be stressed here is that we are not dealing with fixed 'spaces' but more with ideological constructions, ones which are often open to negotiation and challenge.

Thus, for example, it is often maintained that marriage has become more of a 'private' relationship; indeed this is part of the distinction between institution and relationship. There are, however, some paradoxes within this formulation. Most striking, as has already been noticed, is that this 'private' relationship has become more and more the focus of public discourses. Thus even the relational aspects of marriage, both in general and in particular, become open to the scrutiny of others. In some cases, the members of the Royal family, for example, these 'others' may be very numerous indeed. In other cases, the significant others may be members of the caring professions, counsellors or lawyers. At a more general level, the ideas of what constitutes a 'good' marriage – including the intimate details of sexuality – become open for public debate and evaluation. The history of MG reflects these complex, often ambiguous, and fluctuating boundaries between the public and the private. The model of the counselling encounter, based on strong norms of confidentiality, becomes an analogue of the relational idea of marriage itself: a close, developing relationship separated from the scrutiny of others.

Yet, while the particularities of any one specific marriage remain closed to scrutiny from outside the counselling encounter, marriages in general, with their tangles of dependencies, hurts and expressions of sexualities, become more open to public view. Further, in more recent times, as Relate seeks greater public support and a higher public profile, some edited particulars of the marital experiences of couples who have been helped by counselling will be found entering publicity material. Thus, in the interplay between marriage, the marital agencies and changing society, there is not a straightforward shift from the public to the private but rather a re-drawing of the boundaries.

A LIFE-COURSE APPROACH

Formulations such as 'medicalisation', 'movement/agency' or 'institution/relationship' inevitably run into difficulties in the face of actual sets of practices. This is not to say that such formulations are wrong or to elevate a narrowly empiricist claim on the part of the 'infinite complexity of real life' as against the remoteness or abstractness of 'theory'. For one thing, as has been noted at several points, theoretical formulations and understandings are themselves often part of everyday life and practices. What is needed, however, are some sets of concepts or frameworks of understanding that mediate between day-to-day practices and wider generalisations. In this context we suggest a modification of a 'life-course' analysis.

Although the term 'life-course' might seem to have biological connotations it is, in fact, some distance from naturalistic formulations of the birth, maturation and decline of organisations. This is because it explicitly allows for the interplay between historical change and the development of organisations or institutions. It represents not so much a set of law-like statements as a way of viewing and thinking about the relationships between individual, institutional and historical change.

Conventionally, a life-course analysis has been anchored to studies of families and households as they change over time and in the context of a society which is itself undergoing change (Demos and Boocock 1978; Hareven 1978).However, as has been suggested, such an analysis need not necessarily be limited in this way (Morgan 1985: 180). Indeed, such an extension to units outside families and households may have the advantage of proving a reminder that social life is not lived exclusively within such social institutions.

In the present case, the elements of the analysis are as follows:

1 Individuals These enter into marital agencies at various points in their lives and continue their lives with their involvement in such institutions as providing additional strands in their individual life-courses. They may leave such agencies at some later stage. Here we are chiefly concerned with individuals who enter such agencies as counsellors and managers although, in principle, there is no reason why a similar analysis could not focus upon clients (although their acquaintance with such agencies would no doubt be briefer).

2 Agencies In this case we are chiefly concerned with NMGC, later to become Relate. Such a change, together with other changes that have already been discussed and that will bc analysed in greater detail later in this book, forms part of the life-course of this particular agency.

3 Changes in the wider society As has already been indicated, these are often difficult to conceptualise and to measure. Since the concern here is with marital agencies, the chief area of change must be around issues to do with marriage and divorce and associated topics to do with sexual permissiveness, the changing status of women and so on.

Analysis may begin with any one of these elements, the choice often being determined by the kind of data to hand. The point is to conduct the enquiry constantly alert to the interplays between the elements.

To illustrate how this analysis might proceed, let us consider some aspects of the lives of the counsellors and managers who came into NMGC/Relate at different stages. The Coopers and Lybrand report notes: 'It is widely recognised – inside and outside MG – that MG has traditionally attracted a predominance of female, middle-class, white people as counsellors – and as tutors and managers (Coopers and Lybrand 1986: 21)

This comment smoothes over the gender differences between counsellors and managers but generally reflects a widely held view about agencies such as MG. A life-course analysis might begin with such data although it could not remain content with them. For one thing, gender, class and ethnicity should be seen as cumulative and interwoven identities rather than as attributes which people possess or do not possess. More important, we need to look at the *particular* occupational and class backgrounds from which counsellors and managers emerge. For examples, the role of probation work in the background of some counsellors and managers in the earlier years is clearly a matter of some significance, as might be the experience in one or more other voluntary agencies or charities in the backgrounds of some more recent managers.

In focusing upon counsellors there is a matter of some importance that cannot be overlooked. Counsellors and others often remark on the impact of MG work on their own marriages and relationships. This is inevitable. The training process requires that they look critically at their own marriages and relationships, and recognise what they might learn from them or how concern with some aspect of their own marriage might inhibit sympathetic encounter with the marriages of others. In the early days, divorced persons were not permitted to take up training as counsellors. Such effects (clearly reinforced by aspects of the training involving group work) do not of course end with training but continue throughout their involvement as counsellors and, presumably, beyond. While the actual counselling sessions are not in themselves the occasion for the exchange of confidences, this is not to say that counsellors do not experience challenge and change through these encounters and this fact, again, may serve as one further modification of a straightforward medicalisation model where such effects of the 'gazed upon' upon the 'gazer' are not conventionally recognised.

Such effects are not simply of autobiographical importance. Culture, as we have suggested, does not simply develop out of interactions within the walls, as it were, of the agency. Rather, it arises out of the interplay between these experiences and the cumulation of past experiences and expectations, and the reflections upon these that are prompted by the day-to-day encounters. It is a truism to say that organisations are made up of the individuals that compose them. It is also a truism to say that individuals are made by these organisations. In the adoption of the life-course analysis we have the potentiality for exploring how these interacting processes take place.

Rather than continue this particular line of enquiry further at this stage (see Chapter 5 for further developments), we shall change tack slightly and consider instead the question of gender. It is important to recognise that gender is not a subject to be added on to the analysis; rather it should be shown to be a major strand within any analysis, although its impact is rarely straightforward. Several preliminary points should be made at the outset. Firstly, to repeat, gender is not simply an attribute or a 'face-sheet variable'; it is an identity and a process. Secondly, and following from this, gender identities and ideologies are not automatically given for any situation on the basis of biological sex; they are worked at and used to become effective in highly specific contexts. Finally, in the context of a life-course analysis, gender should be seen as a major strand weaving back and forth across the three major elements of individual, agency and society.

Both counsellors and clients come to marital agencies from a world in which there are major assumptions about the natures of men and women and how these are changing. These assumptions may sometimes be shared and may sometimes differ; what is important is that they both inhabit a social world in which gender issues are conceptualised and worked through. Assumptions about and experiences of gender will be both topic and resource for all parties in a counselling session, whether these are recognised or not.

In the majority of cases both counsellors and clients will have experienced marriage and will probably be married at the time of counselling. To varying degrees they will be aware of the variations between the experiences of women and men within marriage (Bernard 1976). In the case of the clients there is some evidence to suggest that they come to counselling with slightly different expectations, the men tending to expect more immediate practical advice, the women responding more positively perhaps to an open-ended counselling style. In the case of sex therapy, men are (at least in one study) likely to present with more obviously physiological difficulties (Bancroft 1984: 62). In the case of counsellors, we are dealing with recruits from a largely female pool of middle class labour. At the same time it is likely that they came from those sections of society which were most exposed to the kinds of tensions and contradictions that produced various waves of feminisms. Further contradictions appeared in the context of training which explored both the idea of the relational properties of marriage (in which gender issues were relatively muted) and the ideas of deep-rooted if not immutable differences between men and women.

That organisations, even those organisations most conventionally associated with impersonal rationality, are gendered is something which is slowly being recognised (Hearn and Parkin 1987; Hearn *et al.* 1989). They are gendered not simply in the more obvious sense of being composed of men and women who are differently located in different offices at different levels but also in that much of the day-to-day conduct is shaped by assumptions about gender. In the case of NMGC/Relate it has been frequently noted that counsellors tended to be women whereas managers tended to be men. This gendering of the 'technical/managerial' division was often recognised within the organisation and was the subject of a certain amount of theorising.

When it is argued, therefore, that gender was a major feature of the culture of this agency, this was not a statement referring to some detached quality that somehow existed 'out there'. It was a resource which was shaped through encounters in the wider society and through theorising about these encounters; it was deployed in day-to-day encounters both with clients and between counsellors and managers and, consequently, provided a major framework of understanding for processes within the agency. While it is doubtful whether this particular agency was in any way unique in this, the fact that its very rationale was marriage perhaps pushed issues of gender, and theories about and understandings of gender, more to the fore than they might have been in other organisations.

CONCLUSION

In part this chapter has been about the theories that arise out of and are part of the world-views of the people who form the subject matter of the following chapters. As has been noted, while all people are theorists in some measure, the people in this study were used to developing theoretical understandings in more or less explicit ways. Here, then, the task of a different kind of theorist is to try to draw out some of these day-to-day theories and to explore their interconnections and implications. Hence, several of the themes dealt with in this chapter – movement and agency, institution and relationship, organisational culture, gender and so on – are part of the way in which members can come to understand their every day practices and changes within their organisation and in the wider society.

In part, also, this chapter has been about theories that have, in the main, developed outside the day-to-day practices of marital counselling and which may, in some cases, be regarded with hostility or amusement by many of these practitioners. The ideas of medicalisation or the clinical gaze may well be of this order. This does not say that these theoretical perspectives are wrong; simply it is to argue for the normal requirements of testing these perspectives against the experiences and understandings that arise in the data. In this case, the idea of medicalisation or the clinical gaze, while it requires some significant modifications in the face of this case study, does usefully point to the way in which marital agencies do not simply respond to individual troubles or social problems but do, in an important sense, constitute these problems and troubles.

These reciprocal processes, whereby practitioners respond to the 'needs' of individuals with troubled marriages while simultaneously constituting these needs, represent one of the main bridges between institution, marriage and society. Yet, at the same time, we require a set of analytical tools which enables us to think about these linkages in a somewhat more concrete manner. If, somewhat generally, we may describe these constructions of marriage and marital problems as being 'ideology' we need to provide ways of describing those groups to whom this ideology is being imputed (Merton 1957: 460–1) or who might in some sense be said to 'own' such an ideology (Sharrock 1974). While, somewhat simplistically, we may describe these groups as 'marital agencies' it becomes readily apparent that this descriptive term signifies a variety of different sets of people (most notably, technical staff and managers) who might not in any simple sense be said to share an ideology or a culture. Further, since marital agencies are not total institutions, and especially since they are voluntary organisations, the individuals described here have a variety of other identities, ways of describing themselves other than as marriage guidance counsellors or managers. Hence, the existential basis of this particular ideological construction of marriage and marital problems is not as straightforward as it might seem.

One way of overcoming these problems is to recognise that, firstly, ideologies and cultures are rarely straightforwardly and unproblematically anchored to clearly identifiable social groups but often arise out of contradictions and tensions between various overlapping groups and categories. Secondly, one way of beginning to understand this fluidity is in terms of a life-course perspective, or at least something which gives full recognition to the interplays both within and outside a particular institution, agency or organisation and sees these interplays as being subject to change over time. In the course of teasing out these interplays, furthermore, a crucial element in the analysis is the recognition that, however else these players in this particular set of dramas may be described, a major identifier is in terms of gender.

NOTES

1 David Mace, first general secretary of the NMGC.
  John Wallis, training officer for NMGC from 1955.
  Nicholas Tyndall, chief officer of NMGC from 1969.
  David French, director of Relate/NMGC from 1987.

Part II
Jane Lewis

Introduction

The aim of this part of the book is to provide a contextualised history of marriage guidance, focusing on the biggest marital agency, the National Marriage Guidance Council (since 1988 called Relate) and referring for comparative purposes to the other organisations doing marital work: the Institute of Marital Studies (IMS), the Catholic Marriage Advisory Council (CMAC) and the Jewish Marriage Education Council (JMEC). The purpose of such a history is to understand the nature and timing of the changes in the NMGC's purpose and ethos, and the way in which it has delivered what kind of service to whom. The overarching aim therefore is to examine the processes of change in a voluntary organisation, something that in the 1980s became a major preoccupation of the 'third sector', which has been told by successive Conservative governments both that its importance has significantly increased and that the level of funding it might expect from the state will decline.

The process of change in voluntary organisations is still subjected to rather crude biological analogy. For example, in a recent text on management in voluntary organisations, Poulton (1988: 158) expresses some hesitation in using the human life cycle to describe organisational systems, but nevertheless feels that it is appropriate to do so because most will face decay and death. Strangely, such biologistic ideas about the life history of voluntary organisations have paralleled the exclusively mechanistic models of the way in which organisations actually work at any particular point in time, with the odd result that prescriptions derived from engineering have been applied to the relationships between the people in an organisation, while the organisation as an abstract entity has been treated as a biological organism. As Handy (1985: 20–1) has noted, the older mechanistic approaches, symbolised perhaps in the 'wiring diagram' of the organisational chart, began during the 1980s to give way to approaches that owe more to political theory, where the emphasis is on 'culture', 'shared values', 'networks and alliances', 'power and influence', 'federalism' and 'compromise and consent'. However, Handy (*ibid.* 83) has little time for history and bemoans the fact that, when asked why something is as it is, the British will give an historical reason while Americans will usually give a functional one, with the result, he feels, that many voluntary organisations are encumbered with inherited cultures and traditions that may no longer be appropriate to the task in hand. Yet, as this part of the book will seek to demonstrate, an understanding of the historical specificity of particular decisions and of changes in direction, which may result in lags and dysfunctions (as when one branch of a voluntary organisation develops more rapidly than another), should prove a valuable input to decisions about future changes rather than an impediment, while inherited cultures and traditions are ignored at the organisation's peril.

It is not that 'history repeats itself' and can thus be used to predict; the conjuncture for decisions and actions is always different, which means that even if a policy is 'reinvented' its outcome will probably be different. Rather, historical understanding of an organisation sensitises analysis of current problems, especially in regard to two areas highlighted by Handy as being of particular importance in voluntary organisations: values and cultures. In the course of our research on the NMGC, we noted how difficult it was for workers in the organisation accurately to perceive the full dimensions of both a problem and the possible range of choices facing them in its solution. Furthermore the management thinking of the 1980s was in danger of making a fetish of change. As Patrick Wright (1987: 9) has observed: 'the cramped old world of social responsibility and historical cause and effect is replaced by the play of "change" and the Megatrend . . .' Human actors are referred to variously as 'product champions', 'winners' and 'risk takers'. Facing a sea change in all aspects of their work, occasioned in large part by the shifts in government policy in terms of both funding and the values attaching to the 'enterprise culture', voluntary organisations have increasingly turned to the new 'witchdoctors' of that culture (*Economist* 1988): the management consultancy companies. The last chapter in this part of the book charts the attempt of one of these large companies to come to grips with the problem facing marriage guidance and suggests that some of its recommendations might have been modified and alternative issues highlighted had a greater historical understanding of the organisation's values and culture been achieved.

The Marriage Guidance Council was founded in 1938 and was reconstituted as a federal organisation – the National Marriage Guidance Council – in 1946. Its mission and its structure were consciously shaped by its social and political context and in particular by the widespread concern about the perceived breakdown in family life; by contemporary relationships between government and the voluntary sector; by current interpretations of the terms 'guidance' and 'counselling'; and by the position of women, who have always comprised the vast majority of marriage guidance's voluntary labour force. The pioneers of marriage guidance were drawn in the main from two of the professional groups most concerned about marriage and family life and sexual morality: medicine and the clergy. Both the MGC and the NMGC in its early years may be seen as primarily *campaigning* organisations, which aimed to use both mass education and counselling to the larger end of promoting marriage and family life. Those attracted to work with marriage guidance through one of the rapidly expanding number of autonomous, local marriage guidance councils described themselves as members of a *movement*. The focus on counselling deepened in large measure as a result of the terms of the Home Office grant received by the organisation in 1949, which provided money for counselling, but none for the work of lecturing and publishing which government felt should be self-financing.

The idea that 'guidance' might be offered to people about the intimate relationship of marriage was highly suspect. Public authorities had long accepted (since the turn of the century) the idea of, first, voluntary organisations and then the employees of local authorities – in the form of health visitors – entering homes to advise on 'mothercraft', but sex and marriage were a different matter and government was quite clear that there was no place for publicly employed officials in this sphere. It was prepared to back marriage guidance's voluntary endeavours, but was concerned above all that a respectable and professional service be provided. The NMGC thus came to provide a national marital counselling service, heavily dependent on state financing, but jealous of its independence of the state. This model, in which the funding and provision of social services were separated, was usual in much of continental Europe, but not so common in the world of the British post-war welfare state. As Brenton (1985: 26) has pointed out, the NMGC was one of the few voluntary organisations to grow rapidly in the 1950s and 60s. In large measure this growth was due to the fact that the NMGC was virtually the sole provider of marital counselling;

the numbers of clients seen by other voluntary organisations were relatively small.

However, 'marriage guidance' in the sense of the work of the marriage counsellor proved difficult to define. In the case of the Family Discussion Bureaux (which became the Institute of Marital Studies in 1968), marital counselling borrowed heavily from psychology and psychiatry and began to feed the approaches and skills of these disciplines into the practice of social casework. (The FDBx were founded by the Family Welfare Association, which as the Charity Organisation Society had been set up to work in parallel with the state, treating the 'deserving' poor, while the 'underserving' went to the poor law authorities.) In the NMGC, the idea of marriage guidance owed more to a public health model until forcibly challenged by the adoption of non-directive counselling (imported from the USA) which began in the early 1950s and became widespread during the 1960s. Guidance was in the main delivered by women to women, although the leadership of the NMGC remained male. Sexual divisions in the organisation in terms both of sexual segregation and of the perceived difference between the 'female' nurturing work of counselling and that of the male directors and managers have remained characteristic of the organisation.

By the late 1960s, the NMGC was beginning to experience conflict between its publicly stated mission to promote marriage and family life and the private work of non-directive counselling, the outcomes of which were impossible to predict. This conflict was exacerbated by changes in public attitudes and behaviour in respect to sex and marriage, and the liberalisation of the law on divorce. The NMGC found it increasingly difficult to take a firm stand both on marriage as the only place for sexual relationships and on the desirability of saving marriages. With its mission to promote marriage and family life no longer so clear-cut, the NMGC sought refuge in the private work of counselling, rapidly becoming an organisation oriented towards the delivery of a *service*. Counselling thus became both the organisation's mission and its primary task. However, the full implications of this crucial shift for the organisation were not fully recognised until the early 1980s.

During the 1970s the NMGC worked systematically to elaborate its own training for counsellors, using its new residential training college in Rugby which also became its national headquarters. From the beginning of the decade, the organisation aimed to carve out a specialist niche for itself alongside the expanding world of local authority personal social services. The idea of voluntary organisations providing either a parallel service to statutory authorities, or top-up services beyond the 'national minimum' on the 'extension ladder' model first articulated by the Webbs (Brenton 1985) was becoming rapidly outdated. As Kramer (1981) observed, the voluntary and statutory sectors were becoming co-existing systems which sometimes worked cooperatively and sometimes not. Taking its cue from the Seebohm Report (PP. 1968, Cmnd 3703), which heralded the setting up of the new local authority social service departments, the NMGC sought to justify its existence by providing a complementary, specialist and professional service. By the end of the 1970s, the organisation was proud of the 'technical backbone' it had constructed, linking counsellor to tutor to tutor consultant to the head of counselling at the national headquarters. The NMGC had developed a strong therapeutic culture of its own, but at the cost of considerable insularity. The world of 'MG' as it was usually referred to still called itself a 'movement', reflecting both its tendency to look inward and the strength of its home-grown therapeutic culture. However, this 'cosiness' served to mask certain crucial failures in the development of the organisation as a professional service agency, particularly in regard to its capacity to evaluate its work, assess new needs and manage the changes required to meet them. Just as the transition to a service agency had been but partially recognised, so professionalisation within the agency was less than complete, being largely confined to the business of training counsellors. These weaknesses became increasingly significant with, first, the rapid expansion of the organisation and the number of clients it served during the 1970s and, second, the sea change in the relationship between government and the voluntary sector following the election of the first Thatcher administration in 1979.

During the 1980s, as the NMGC's costs increased, so the real value of the grant it received from the Home Office declined. For while successive Conservative governments promoted the importance of the new 'trinity' of the voluntary sector, the market and the family as the sources of welfare in society (rather than the state), so public expenditure cuts also adversely affected the grants received both by the NMGC from central government and by the local marriage guidance councils from local authorities. Instead, the Home Office urged marriage guidance to raise more money by way of client contributions. Problems with intimate relationships, whether concerning marriages or childcare, were deemed more firmly than ever to be 'private troubles'. Thus even an organisation claiming to foster self-reliance among families was itself expected to be independent. Whereas forty years previously the Home Office had been concerned above all about the respectability of marriage guidance, insisting that it behave with discretion, in the 1980s it encouraged the organisation to adopt a more entrepreneurial approach, including, for example, advertising. The NMGC was not alone among voluntary organisations in finding much that is tempting about the 'enterprise culture'. It had always emphasised its desire for independence from the state and welcomed the new importance attached to the voluntary sector. However, the restructuring demanded by the new financial circumstances with the emphasis on 'management' and financial accountability proved painful. Similarly ambiguous feelings have been aroused by the emphasis, also linked to New Right ideas, on the importance of traditional family values and the importance of the stable, two parent family form. In many respects, this might seem to herald the possibilities for a return to marriage guidance's public commitment to marriage and the family which characterised it during the 1940s and 50s. However, there is a gap between such prescriptions and the reality of behaviour in the 1980s, with high divorce rates and increasing numbers of one parent families and cohabiting couples.

At the end of the 1970s, *Marriage Matters*, the interdepartmental consultative document on the marital agencies (the NMGC, the IMS and the CMAC), which was largely engineered by the NMGC, gave marriage guidance reason to hope that it had indeed been successful in securing government blessing for its work and for its continued existence outside the state, while receiving substantial state aid. This made adjustment to the rapid changes of the 1980s all the more difficult. The 1986 review of the NMGC by Coopers and Lybrand, a large management consultancy company, and in particular its recommendations emphasising the importance of setting up a new management structure, was viewed by the technical staff of the organisation as threatening to the organisation's ethos and as the imposition of 'male' management on a 'female' therapeutic culture. Certainly, the gender divisions within the organisation between male administrators (later, 'managers'), and female counsellors and tutors were real enough. In addition, the financial crisis has made the weaknesses exposed in the 1970s more evident. In particular the organisation's purpose in terms of the kind of counselling it intends to deliver, to whom and in which types of settings, was not made a priority until 1989. The place of volunteers within a professional service agency has also become a more acute issue. Not many service agencies continue to rely on volunteers for their core workers as marriage guidance does for the most part with its counsellors (the Royal National Life-boat Institution and the Samaritans share this characteristic). The trend is rather to employ paid workers because of the need to secure an efficient and effective service and the increasing desire of married women to work for pay.

An influential American volume (Bellah *et al.* 1985) has stressed that the ability of voluntary organisations to express the core values of human concern is their greatest value. The ethos of such organisations, in terms of their values and their commitment both to their members and to serving their clients irrespective of means, is thus portrayed as the core of a voluntary organisation's meaning and identity. But elements forming that identity were set in flux during the 1980s as never before since the founding of the marital agencies, and the struggle for direction became acute. This part of the book shows that the life history of marriage guidance has not been a process of steady growth and decay. Rather the organisation has attempted a radical change in direction both in the late 1960s and the 1980s, and heads have rolled in the process. Achieving change in the organisation has proved problematic and it is hoped that a better understanding of the factors that have determined NMGC's central purpose and organisational ethos will prove of use in the assessment of future options.

2 Marriage mending, 1920–50

The idea of providing marriage guidance was first given formal expression in the form of a Marriage Guidance Council in 1938. Writing in 1948, just after the establishment of the National Marriage Guidance Council, David Mace (1948a: 12), the NMGC's first General Secretary, remarked that it had been 'clever' of those who came together in 1938 to sense the approaching crisis in marriage. He was referring to the widespread perception in the late 1940s that the family had suffered dislocation and breakdown as a result of war, and to the alarm at the rapid rise in the divorce rate. The pioneers of the 1930s were not however psychic. They were concerned about marriage and family life, but in the context of, first, the 1930s debates about the role of birth control and late marriage as factors determining the quality and quantity of population and, second, the morality of sexual relationships between men and women. The latter encompassed the issue of divorce – especially in the light of the concern about 'hotel divorces' and the relaxation of the divorce laws in 1936[1] – but also included discussion of the basis of traditional Christian morality in the light of the ideas of radical sex reformers of the 1920s.

The precise origins of marriage guidance are hazy, but groups promoting the idea appeared in Birmingham and in London simultaneously in the late 1930s. The membership of the groups comprised two distinct strands, one personified in the figure of the Reverend Herbert Gray, a Presbyterian minister and activist in the Student Christian Movement. Gray was widely recognised as the founder of marriage guidance. He represented those who were attempting to rethink the spiritual and religious aspects of sexual relationships, and who, while rejecting the views of the sexual radicals, were also determined to provide a new and more positive basis for traditional Christian teaching on chastity and fidelity. The other strand was personified in Dr E.F. Griffith, who came to marriage guidance via his interest in birth control and eugenics, and who represented the medical response to the challenge of the sexual reformers. Accepting the importance of lifting the taboo from issues such as birth control and sexual technique and of opening sex up to scientific inquiry, doctors like Griffith were also concerned to preserve traditional sexual morality. Gray and Griffith were additionally concerned about the national implications of healthy marriage and parenthood. Griffith was an active member of the British Social Hygiene Council, originally an offshoot of the Eugenics Society (Rolfe 1949a), whose sub-committee on marriage was largely responsible for developing the idea of marriage guidance.

The religious and medical strands within marriage guidance came together during World War II when David Mace, a former Methodist minister who had spent the early war years at Cambridge writing his PhD thesis on Christian sexual ethics, and Griffith independently developed proposals for a marriage guidance centre. War-time conditions fed a more generalised commitment to planned reconstruction, which included marriage and parenthood. Education for marriage became part of the new-found commitment to education for citizenship and the movement for marriage guidance gained strength as a publicly identified defender of marriage and family. This represented something of a departure from its rationale in the 1930s. In their prolific writings during the 1940s, Gray, Griffith and Mace pursued the themes identified in the previous decade – in particular the function of sex and the meaning of marriage for men and for women – but developed them so as to constitute a defence of traditional morality that was at one and the same time believed to be essential for the welfare of race and nation. Mace in particular played a crucial role in popularising the ideas of marriage guidance within the context of war-time concerns about marriage breakdown.

By the end of the war, anxiety over the family pervaded the government as well as the professions and the press, and it was a government committee of inquiry into matrimonial breakdown, chaired by Lord Denning (PP. 1947, Cmd 7024), which first proposed that marriage guidance be given a government grant. Because it had attached its flag firmly to the importance of the family and the national interest, marriage guidance's request for grant was hard to refuse. However, leaders of marriage guidance were prepared to discuss topics such as sex in marriage which were still risky in terms of respectability. Thus the debate over government commitment to the organisation continued for almost two years after the Denning

Report and encompassed issues of the organisation's expertise and respectability.

Marriage guidance secured its grant in 1949 and emerged from the 1940s to all intents and purposes as a successful, respected and energetic organisation. However, it owed its early success to the way in which it articulated, and promised to help solve, a set of concerns about marriage and the family that were the product of a particular historical moment. These concerns were embedded in the formal 'principles' that were incorporated into the constitution of the National Marriage Guidance Council when it was set up in 1946 (see Appendix 2). To this extent, the movement's philosophy, if not its practice, was frozen in time.

RETHINKING SEXUAL MORALITY IN THE 1920s AND 1930s

During the 1920s, many taboos were lifted from the public discussion of sex, sexuality and the proper regulation of relationships between men and women. Not only were general issues, such as birth control, referred to relatively openly, but their implications for personal relationships were also discussed. The major significance of Marie Stopes' famous text, *Married Love*, published in 1918, was the way in which it discussed sexuality in marriage rather than the vague information it contained about birth control. While the consistent downward trend in both the birth rate and family size since the last quarter of the nineteenth century was achieved by the use of artificial contraception, the broader implications of the possibility of separating sex from reproduction remained taboo until after World War I. After the war, the whole tenor of the discussion was changed by the acknowledgement of two further crucial factors. The first was the work of psychoanalysts and sexologists on human sexuality, which attached great importance to the creative potential of the sex drive and re-evaluated female capacity for sexual pleasure. The second was the changing social position of women, which meant that marriage was no longer virtually the only means of financial support open to women, as had been the case in the late Victorian period, when the separation of public and private spheres had been rendered most complete for women of the middle classes (Davidoff and Hall 1986).

War loosened the traditional means of securing female purity, namely surveillance in the form of chaperonage, and ignorance. Thousands of young women, like Vera Brittain, who became nurses or joined the armed services gained information about both sex and birth control (Brittain 1933, Summers 1988). This, together with the greater range of career options open to single women, ensured that the kind of equal moral standard favoured by late nineteenth century social reformers and most feminists was not to be. Ideas about women's right to sexual pleasure also began to filter into public discourse, such that by the 1930s women's magazines could refer to the way in which Freud had made it possible for women to stake a claim to 'loverhood' as well as wife and motherhood. Remaining social purity campaigners, such as those working within the British Social Hygiene Council, observed a diminution in prostitution, but attacked what they viewed as a new menace: 'the amateur' (Rolfe 1935, 1949). Moral standards were becoming more equal between the sexes, but many commentators glumly regarded the process as having been one of levelling down rather than levelling up.[2]

Sexual radicals in the 1920s used the literature on sexuality and the evidence of changing social mores to demand sexual reform, particularly in respect of premarital relationships. The challenge to traditional Christian morality was profound. Church teaching had focused primarily on marriage as a means to legitimise procreation and as a remedy against sin. It was the latter which in the new climate became particularly hard to defend. The negative equation of sex with sin not only flew in the face of the findings of Freud and Havelock Ellis as to the creative expression of sexuality, but made many churchmen uneasy because it implied a certain denigration of the married state: better to marry than to burn. Those medical doctors who were as prepared as the sexual radicals to line up on the side of science rather than religious orthodoxy were happy to endorse a more frank and open discussion of sex that would, they hoped, pave the way for the acceptance of sex education and the free dissemination of birth control information, but they were not necessarily prepared to see all notions of traditional sexual morality thrown into the melting pot. Like many churchmen, they too engaged in a search for a new rationale for the old concepts of chastity and fidelity and by the 1930s there were as many signs of an urgent attempt to find a middle way that would combine science and religion in terms of sexual morality as there were in terms of politics (MacMillan 1938).[3]

Sex radicals

The small number of sex radicals – the British Sexology Society numbered about 250 members during the 1920s (Weeks 1981) – were anxious to promote the new understanding of sex and sexuality and to spearhead sexual reform. The most comprehensive volume on sex, written by the Dutchman, Van de Velde (1928), was translated into English by Stella Browne, a feminist, who campaigned strongly for access to abortion as well as for more sex education (Rowbotham 1977). Van de Velde's text, while explicit on all aspects of sexuality, was nevertheless conservative in its aim to celebrate 'married love'. This was the position commonly adopted by birth controllers, like Stopes, and those promoting sex education of all kinds, including E.F. Griffith in the 1930s. But the issue of premarital and extramarital sexual relations could not be wholly avoided.

The question of premarital sex was brought to the fore by an American judge, Ben Lindsey, who advocated something he called 'companionate marriage' as a means of regularising relations between young people who could not marry until their mid or late twenties for financial reasons (Lindsey and Evans 1928). The English edition of Lindsey's book was introduced by Dora Russell, another leading sex radical. Lindsey's position was above all pragmatic, but his ideas were used in Britain to open up the whole debate about the regulation of sexual relationships and marriage. Lindsey defined companionate marriage as 'legal marriage, with legalised birth control, and with the right to divorce by mutual consent for childless couples, usually without payment of alimony' (*ibid*. Preface). He took pains to emphasise that he was not advocating 'trial marriage' or 'free love'. His idea was merely to regulate childless marriage differently from marriages with children. However, the book was written in a singularly racy style, replete with illustrative stories about, for example, the fates of Hortense, Herbert, and Hattie the Home-breaker, and tended to stress rather than play down the case for experiment in relationships between men and women. Eustace Chesser (1952), one of the many doctors writing manuals on sex during and after World War II, was one of the few to point out that Lindsey's proposals were essentially designed to impose more rigorous control of sexuality among the unmarried. Like the English divorce reformers of 1909, Lindsey's chief goal was to secure the institution of marriage.

Bertrand Russell (1929: 108) hailed Lindsey as a 'wise conservative' and also argued for treating relationships with children differently from those without. But, as a radical, Russell went further by arguing that because children, rather than sex, were the purpose of marriage, there was in fact no need for any regulation of relationships not involving children. His definition of the purpose of marriage also enabled him to make radical proposals for divorce reform: desertion, insanity and mutual consent should be grounds for divorce, but adultery in and of itself should not. Only if birth control was practised unsuccessfully and an illegitimate child was born should grounds be given for divorce. Russell advocated stable marital relationships where children were involved, but believed these were best sought by distinguishing between marriage and merely sexual relationships and by emphasising the biological as opposed to the romantic aspect of married love. Proposals such as these, which were typical of the progressive case, relied on the use of scientific contraception, sex education and equal sexual freedom for both male and female partners. However, Russell, in a manner that was to become increasingly familiar, expressed major reservations about changes in the social and economic roles of husbands and wives, being particularly concerned about the erosion of the functions and authority of fathers.

Many of those who, like Russell, attended the Congresses of the World League for Sexual Reform engaged in practical efforts to further the cause of sex reform. Janet Chance, for example, opened a 'marriage education centre' in the East End in 1929, an experiment which came out of her work in the Walworth Birth Control Clinic and the lectures that she gave to Women's Cooperative Guild members. The new centre concentrated on providing women with information about 'marital hygiene' and information that would enhance their sexual satisfaction (Chance 1930, 1935a, 1935b). Chance's contacts with working class women confirmed the overwhelming impression conveyed by letters from members of the Women's Cooperative Guild, published in 1915 that few women either expected or found sexual pleasure in their marriages (Davies 1915). With the new-found emphasis on sexual pleasure as a crucial component of marriage, sex reformers set out to remedy this situation. In large measure, working women's negative view of sex was a product of fear of pregnancy, hence the close connection between sex reform and the birth control movement in the inter-war years. A centre such as Chance's added sex education and information on sexual technique to the information already being given by birth control clinics. This meant that opposition was incurred not just from traditionally minded churchmen who condemned artificial contraception and feared the kind of prescriptions for a new sexual morality being drawn up by progressives which were premised upon its use, but also from those who were anxious about any movement that might promote a further decline in the birth rate. Most sex reformers, moderate as well as radical, were forced to defend their proposals as ones that would promote a better quality, if not quantity, of population.

Moderate churchmen

Moderate churchmen answered the radicals' rationalist proposals to deregulate sexual relationships by redefining the nature and purpose of sex such that it became both positive and capable of its highest expression only within marriage. Moderate sexologists followed by devoting themselves to the promotion of sexual fulfilment within marriage. Herbert Gray, who became recognised as the founding father of marriage guidance, was a clergyman working with the Student Christian Movement in the 1920s, and became particularly influential in reconstructing the fabric of Christian sexual morality in the face of radical attack. In particular, his *Men, Women and God*, published in 1923, was successful in articulating an attractively positive and warm view of sexual relationships between men and women which had considerable influence.[4]

As a chaplain to the forces in World War I, Gray had written advice for young conscripts in accordance with the usual canons of the contemporary social purity movement, counselling the road to chastity via cold baths, early rising, exercise, sobriety, pure mindedness and refraining from rich food (Four Chaplains to the Forces 1919). The preoccupation of social purity campaigners, who worked through the British Social Hygiene Council during the inter-war years, with chastity and fidelity as the means to preventing venereal disease (VD) continued to constitute a major strand in Gray's writings, but in *Men, Women and God* he took a wider and more reflective view of male/female relationships. Addressing students, he began by stating that he did not believe 'in the power of fear to deliver us' (Gray 1923: Preface). Sex was God-given and should therefore be regarded as something beautiful to be studied and 'rightly understood' rather than as something sinful: 'I start in fact, with the faith that the sexual elements in our humanity once rightly understood and finely handled, make for the enrichment of human life, of the increase of our health and efficiency and the heightening of our joy' (*ibid*. xi). Traditional Christian morality had, he believed, made the mistake of separating the body from the spirit. Following the sexual psychologists, Gray argued that, correctly handled, sexual passion provided the driving force for life. It was crucial that sexual expression be the fruit of body, mind and spirit and it was this that distinguished love from lust. Love in turn was properly unselfish and permanent. Thus Gray arrived at the purpose of sex as an expression of married love. As such it had a procreative function – a baby made love perfectly unselfish and a 'call to service' (*ibid*. 37) – but also served to express the perfect union of the couple as one flesh. Gray stressed that this meant that both husbands and wives should enjoy sexual pleasure. While the functions of men and women biologically and socially were different, they were, he argued, equal in terms of their value as persons before God and in the expression of their sexuality as integral to their personalities. Gray was also advanced in his view of the possibility of 'comradeship' between men and women, which was essential if mutual understanding of sexual needs was to be furthered. Many contemporaries believed that sexual attraction made friendship between men and women a virtual impossibility; indeed this had been a major factor in the arguments of anti-suffragists, who did not believe that women would be able to mix freely with men in politics (or in paid employment) without catastrophic results.[5]

Gray thus painted a positive picture of sexual fulfilment, mutual support and equality (interpreted as respect for their different roles) between men and women. The idea of the matrimonial relationship as a microcosm of the polis, that was inherent in this vision, was not new. Edwardian writers had stressed the importance of marriage as an arena in which things might be arranged to provide mutual satisfaction as part and parcel of their arguments against any relaxation of the divorce laws. But in their writings the picture tended to be the more negative one of marriage as a necessary social discipline (e.g. Ward 1909). In Gray's view, responsibilities arose naturally from the attainment of a perfect love and the emphasis was placed on mutual satisfaction. It was an image that also pervaded the progressive sex manual literature. For example, Eustace Chesser (1952: 19) described marriage as the coming together of two free individuals to share their lives to their mutual enrichment: 'Thus the ideal marriage is an ideal community in miniature'. Gray made a point of acknowledging the writing of a leading post-war feminist and lay preacher, Maude Royden (1925, 1922), who also welcomed the way in which psychology had succeeded in 'lifting the veil' from sexual repression and had provided unmarried women in particular with a rationale for socially useful work (through the sublimation of their sexual energy) and married women with a recognition of their sexual needs. Like Gray, Royden argued that sex outside marriage must be motivated by the desire for bodily gratification, rather than by love, which was a product of mind, spirit and body. But Royden also admitted, as such revisionists were bound to do, that the institution of marriage did not necessarily make an immoral relationship, that is one without love, moral. Having defined sex as the expression of love, there was no logical reason why unselfish, longlasting love, uniting body, mind and spirit, could not be found outside the institution of marriage.

Both Gray and Royden were forced to admit this. Gray (1923), however, warned that while such non-marital sexual relationships were possible, they would be a mistake, because love could only be perfect when it issued in responsibilities (by which he meant children), and relationships with children required the governance of marriage. But in this he was forced back on reasoning not so dissimilar from that of Russell. Similarly, neither Gray nor Royden was able to deny the possibility of divorce for an impossibly loveless marriage. The problems faced in constructing a morality based on love rather than fear were to continue to set the terms of the debate about sexual relationships throughout the 1930s and the post-war years. John MacMurray's influential work of moral philosophy, published in 1935, which called for the development of emotional life, argued that the moral problem of sex was 'the problem of subordinating the functional relation of the sexes to their relation as persons' (1935: 113). He argued that sex was the expression of personality and could not be regulated by social institutions. Sexual morality had to come from within and could not be externally imposed. While MacMurray envisaged fully developed personalities practising a more deeply founded morality, his views were as likely to result in greater freedom in sexual relationships. Medical authors of sex manuals were also soon pointing out that marriage alone would not secure a moral sex relationship (e.g. Walker 1935).

Some of the thinking of moderate religious reformers like Gray penetrated the mainstream of the Church of England. The influential 1924 Conference on Christian Politics, Economics and Citizenship, which produced a number of volumes on a wide range of issues, certainly absorbed some of the new ideas. Gray sat on its committee charged with the task of considering 'the relationship of the sexes'. Its report accepted the crucial idea of sex as an expression not of sinful desire, but of love; acknowledged the desirability of men and women achieving sexual pleasure through the unity of mind, body and spirit, as well as engaging in sex as the means to procreation; and emphasised the creative possibilities of sexual energy in sublimated form (COPEC 1924). The report argued that sex could only properly be the expression of married love, and sex outside marriage was condemned as selfish and hence destructive to personality. The authors also felt optimistic about the possibility of genuine comradeship between men and women and hoped that this would eventually result in a lessening of sexual desire (see also Ingram 1930: 102). This had also been the hope of late Victorian social scientists, such as Herbert Spencer, who believed that as mankind became more completely evolved so 'animal passions' would be subdued. However, not all members of the committee could accept that the 'secondary ends', that is sex as a means to pleasure as opposed to purely procreation, were important enough to justify the use of birth control. The committee was also split on the issue of liberalising the divorce law. In regard to birth control, the Lambeth Conference of Bishops of the Church of England was prepared to go somewhat further in 1930 when it gave cautious approval to the use of artificial contraceptives in marriage, accepting that 'intercourse has also a secondary end within the natural sacrament of marriage', and recognising the rightness of sex in marriage emerging 'from the mists of shame' (Lambeth Conference 1930: 92, 85).

Moderate sexologists

The doctor who wrote and lectured on issues to do with sex and sexuality in the inter-war years, especially in the 1930s, were sympathetic to groups such as the World Congress for Sexual Reform in so far as they desired to lift the taboo from all aspects of sexual behaviour and to make it the legitimate focus for scientific concern. The editorial introduction to the new journal *Marriage Hygiene*, which published from 1934–37 and served as a forum for many sex reformers, both radical and moderate, stated its aim as securing 'for the science of conjugal hygiene a proper place in preventive medicine' (Editorial, Aug. 1934: 1). However, moderate sexologists tended to be more interested in various aspects of sex technology and technique than in reflecting on relationships between the sexes. They were radical in their willingness to discuss sex; in many of their proposals for sex reform, especially in terms of sex education and access to birth control information; and in their often strong opposition to traditional Christian views on sex and sexual morality. But their purposes were more often than not conservative. Van de Velde's important work on sex might have been translated into English by a sexual radical, but it condemned those whose political views threatened to bring sexology into disrepute (Van de Velde 1935). Nor was Van de Velde (1928) at all radical in his views as to male/female relationships. He acknowledged women's capacity for sexual pleasure, but saw husbands as the initiators and the 'natural educators' of their wives in sexual matters. Similarly, the American psychologists investigating sex and personality in the 1930s proved extremely hostile to Margaret Mead's ideas that nurture rather than nature explained sexual difference in personality (Terman and Cox Miles 1936: 461–2).

The doctors popularising ideas about the importance of sex education eschewed the church's traditional condemnation of sex as sin. But they accepted the essence of traditional Christian morality and were often motivated more by eugenic concerns to improve the quality of population – for example by the selective use of birth control by the unfit and by better mating to be secured by the premarital medical examination – than by anything else. Writers such as Griffith were as concerned as Russell to de-romanticise sex and marriage and to make it the subject of practical information, but as a means to securing more sexually satisfied couples with more, well-spaced, healthy children rather than as a step towards a new sexual morality. Nevertheless, it was not uncommon for moderate sexologists to suffer public condemnation. Eustace Chesser, for example, was prosecuted for publishing *Love Without Fear* in 1941. As he commented, it was assumed that because he wrote about sex he must be a radical in terms of his views on sexual morality, but this was not so (Chesser 1952). Chesser no more believed in free love or indeed in any fundamental reordering of male/female relationships than did any of the moderate sexologists.

E.F. Griffith was one of the leading moderate sexologists in the 1930s and 1940s. His *Modern Marriage* went through nineteen editions between 1935 and 1946. He was particularly committed to furthering sex education (including education in birth control technique) and stressed the importance of premarital medical examinations, which critics feared would inevitably increase premarital sexual activity. Reflecting on the opposition he encountered in trying to introduce premarital instruction as part of the work of the Guildford Birth Control Clinic during the 1930s, he wrote angrily: 'Nothing the day before marriage; anything afterwards. Completely illogical and unscientific of course. It even went so far that the County Council authorities thought it wise to limit our cases to married cases if we were to use their clinic'.[6]

Griffith followed other sexologists in making sex central to marriage (for example, Helena Wright, whose book, *The Sex Factor in Marriage* (1930), was also endorsed by Herbert Gray). Van de Velde (1928: 6) had concluded that sex was the 'foundation' of marriage. Kenneth Walker (1940), another doctor who wrote sex manuals over three decades, reported a Los Angeles study of 500 consecutive cases of unsuccessful marriages in which all but one had experienced problems of sexual maladjustment. Eustace Chesser, in *Love without Fear*, stated firmly that sex was both the 'foundation and motive power of marriage' (1941: 20). Maude Royden (1922: 179; 1925) had also begun to address the issue of sex technique in her comments on 'the sin of the bridegroom', concerning men's behaviour towards their often sexually ignorant wives on their wedding nights, and Gray had both commended her views and applauded efforts to give more information on sexual technique. But it was the sex manuals of the 1930s and 40s which gave explicit information on the technique of 'married love'. Griffith believed that sexual difficulties were the most common stumbling block to successful marriage and he devoted considerable time during the 1930s to lecturing for the British Social Hygiene Council, and after 1938 for the new marriage guidance council, on male and female anatomy and physiology, sexual morality, infertility problems, birth control, eugenic issues and sex technique.[7] Griffith and Walker agreed with Gray's position on sexual morality and opposed both trial and companionate marriage. But, placing as much emphasis as they did on sexual energy, they both favoured early marriage and the use of birth control until the couple had achieved 'full sexual adjustment' (Walker 1940: 110).

In the 1930s, the British Social Hygiene Council set up a number of sub-committees, including one on physical training and recreation and others on positive health and on marriage. In 1932 the Council produced a volume on *Preparation for Marriage*, edited by Kenneth Walker. It cited the view of the psychologist and eugenicist Crichton-Miller that a marriage was more likely to be successful if the partners had not 'kissed [anyone else] with significance' before marriage in support of its stand against premarital and extramarital sex, which was motivated as much by concern about VD as moral values (British Social Hygiene Council 1932: 57 and Crichton-Miller 1921). It emphasised sex in marriage as a 'positive ideal' and stressed the importance of education for marriage, urging that more attention should be given to preventing the beginning of marital disharmony than to its outcome in the form of divorce.

The British Social Hygiene Council's committee on marriage stressed a biological approach to sex and marriage: 'The modern conception of positive health which our Council can justly claim to be doing much to popularise, is based on a frank recognition of the fact that mental fitness and physical fitness are inextricably linked'.[8] Furthermore, 'fitness' depended in 'no small measure on the person's attitude to sex'. This was very much in line with the Council's predominant concerns about racial hygiene, but also consciously echoed the approach of the Peckham Health Centre, which was set up as a research experiment to test the ideas of its founders (George Scott Williamson and Innes Pearse) regarding the nature of health and the conditions necessary for its maintenance. It operated between 1926 and 1930, 1935 and 1939, and 1945 and 1950 as a family club, whereby each family paid a weekly subscription and all family members agreed to submit themselves to periodic 'health overhauls'. The Peckham Health Centre insisted that the married pair constituted the basic biological unit of society and the Centre's efforts were dedicated to promoting the orderly growth and development of family life. Williamson and Pearse claimed to be disinterested in the moral aspects of marriage, but were as concerned as the moderate sexologists to inject marriage with new purpose. They too stressed sexual fulfilment and planned families, but also hoped that the Centre would provide a means to 'social integration' combating the 'dissociated urban existence' of young families. A richer environment for the married couple would prevent 'disharmony, neurasthenia, inebriety, "suburban neurosis", causes for divorce, [and] parental neglect and incompetence' (Pearse and Crocker 1943, Pearse 1979, Lewis and Brookes 1983).[9] Williamson and Pearse also became interested in marriage guidance and became involved in the Family Welfare Association's war-time experiment in counselling, set up under the auspices of the Tavistock (see below).

Ideally, E. F. Griffith wanted to set up a Peckham-style centre for the teaching of birth control, general sex education, marriage preparation and sex research. In his early formulations for such a centre, Griffith took up the Peckham Health Centre's idea of a club with members paying a subscription and getting regular medical examinations, and envisaged the centre as an adjunct to the activities of the National Birth Control Association. He was anxious that it should serve the cause of eugenics and wrote to Paul Popenhoe, the director of the Los Angeles Institute of Family Relations for advice and information.[10] Popenhoe was a eugenicist who went so far as to suggest that there was strong evidence from the cases seen by his Institute that those divorcing were the less fit members of the community (Popenhoe 1935). By 1938, Griffith's ideas for a marriage centre had crystallised into a proposal to establish an Institute of Marriage and Sex Hygiene.

In the meantime, the British Social Hygiene Council's (BSHC) committee on marriage, of which Griffith was a member, had decided to break away from its parent body and rename itself the Marriage Guidance Committee, chiefly because the BHSC refused wholeheartedly to endorse the use of birth control (according to Griffith this was because it received considerable financial support from the Roman Catholic community (Griffith 1981)). The Committee endorsed contraception in the leaflet it produced early in 1938 addressed 'To Those About to Marry'. This was based in large part on the leaflet entitled 'To Those Thinking of Marriage' produced by the Birmingham group on marriage, which had been organised by Herbert Gray.[11] The Birmingham leaflet consisted of sixteen points, chief among which were: the idea that marriage was based on love and required self-control, which became a justification for arguing strongly against sex before marriage; that marriage was 'naturally' for children, but that the newly married couple would be well-advised to use birth control at first until they had weathered the period of sexual adjustment; that marriage was a partnership with husband and wife playing equal but different parts; and that both husband and wife should have a medical examination before marriage. The Marriage Guidance Committee leaflet, which according to Griffith proved difficult to draw up, started similarly by stating that 'marriage is not the goal but the starting point of a great adventure. It is union of body, mind and spirit, and its only true foundation is real love and mutual respect'. But it went on to place considerably more emphasis on premarital medical examinations, on the importance of birth control in spacing children, and on learning 'how sexual intercourse can be happily and healthily managed: Its mismanagement is a common cause of unhappiness in marriage'.

The members of the new Marriage Guidance Committee included Gray and Griffith; and the vast majority of the rest were medical.[12] The Committee carried on its work with a £75 grant from the Eugenics Society.[13] Late in 1938 the Committee issued a Memorandum on its work and stressed the need for 'scientific preparation for marriage' and for help with matrimonial problems. The main activity of the organisation was lecturing and all lectures had to be approved by the Committee.[14] As a charitable body, the Marriage Guidance Committee said that it hoped to demonstrate how such work might be carried out with the ultimate aim that it be recognised as part of a national scheme of preventive medicine.[15] This reflected both the preponderance of doctors on the Committee and the tenor of thinking of moderate sexologists such as Griffith. Griffith approached both Sir Farquhar Buzzard, Regius Professor of Medicine at Oxford, and John Ryle, Professor of Social Medicine, also at Oxford, to become president and vice-president respectively of the Marriage Guidance Council, but without success.[16]

Provincial branches of marriage guidance began to be established in 1938 and 1939, for example in Bath, Bristol and Sheffield. Griffith's correspondence showed that suspicion about the connections between marriage guidance and the birth control movement were strong, particularly among local clergy, but also among members of the medical profession opposed to contraception.[17] When speaking in public for the marriage guidance cause, as he did in Sheffield in 1939, Griffith stuck to the idea of sex education before marriage and information about birth control as providing the foundations for breeding a better quality race.[18] Thus at the outbreak of war, despite marriage guidance's roots in efforts to rethink the basis of traditional sexual morality, it was associated in the public mind more with contemporary concerns about the quality and quantity of population and with the work of medical experts on sex. The press tended to make fun of the latter. Reporting the establishment and the first conference of the marriage guidance council, the *Evening News* produced the headline 'The "Marriage Doctors" meet'; the *News Chronicle*: 'Scientists Plan to Make Happy Homes'; and the *Daily Mirror*: 'School of Marriage Founded to Teach Britain Happiness'.[19] But during World War II, the idea of marriage guidance was further legitimised by reference to the needs of race and nation in terms of population and stable families.

RATIONAL MARRIAGE AND POST-WAR PLANNING

World War II produced, first, a renewed concern about both the falling birth rate and the welfare of those children born and, secondly, as the war continued, profound anxiety about the effect of war-time dislocation on family life. Literature on sex education, including education for marriage and parenthood, as well as the more traditional warnings about VD, were distributed widely, especially among members of the armed forces; incentives to parenthood, particularly financial, in the form of family allowances, were widely canvassed; and problems of re-establishing relationships between women and children and returning male combatants were discussed. During the war Griffith was told by Lord Horder, who became the joint president of the reconstituted Marriage Guidance Council in 1943, of a request from the army for names of people to lecture on marriage and the family.[20] Similarly, the Probation Training Board approached marriage guidance about the possibility of providing regular training for its probation officers.[21]

In the later stages of the war and in the immediate post-war years, concern focused more centrally on problems of re-establishing family ties after the war. Child psychologists, particularly Bowlby (1951), stressed the importance of 'adequate' mothering, and increasingly the attention of the media, the church and politicians swung towards the 'epidemic' of divorce. Leading members of the medical profession, politicians and established pre-war commentators on the family, such as the founders of the Peckham Health Centre, warned of the imminent 'disintegration of the family' (Lewis 1986b). The marriage guidance movement was quick to portray itself as a valuable means of addressing these concerns.

Re-forming marriage guidance, 1941-43

The Marriage Guidance Committee was effectively disbanded at the outbreak of war, but the members did not lose touch with one another and by 1941 Gray was suggesting to Griffith that war-time conditions demanded the resuscitation of the Committee.[22] Griffith agreed and returned to his idea for establishing a marriage institute, now referred to as an Institute of Marriage and Parenthood and advocated by Griffith as a crucial part of post-war planning. Late in 1941, Griffith wrote to an American colleague that '. . . one of the major problems which we shall have to concern ourselves with after the War are the steps which have to be taken to increase the population and the methods by which parenthood can be encouraged'.[23] In his formal proposal for the Institute, he wrote that 'we have no policy regarding this vital problem [of population quality and quantity] which is one which strikes at the very root of the whole country and indeed the whole empire'. In addition he acknowledged 'an extensive alteration in the attitude of the general public towards social morality', which had emerged during the war:

On the one hand there is a greatly increased knowledge of certain aspects of sex, whilst on the other there is great ignorance, lack of understanding and a poor social conscience. We are living in a transition period when ideas are fluid and lacking in purpose or direction . . . the family unit would be strengthened if our young people received adequate instruction in social biology and psychology and were more effectively prepared for marriage.[24]

Gray welcomed Griffith's new initiative but felt, first, that his proposal should include more explicit reference to the intention to include clergy – as it stood the Institute sounded too exclusively medical – second, that cooperation with the British Social Hygiene Council would have to be sought in respect of sex education and, third, that Griffith's insistence on a thorough premarital examination, including stretching the hymen, would prove off-putting to many supporters.[25] Certainly Paul Cadbury, whom Gray approached with regard to the financing of Griffith's institute and who gave generously to marriage guidance after 1948, serving also on its Executive Committee, felt a more modest experiment involving both doctors and clergy was what was needed.[26]

A more modest proposal was put forward in the middle of 1942 by David Mace, a former non-conformist minister and associate of Gray and Griffith. Mace wrote to Griffith to say that he had asked Gray and the secretary of the old Marriage Guidance Committee, Marjorie Hume, to call together the remnants of the Committee to discuss his proposal, which he also wanted to compare with Griffith's own ideas for an Institute. Mace explained that he had completed his PhD research on the 'Christian Sex Ethic' and was anxious to get involved in a project that would be of practical use to married couples: 'My idea is roughly a movement parallel to that which has established the Child Guidance Clinics', he wrote.[27] But Mace did not envisage 'marriage guidance clinics' as resting firmly in the hands of professionals. Rather, he proposed that the staff should include a minimum of a doctor and a parson, the latter taking the place of the educationist on the child guidance clinic staff.

Mace thus proposed uniting the two main groups that had been involved in rethinking marriage in the 1920s and 1930s. Griffith replied: 'I think your idea is excellent, but I don't think we shall get anything through the MGC. They are full of nice ideas, but they have no money. We need a combination of businessmen, doctors and parsons to run this show, the fewer the parsons the better (with due deference to yourself!)'[28]. Griffith's suspicion of the more traditionally minded clergy, amply reinforced by his experience in helping to set up local marriage guidance committees in 1938 and 1939, together with his more ambitious medical aims, made him lukewarm about Mace's proposals.

However, when members of the old Marriage Guidance Committee met again in late 1942, they agreed to try Mace's humbler scheme. Griffith, after all, was no nearer finding financial backing for his Institute than he had been in 1938. Mace proposed that the committee be reconstituted as a Marriage Guidance Council, with considerable effort going into securing influential presidents and vice-presidents ideally representing both medicine and the church. The Council would oversee the delivery of a very similar range of services to that of Griffith's Institute: premarital guidance and medical examinations, guidance to married people concerning 'marital disharmonies based on physical causation', together with legal and spiritual advice. However, Mace planned to operate the marriage guidance centre itself with two co-directors, a parson and a doctor, one of whom would be full-time, and a voluntary panel of medical, legal and spiritual consultants. When the Centre was finally established in Duke Street, London, in 1943, it consisted of two rooms sandwiched between a chemist's shop on the ground floor and a flat used by a prostitute above. Mace, however, was clear that further monies would have to be found – he hoped by the influential members of the Council, who would provide marriage guidance with valuable publicity. He envisaged an organisation that was less exclusively medical and more a movement designed to capture the widespread war-time concern about marriage and the family: 'One of the vital tasks with which this country will have to concern itself after the War is the establishment of a social organisation directed towards the safeguarding and strengthening of the family unit'[29].

From the middle of 1942, Mace and his wife became the energetic directors of the new venture at a joint salary of £300 a year[30] and were in large measure responsible for the extraordinarily rapid growth in both the interest in and activities of marriage guidance. Those involved swiftly identified themselves as part of a 'movement' and Mace soon reported to Griffith that Dr Ethel Dukes, the pioneer of child guidance clinics, was ready to join the Marriage Guidance Council. Dukes represented another important motivating force within the MGC of the late 1940s, especially among the women who joined the Council. Her primary interest was in the welfare of children and the importance of both preventing divorce and promoting harmonious marriage. 'Problem children', she felt,

were produced mainly by stressful marriages, which offered little
by way of security or role models for the child (Dukes and Hay
1949: 41–3). While marriage guidance gained broadly based
support as an organisation which promised to strengthen marriage
and family, it would be wrong to conclude that it also achieved
overnight respectability. The services Mace planned to deliver were
still controversial. Many could not support any reference to birth
control, for example. Gray, Mace and Griffith were firm supporters
of contraception, but it became clear during the 1950s that not all
those attracted to the marriage guidance movement shared their
commitment. Mace also experienced difficulty on this score when
he tried to get the Archbishop of Canterbury to become one of the
new Council's presidents (together with the representative of the medical profession, Lord Horder). Eventually the Bishop of London
agreed to be associated with the new organisation as long as the
Council made it clear that scientific birth control was neither the only
nor the universally approved way of regulating families.[31] Marriage
guidance's purpose made it the subject of approbation and support,
but insofar as it insisted on addressing questions to do with sexual
relations and on counselling couples on these issues, it remained an
organisation on the edge of respectability.

The philosophy of marriage guidance, 1941–49

Gray, Griffith and Mace wrote extensively on marriage, sex and
marriage guidance during the 1940s. Gray (1938, 1941) and Mace
(1943) contributed between them three volumes to W. E. Boardman's
'Needs of Today' series. Mace also did a series of radio broadcasts
for the BBC, which was subsequently published, began a weekly
column for the *Star* newspaper, and published several books and
pamphlets on marriage guidance, aimed at 'the lay reader'. Griffith
continued to produce manuals on sex and marriage which, as his
titles indicated, were tied more closely to war-time concerns: *Sex
and Citizenship* (1941) and *Morals in the Melting Pot* (1948). By
1949, these three writers had succeeded in, first, drawing together and
publicising the strands of a distinctive marriage guidance philosophy
and, second, popularising it by relating it firmly to war-time anxieties
about divorce, the birth rate and the principles of sexual morality.

The first Appeal leaflet produced by the reconstituted MGC in
1942 urged that it was not enough to repair bombed houses;
homes needed mending too.[32] As early as 1944, Mace was using
the evidence provided by the 800 people who had visited the

London Marriage Guidance Centre over its first two years in support of the need for a new 'social and personal service' which he maintained would prove crucial to the work of post-war reconstruction.[33] Mace made a point of addressing explicitly the problem of marital infidelity in war-time in his books, journalism and in his radio broadcasts published under the title *Coming Home* (1946a), arguing that the rebuilding of marital relationships and family life, if necessary by the setting up of a Ministry of Family Welfare, was central to the task of reconstruction (Mace 1943: App. II; 1945a and b; 1946a). Similarly, Griffith (1947a: 14) insisted that 'the home and all that it stands for, must be the pivot of social reconstruction'.

By 1945, Mace was beginning to highlight the problems of extramarital conceptions and of divorce. Looking at the Registrar General's data on premarital conceptions for the period 1938–1943 (the 1938 Population Statistics Act had required the mother to register her age at the birth of the child for the first time), Mace (1945c) estimated that one woman in six had abandoned the idea of premarital chastity. His findings, published by the MGC, fuelled anxiety about sexual morality and the family and were discussed in the House of Commons in May 1946. In 1940, 56 per cent of divorces were granted on the grounds of adultery; by 1947, when the divorce rate peaked, this figure rose to 71 per cent (Phillips 1988). Mace also began to stress the increase in the number of marriage breakdowns, their cause and their cost to the Exchequer in terms of legal aid (freely available after 1946) and welfare benefits (1948a: 70, 79).

Griffith's lectures during the 1940s took as their main theme the importance of 'marriage and parenthood in a planned society'.[34] Griffith's ideas fitted easily with the new stress on planning. In 1941, he urged that planning did not necessarily involve Nazi-style 'regimentation' and went on to reiterate his eugenically inspired faith in education for marriage and parenthood as a necessary component in population planning: 'A sex relationship may be the private concern of individuals, the same cannot be said of marriage and children' (Griffith 1941: 160, 165). Griffith became increasingly forthright in his condemnation of couples who deliberately opted for childlessness at a time when demographers were issuing dire warnings about the future size of the British population in the light of population projections based on simple extrapolations of the falling birth rate (Griffith 1949: 330). And he became increasingly confident in his claims for the kind of rational sexual relations that could be produced by universal sex education: 'In a well-organised, intelligent society there would be no need to have abortions, illegitimacy, VD and all the rest for the simple reason that society wouldn't tolerate that sort of behaviour' (Griffith 1948: 48). 'Failures', as Griffith termed them, would be dealt with in a kindly manner, but his enthusiasm for state control was nevertheless chilling. In the case of those indulging in sex before marriage: 'I would like such people isolated from society and given a course of re-education and would not allow them to mix with the general public until they presented evidence of knowlege and stability' (*ibid.* 77).

Mace (1943: 99) was rather more in tune with the British and Allied language of post-war planning when he stressed that the family of the future would be more democratic and concerned more with fulfilment than duty. Ideas about freedom, equality and cooperation would make the family 'not so much an institution as a fellowship'. Government and voluntary organisations, he argued, should play a part in furthering these ideals by establishing a network of services for families, available at critical periods during the life course when the couple needed help. Mace was no less interventionist than Griffith, but he couched his ideas in a democratic rhetoric that had more in common with that being developed in other western countries during World War II, particularly by Gunnar and Alva Myrdal in Sweden (Myrdal 1941, Kalvemark 1980), than with the language of pre-war eugenics. The fact remained that Mace shared Griffith's views as to the proper ordering of sexual relationships.

The writings of Griffith, Gray and Mace all addressed the issue of sexual morality at great length during the 1940s. For Griffith, the emphasis on questions of morality was something of a new departure and it reflected the urgency of war-time concerns. The fundamental themes stressed by all three writers were those identified by Gray in the inter-war period: first, that the purpose of sex included pleasure as well as procreation, and indeed in its highest form became a measure of the development of personality; and, second, that man and woman, being equal in personality, derived equal sexual enjoyment, although sex was believed to mean something different to each, just as their roles and functions in society were different in the literature of the 1940s. These positions were developed further and tied more firmly to the needs of race and nation in order to justify the prohibition all these writers wished to make on premarital and extramarital sex. There were few dissidents from the line of argument developed by Griffith, Mace and Gray during the 1940s. One, Kenneth Ingram (1922, 1940, 1945), a lawyer and long-time writer on sex questions, underwent a major shift in views from that of an Anglo-Catholic (in the 1920s) to a socialist (by 1945), and began to argue a position that derived logically from much of Gray's early writings and that would become the focus for debate in the late 1950s and 1960s: that because sexual behaviour was based on love, then the presence or absence of love, rather than the presence or absence of the institution of marriage was the crucial thing.

War and the nature of Nazism gave additional impetus to those calling for more attention to be paid to the development of personality. Writing in the wake of the Munich Crisis, Peter Fletcher (1938), who in the 1960s was to write on marriage and sex with Kenneth Walker, condemned the intense individualism and lust for power that characterised modern western society and called for 'spiritual reconstruction'. He believed that in the family and the 'cement of personal affection' lay 'the way out of individuality into personality' and a means to social integration (*ibid*. 32). [Ten years later, the Reverend Kenneth Ball (1948) urged a spiritual approach to marriage preparation such that selfish and vacillating people might be turned into loving and dependable people.] The medical profession was also influenced by the renewed emphasis on the importance of integrating physical, mental and spiritual health, as was reflected in the brief but dramatic flowering of social medicine (Lewis 1986a; Jenkins 1949), to whose leaders Griffith (1947b) appealed on behalf of marriage guidance, asking them to prevent sexual maladjustment and thereby save marriages. But, paradoxically, war also provided impetus to sociobiological approaches to the family. When F. A. E. Crewe (1949), a professor of social medicine whose primary interest was in the question of population quantity and quality, wrote of sexuality in relation to self, society and the species in 1949, he stressed the overwhelming importance of reproductive sex.

Griffith's writings of the 1940s reflected both the absorption of much of Gray's earlier work and a greater urgency in tying these ideas to arguments about racial and national needs. He urged that those concerning themselves with marriage guidance work should have 'a clear idea of the most desirable qualities necessary for eugenic breeding' (Griffith 1947b: 10). For, the vast majority of people cannot see that the problems of our sex lives affect the whole structure of our civilization; that our attitude to sex colours the whole of our outlook on life. If our attitude to sex is creative our attitude to life is positive. If our attitude to sex is negative, our attitude to life is warped . . . If the war has done nothing else, it has presented the social problem in a new light illustrating the barreness of our moral structure, the hypocrisy of our behaviour and the confusion of our thinking . . . War by encouraging a materialistic outlook which pays little attention to the deeper values of life and often ignores the personality of those around us, merely accentuates selfishness and the desire to live in and for the present . . . There are six unsatisfactory conditions in social morality which owing to the fact that they have never been tackled satisfactorarily by the individual or the state, are undermining the family. They are: divorce and separation, sexual relations before marriage, extramarital relations, illegitimacy, abortion and VD.

(Griffith 1948: 73–4)

In this breathless summary of his case, Griffith showed how he too was now linking sexual enjoyment as one of the legitimate purposes of sex to the expression of a mature, well-developed personality, which by definition could be relied on to act selflessly. This would prove the guarantor of sexual morality as well as inspire a more communal and less individually oriented society. Non-marital sex as the selfish expression of bodily lust could only prove destructive of personality: 'To embark on any course of action which is intended to separate sexual energy from the whole personality is to cause disruption and tension' (Griffith 1941: 90). This was very similar to Gray's thinking during the inter-war years. By 1945, Gray in his turn was seeking to tie his views on sexual morality more firmly to national concerns, arguing that any sexual behaviour was wrong if it was based 'on a principle of conduct, which could not be made universal without social disaster' (Gray 1945: 1).

Gray also stressed that any sexual experimentation outside marriage was inevitably more perilous to women: 'many, including the writer, believe that the Christian rule which calls for chastity before marriage was made chiefly for the protection of women, who will discard it at their peril'. Gray conceived of marriage in a similar way to William Beveridge, who was considering the family in relation to social service provision, as an equal but different partnership of a male breadwinner and dependent female housewife and mother, and insisted additionally that the meaning of sex was fundamentally different for men and women. Whereas men desired gratification of bodily desire, women desired home and children. In the view of Griffith and most medical commentators (e.g. Spence 1946), the old idea that women could not be either physiologically or psychologically complete until they had born children was significantly reinforced by the discovery of hormones. Given his faith in the powers of sexual sublimation, Griffith no longer denied, as had his Victorian and many of his Edwardian predecessors, that childless women could be happy and useful, but the frustration of maternal desire was, he felt, an individual and a racial tragedy (Griffith 1941). In premarital or extramarital affairs women's desire for home and children was usually doomed to disappointment.

This line of argument, which was shared by Mace and by most writers on sexual questions in the 1940s, 50s and 60s, made women the guardians of sexual morality just as effectively as had the late Victorian double moral standard. Arising from deeply felt beliefs as to sexual difference, which had not been in the least eroded by the recognition of women's right to sexual pleasure, this interpretation of the meaning of sex fitted neatly with the late 1940s concern to encourage a higher birth rate and better quality mothering. As Gray wrote in 1941, on the modern 'dilemma' facing working women who married: in the case of those women who resented giving up their careers there was no solution other than for them to realise that motherhood and keeping a home were in themselves a career 'and a very high and lofty one for those whose eyes are opened' (1941: 74). Griffith went further, expressing the pious hope that

> when equality of personality and difference of function [between men and women] is admitted and respected, women will cease to be dissatisfied with the feminine role. We shall cease to see women endeavouring to evade their feminine responsibilities by adopting a masculine outlook to compensate for the supposed deficiencies of their own sex.
>
> (Griffith 1941: 65)

Like Beveridge, Gray and Griffith assumed that the inter-war pattern, whereby women quit work on marriage (in the professions, because marriage bars obliged them to do so) would continue in the post-war world. Even during the war, women with children under fourteen years of age were never conscripted (Summerfield 1984). These views as to the meaning of sex and sex roles would prove of fundamental importance to the nature of counselling offered by the marriage guidance movement in the 1950s and 1960s.

David Mace stated the same case as Griffith and Gray in a more robust fashion, with considerably more zest, and with more popular appeal. Whereas Gray's titles in the 'Needs of Tomorrow' series struck his usual moderate tone with *Successful Marriage* (1941) and *Love the One Solution* (1938), Mace asked bluntly in a 1943 title, *Does Sex Morality Matter?* He explained that he aimed to give a reasoned defence of Christian standards of chastity and fidelity and proceeded to deplore the way in which a single standard of morality had been achieved by 'levelling down' to that of men rather than 'levelling up' to the standard demanded of middle class women by the Victorians (Mace 1943: 17–20). In large measure, he blamed women themselves for this and particularly their apparent reluctance to concede to men any liberties they did not share, including promiscuous behaviour. Mace took for granted the basic rethinking of sex as having a secondary pleasurable function for both women and men, and addressed his argument to the need he perceived 'to regulate the balance between pleasure and responsibility in the realm of sex' (Mace 1943: 48). In this he was more explicitly backward looking than either Griffith or Gray, urging that more regard be paid to the way in which traditional Christian morality insisted on marriage as a long disciplinary process by which the urge to selfish sexual gratification was transformed by combining it with altruism – the unity of *eros* and *agape*. Nevertheless Mace agreed that the enforcement of the old morality by an appeal to fear would not do. New principles needs must be positive. This view was neatly summarised by Marjorie Hume, the first secretary of the MGC, in an article she wrote on sex education in 1949: 'There is a great need for a new moral standard of chastity outside marriage and faithfulness within, but based on "Thou shalt" rather than "Thou shalt not" . . . Unlike the old morality, it will have sympathy and understanding for those who fail but no lowering of the high level to be striven for' (Hume 1949: 239).

Mace therefore argued in favour of chastity and fidelity as high ideals necessary for individuals, but also for human welfare and national well-being. This nevertheless slipped easily into dire warnings of racial ruin if chastity and fidelity were abandoned. Similarly, when Mace took up the idea that women lose most in the practice of sex outside marriage, he tended to rely on scare tactics. If men were able to obtain sexual pleasure without incurring obligations, women should not complain if in future they were forced to bear the burden of parenthood alone. He concluded briskly on this theme in

1948: 'So really the woman defeats her own best interests by all this demand for sexual freedom . . . the true woman cheats herself out of her destiny if she is taken in by this sex equality stuff . . . it's only the unnatural masculine woman who can be satisfied for very long with sex alone' (Mace 1948a: 42–3: see also 1943: 54). 'Normal' women wanted homes and children.

Mace's position was not dissimilar from that of Eustace Chesser (1952: 89), who felt that the aim should be to re-establish the old morality, but also to ensure a better quality sex life in marriage. Sexual fulfilment in marriage represented the best guarantor of sexual morality. Like Griffith, Mace therefore devoted considerable attention to sexual difficulties in marriage: 'The sex life in marriage is like the base in a musical opposition; it should form a background which, while drawing no attention to itself, throws the melody into due prominence' (Mace 1943: 93). This meant that Mace was to teach that 'no normal marriage can in practice become satisfactory or stable at other levels until a reasonable degree of sexual harmony has been achieved' (1948: 122). And while 'sexual adjustment' meant satisfying orgasm for both the husband and wife, the sex needs of men and women were believed to be fundamentally different, reflecting the woman's need for protection and motherhood and the man's for urgent gratification of bodily desire, which in turn were symptomatic of their differing social roles. While Gray had stressed that sex was but one aspect of the expression of love, the reformulation of the basis of sexual morality had involved above all rethinking sexual behaviour. Thus a fundamental tension remained that became ever more apparent in the writings of Griffith and Mace: while they deplored any tendency to overemphasise sex, they believed sex to be fundamental to marriage.

Mace was often slipshod in his writing and unorthodox in his views, for example in his admiration for J. D. Unwin's (1934) doubtful thesis concerning the positive relationship between traditional sexual morality, the sublimation of sexual energy and levels of civilisation (Mace 1943: 44). Griffith expressed uneasiness about Mace's willingness to employ scare tactics, fearing that this would brand marriage guidance with a negative image. But Mace's approach was influential. His book *Does Sex Morality Matter?* was, for example, to convince Samuel Courtauld of the importance of marriage guidance and make him a wealthy patron of the movement (*Marriage Guidance* Feb. 48, p. 6). More than either Griffith's 'expertism' or Gray's moral philosophy, Mace's combination of robust views on the importance of traditional sexual morality and of sex in marriage embodied marriage guidance. Having recognised sex as a creative force and as having a purpose beyond procreation, the genie had somehow to be forced back into the bottle. Otherwise there was no reason why the ideas that Ingram had begun to formulate during the 1940s and which Middleton Murry took further in 1944, regarding morality vesting in the presence or absence of love rather than marriage, should not take hold. Mace provided the means of achieving this with his clear-cut, no-nonsense stand on chastity and fidelity, together with his willingness to be radical when talking of the importance of sex *in* marriage and of the allied issues of birth control, sexual technique and even divorce.

For while Gray, Griffith and Mace were all strongly opposed to sex outside marriage, they expressed less public opposition to divorce, believing that if more attention were given to marriage preparation and to the quality of married life, particularly in its sexual aspects, there would be less divorce anyway. Despite this, in his popular journalism, Mace (1946) adopted a position that has recently become fashionable again among social psychologists (Burgoyne, Ormrod and Richards 1987) – that it is worse for the children for their parents to part than to live with them, however conflict-ridden the home might be (Mace 1946b: 6). Gray also preached, as part of his emphasis on love, the importance of forgiveness. Even infidelity did not necessarily mean the complete loss of love (Gray 1941: 116). Griffith (1948: 100) went furthest in suggesting that the divorce law required reform. Believing that infidelity was 'often merely a cover for some deep-seated psychological disharmony', Griffith argued cogently against the idea that there had to be a guilty and an innocent party, and suggested that once marriage guidance was introduced into the picture it would bring an end to a situation in which one spouse often had to collude with the other in order to produce grounds for divorce in the form of adultery. Mace and the marriage guidance movement of the late 1940s did not get more generally involved in the controversy over divorce law reform, but rather stressed that

> we get the whole thing wrong when we talk as if divorce and separation were the real enemies we're up against . . . The real trouble lies further back. The true enemy we have to fight is the marriage which has got stuck and stopped growing.
>
> (Mace 1948 a: 111)

Thus, despite his scare tactics and repeated warnings about the rising divorce rate and number of premarital conceptions, Mace nevertheless managed to strike a positive note. Above all, at a time of moral panic about the disintegration of the family, he promised to mobilise an organisation that would both preserve traditional values in regard to sexual morality and make marriage more exciting and attractive. In his journalism he stressed the need to address the problem of dull marriages (Mace 1948c: 6). While both Griffith (1948: 284) and Mace (1948a: 53) stressed the importance of discussing questions of sexual morality in relation to religious and spiritual life, their spirituality manifested itself in the sense of mission that pervaded the marriage guidance movement of the late 1940s rather than in any fundamental rethinking of the Christian ethic, such as Gray had begun. More fundamental to both Griffith and Mace was the location of their commitment to the package of activities that they labelled marriage guidance within contemporary anxieties about the family. As Mace described it in the opening issue of the *Marriage Guidance Bulletin* in May 1947 and in his book *Marriage Crisis*, published in 1948: 'the battle of the family isn't going to be fought out in the end, in the realm of methods and techniques. It's going to be fought out in the realm of ideas – of standards and values' (Mace 1948a: 135–6). He believed marriage guidance had an important role to play in shaping these: 'Ranged against the disruptive forces of our time are certain organisations which stand for sound, stable family life' (Mace 1947a).

THE NATIONAL MARRIAGE GUIDANCE COUNCIL, 1947–49

Marriage guidance had proved its capacity to stand among such organisations by growing in four years from a handful of people in London to a movement with over one hundred active groups all over the country. Nor was it alone in its efforts. Graham J. Graham-Green started the Catholic Marriage Advisory Council in 1946 after coming in contact with the marital problems of servicemen in his work for an advisory organisation set up by the army, while his wife recognised a similar need in the course of her work among London's bombed out civilians. Graham-Green acknowledged the inspiration and encouragement of Mace, whom he referred to as 'a true Christian', but faced opposition from the Catholic hierarchy. In the event, a personal appeal to the Cardinal Archbishop of Westminster was successful in providing the necessary church backing for a separate Catholic Association that would take a sacramental view of marriage and oppose artificial contraception (Graham-Green 1967). At the same time, workers in the Citizens' Advice Bureaux (CABx) run by the Family Welfare Association (FWA) (called the Charity Organisation Society until 1946) urged the development of a service 'to help in rebuilding the large number of marriages which were on the verge of complete breakdown and by educative methods, to prevent such conditions arising' (Family Welfare Association 1946). The establishment of some local marriage guidance councils, for example in Liverpool, was similarly inspired by the experience of personal social service associations with marital problems.[35] During 1945–6, the MGC helped the CABx to train 30 workers for six centres and received £150 from the FWA in fees for so doing; however, developments in training for marital work were soon to mark out the programme initiated by the FWA as superior to that of the MGC.

The London-based MGC had become an incorporated society in 1944 with provincial groups affiliating to it as branches.[36] By 1946, proposals were on the table for the formation of a National Marriage Guidance Council (NMGC) to provide a coordinating headquarters, to campaign for new members, publish marriage guidance literature, advise and encourage local centres, convene meetings, undertake publicity, cooperate with other organisations, and organise the selection and training of counsellors. From the very first, it was clearly stated that the local centres must in time become 'the real strength' of the movement and must therefore retain autonomy of action.[37] The NMGC was set up in March 1946 with eight of the founder members of the MGC joining it to provide continuity. The funds of the MGC were split between the new body and the London MGC.[38] Local centres were expected at this stage to be self-supporting. The national body suggested that this be achieved through client contributions, the need for which should be 'communicated either on a card put up in the waiting room, on a slip of paper sent through the post when the appointment is made, or by word of mouth at the end of the interview'.[39] While the experience developed by the organisation to this date was vested firmly in the membership of the national body, the NMGC took upon itself responsibility only for standards of training and for providing marriage guidance with a public voice. It was left to local members of the movement to shape their own constitutions and to develop their own modes of working. At the inaugural conference in 1947, it was reported that 60 local centres had agreed to accept the principles and aims set out by the national body and thus qualified for 'constituent' status.[40]

The aims and principles of marriage guidance were set out clearly in a memorandum on its work issued in 1949. These remained essentially unchanged until 1968 (see Appendix 2). The first principle tied marriage guidance firmly to contemporary anxieties about the family: 'That the safeguarding of the family unit as the basis of our community life is of vital importance to the future welfare of the nation'. Subsequent principles stressed that 'the right foundation' for the family unit was monogamous marriage, which it was the 'public duty' to build up and protect. The most controversial principle, regarding birth control, was finally worded so as to support its use to assist the spacing of children, but to warn that it became 'a danger when misused to enable selfish and irresponsible people to escape the duties and disciplines of marriage and parenthood'. As a means to promoting marriage and the family, the NMGC envisaged three types of activities: first, educational work, emphasising the need to encourage a right attitude to sex in the young, to prepare young couples for marriage and to provide lectures for doctors, clergy and social workers; second, personal service work to provide help and guidance to the married and to refer them for treatment when necessary; and, third, research (NMGC 1949a). The second of these activities was the one that captured most public and political support, in large part because it was directly connected with the task of 'marriage saving'. Mace (1948b: 17) called the work of the London Marriage Guidance Council 'the constructive answer to the divorce court' and presented marriage guidance's task to the public as one of preventing and remedying 'the mediocre marriage'. However, in many respects, the public voice of marriage guidance, especially in the form of Mace's writing, amounted to a campaign to make marriage the subject of serious political social debate during the early years. To this extent, public education was an overarching preoccupation of the early marriage guidance movement. This was also true of the CMAC and to an even greater extent of the Jewish Marriage Education Council, which was formed in 1948, with an emphasis less on relationships and more on the cultivation of 'Jewish marriage', the 'Jewish home', and 'Jewish family life'. Marriage counselling *per se* did not begin in the JMEC until 1960.[41] The Scottish Marriage Guidance Council was also founded in 1948.

The NMGC still lacked an assured source of funding. An appeal through *The Times* correspondence column in 1947 raised £600, but, capitalising on the importance of its work to race and nation, Mace began to campaign in earnest for government support. The 'disintegration of the family' and in particular the high rate of divorce was the subject of Parliamentary debate and government inquiry in the late 1940s, and Mace's own writing in the form of his weekly articles in *The Star* and his scaremongering use of statistics on premarital conceptions and the cost of divorce were picked up in debate in the House of Commons in 1946. In the same year the government appointed a Committee of Inquiry under the Chairmanship of Lord Denning to look into procedure in matrimonial causes (PP. 1947, Cmd 7024). Its report made explicit reference to the need for reconciliation and to the work of both the probation service and the voluntary organisations active in the field.[42] Denning favoured the establishment of a 'marriage welfare service', sponsored by the state, but not a state institution, a common enough form of provision in many European countries, but rare in the British post-war society, where financing and provision were usually both tied to the state. Denning envisaged this as a new social service, evolving gradually in the manner of child guidance from the child welfare clinics, and the probation service from the court missionaries, with the aim of advocating marriage preparation, encouraging couples in trouble to seek help early, and of effecting reconciliation. While initially favouring a merger between the CMAC and the NMGC, Denning was persuaded by the verbal evidence of the Cardinal Archbishop of Westminster together with the written evidence of the CMAC, which stressed the organisation's different approach to both marriage and contraception, and its firm position on divorce, to recommend funding for both organisations. The CMAC suggested that a petition for divorce should not be permitted unless accompanied by a certificate from an approved 'Reconciliation Centre'.[43]

The House of Lords debate on the Denning Report encapsulated contemporary anxieties. Introducing the debate, the Marquess of Reading criticised the efforts of some government departments to encourage married women to remain in paid employment, fearing that without the re-establishment of traditional gender roles 'you will require greatly to enlarge the sphere of your reconciliation machinery, and even then it is unlikely to succeed' (Hansard, House of Lords, 23/3/47, col. 883). The Archbishop of Canterbury referred to the way in which each divorce created 'an area of poison and a centre of infection in the national life' (col. 887). The Archbishop told their Lordships that the church was virtually alone in struggling to stem the tide of divorce, but the Denning Committee's proposals to grant funds to marriage guidance organisations opened up the possibility of enlisting 'every citizen who cares for our national character and stability to re-establish the institution of marriage in our midst' (col. 888). Education for marriage, he concluded, was a crucial part of education for citizenship. Participants in the debate were enthusiastic at the prospect of marriage guidance organisations engaging in the battle for the family and explicitly assumed that marriage guidance volunteers would affirm the obligations of marriage. The Marquess of Reading pictured 'professional people' doing the work of helping and guiding, a view confirmed by Mace (1948b: 105) who stated simply: 'Obviously he [the counsellor] must be a person of some education and culture'. Mace also welcomed the idea of married women who had had to give up careers as social workers or doctors on marriage returning as volunteer marriage counsellors.

Despite the enthusiastic reception accorded the Denning Report, the government dragged its feet in providing money for the voluntary marriage guidance organisations. In the first place, as the Lord Chancellor warned in the course of the 1947 House of Lords debate, government was wary of intervening in marriage and of providing voluntary organisations with funding such that they might become arms of the state. The desire to preserve the voluntary character of marriage guidance work continued to pervade debates over the level of funding for it long after the principle of government grant had been finally established in 1949. The Archbishop of Canterbury also feared that state subsidy might be used to promote birth control, while the Lord Chancellor did not want to build up an organisation to cope with 50,000 divorces a year, a figure he considered quite exceptional. Furthermore, there were other issues concerning the competence and respectability of marriage guidance organisations, especially the NMGC, which caused government to hesitate over the question of funding. While the aims of marriage guidance appeared inherently respectable and in line with established thinking, both its capacity to carry them out and the respectability of its actual activities remained in doubt.

The much vaunted voluntary nature of the marriage guidance movement was both its strength and weakness. For it could provide government with little idea of either the precise ways in which it intended to carry out the aim of personal counselling, which had captured the imagination of the Denning Committee, or of the efficacy of its work. Marriage guidance had begun in the late 1930s with a firm medical orientation. A leading medical figure had been sought to become president of the Marriage Guidance Council and Griffith had wanted to see a marriage guidance service become part of the new National Health Service (Griffith 1944). In 1943, Griffith drew up a detailed medical case sheet for use in marital 'consultations', which was not unlike that used by the Peckham Health Centre and which required the collection of data on family and parental history, previous medical history, physical condition, sexual knowledge and psychological condition.[44]

Mace was quite prepared to give precedence to the medical approach.[45] In his own book on marriage counselling published in 1948, he stressed the importance of referring clients to the appropriate medical consultant and described marital disharmony as a 'disease' with two phases, the first of which he described as an unresolvable tension which remained an 'infected zone' and the cause of further trouble, and the second a 'chronic phase' (Mace 1948: 11, 50–1). However, Mace was the only full-time staff member of the London marriage guidance centre and he was not medically or otherwise professionally qualified. He nevertheless felt equipped to deal with psychological problems in particular and early on this raised the issue of professional competence within the marriage guidance council itself. Being constantly short of money Mace even asked Griffith to send him some of his private patients: 'I reckon on the psychological side I'm as well equipped as most people who are doing this work'.[46] Griffith, however, grew increasingly impatient of Mace's confidence in administering 'treatment' to couples 'presenting' with 'marital disharmony' and complained to Gray that Mace was overstepping his authority, suggesting that all cases should be reviewed by either the doctors or lawyers connected with the Council.[47] Gray agreed that Mace should have used the services of Griffith and Dr Ethel Dukes more, but pleaded that Mace was overworked. The controversy was serious enough for Mace to offer to resign but, as Gray observed, where would the movement have obtained another leader as energetic.[48] Adequate standards of marriage guidance work were initially hard to secure. At the end of 1945, the Home Office prohibited its probation officers from serving on local marriage guidance councils because of the incompetence shown by some councils, a position Mace had to work hard to reverse.[49]

Mace cheerfully acknowledged that marriage guidance in the late 1940s was feeling its way and had no real notion of what to do or how to do it. He reported that, among themselves, the pioneers of marriage counselling adopted the motto '"*solvitur ambulando*" – "you find the answer by getting on with the job"'. But this was hardly comforting to officials in the Home Office who were contemplating giving substantial sums of public money to an organisation working in the highly sensitive area of personal relationships.

The NMGC rapidly evolved both a method of counselling and a training for counsellors. Training began in 1946 with residential selection procedures based on a combination of the methods used by the War Office in selecting civil servants and by the Church of England in selecting ordinands (Wallis 1968: 174). The War Office

Selection Boards had come to regard personality as quantifiable and manageable, and had developed techniques of personality assessment (Miller and Rose 1988: 180). By 1947, candidates for marriage guidance work attended 48 lectures and worked for one year on probation before being finally accepted by the selection board, which always included one psychiatrist[50], although in practice a staged selection and training programme remained an ideal. Early in 1947 the Home Office commented wryly that it was to be 'the object' of the NMGC 'to select before, not after training in future'.[51] Marriage guidance volunteers could thus claim a degree of expertise, but their professional status remained in doubt and while they were soon able to settle on a name for themselves – marriage counsellor – their lack of medical expertise made it difficult to attach a label to those seeking their help. 'Patient' would not do and Mace (1948b: 37) initially felt that 'client' was too cold and impersonal. Marriage counsellors gradually passed from aiming to diagnose and refer to appropriate specialists, to offering some 'treatment' of their own. Mace described this in 1948 as essentially a process of adjudication. The counsellor listened to both the husband's and the wife's accounts of the marriage and 'guided' according to his/her interpretations of the cause of the trouble (Mace 1948b: 38–9). That interpretation was derived above all from assumptions as to the 'natural' differences in roles of men and women and of their understandings of the meaning of marriage.

Notwithstanding the emphasis marriage guidance attached to the development of its training programme, this approach appealed above all to a belief in a 'common-sense' rather than a 'scientific' approach to the solution of marital problems. To this extent, under Mace's leadership, marriage guidance avoided the 'expertism' advocated by the 1930s sexologists and envisaged by Griffith in the plans for his institute. The warmth and energy of marriage guidance and its readily accepted sense of mission and purpose made it a popular movement and attracted the criticism of the medical profession as the struggle for government funding intensified. Both Gray and Mace in particular felt 'called' to the work of marriage guidance. As Gray put it when writing in *Marriage Guidance* at the end of 1949: 'I have said that my belief in the marriage guidance movement came into being because a divine urge came upon a group of us – in other words because God called us to do this thing' (Gray 1949: 2). He added with equal fervour: 'If we do our work well, the divorce rate will go down in Britain'. Later, marriage guidance was to become less fervent and less certain, both as to the effect of its work on the divorce rate and indeed as to whether saving marriage was properly part of its concern. But in the late 1940s, this aspect of its character was very popular. Sir Stafford Cripps, for example, welcomed marriage guidance as 'a great spiritual adventure' (*Marriage Guidance*, July 1947, p.3).

Expertise was not always welcomed or thought necessary in 1940s British society, especially when dealing with personal relationships. In the House of Lords debate on the Denning Report, Viscount Simon gave his opinion that: 'Frankly I do not believe – this is perhaps a mistake – that it requires quite so much technical expertness [to counsel] as some people suppose . . . persons of good sense and sincere affection may be helpful here' (Hansard 27/3/47, col. 896). After all, as the Viscount pointed out, most people had offered advice to a friend in marital distress.

Common sense and zeal appealed to the public and politicians, but less so to the Home Office. In evidence to the Denning Committee, Home Office officials were scathing about the National Marriage Guidance Council's capacity to fulfil its aims, describing it as 'all brains and no body'.[52] These officials were attached to the Probation Department, which figured centrally in the decision to fund the voluntary marriage guidance organisations. The Probation Department was itself already involved in marriage guidance work and it is possible that there might have been an element of rivalry present in the judgement of its officials; later on in the 1950s there is evidence to suggest that probation officers felt that while they did more counselling than those working with the marriage guidance agencies, they were given less recognition. Certainly the claims of the NMGC must have appeared inflated to the Probation Department given the much greater volume of work being handled by probation officers.

Early in 1948, the Home Office appointed a Departmental Committee under the chairmanship of Sir Sidney Harris to investigate the whole issue of grants for the development of marriage guidance (PP. 1948, Cmd 7566). The Committee recommended unanimously that government grants be made to the NMGC, the FWA and the CMAC, but the Home Office remained unconvinced as to the competence of the NMGC in particular. Mace's submissions to the Home Office appealing for funding on behalf of the NMGC during 1947 had been extremely disorganised, especially in respect of the Council's balance sheets.[53] A Home Office official reported that Mace knew next to nothing about the finances, employees, or even the numbers of local marriage guidance councils.[54] However, he apparently made a favourable impression on the Lord Chancellor, who admired his energy, but who nevertheless had no faith that marriage guidance was the answer to the problem of divorce and was prepared only to give marriage guidance 'a try' in view of the fact that the churches apparently could not cope.[55]

In comparison, the Home Office officials were much more impressed by the work of the FWA. After a year's experience with its five marriage guidance centres, the FWA's Marriage Welfare Committee had decided not to continue that particular form of work, feeling that it put too great a strain on the CABx workers involved.[56] Instead, with the help of a Goldsmith's Company grant, the FWA opened two new centres in Hendon and Fulham which it hoped would focus on 'preventive' work. The direction of the centres was put in the hands of a Marriage Guidance Sub-Committee, consisting of FWA members, the two directors of the Peckham Health Centre, Scott Williamson and Innes Pearse, and two Tavistock staff, Professor A. T. M. Wilson and Isobel Menzies, a lay analyst. The work of the centres was tied firmly to the principle of family casework that informed the activities of the FWA as a whole, and it was decided to train staff, using the members of the Sub-Committee, to deal with a small number of cases in the early stages of marital breakdown. The work was envisaged as experimental in terms both of determining the causes of breakdown and the methods to prevent it. In keeping with the Peckham Health Centre's emphasis on the importance of studying 'normal' families, the centres approached their work from 'the angle of the healthy marriage' in an effort to find out at what stage tensions and difficulties arose rather than 'to try to cure marriages already at breaking point'. In its first formal report the Marriage Welfare Sub-Committee echoed the findings of the Peckham Health Centre in the stress it placed on the isolation of families, the lack of 'real' family life and the general 'malaise' in the two communities.[57] Initially called Family Advice Centres, they were eventually called Family Discussion Bureaux (Family Welfare Association 1949), which the Sub-Committee felt more accurately described their preventive work, as well as avoiding the stigmatising connotations of 'welfare'.

While Mace had urged the FWA to join the NMGC in applying for government funding at the end of 1947, the shift in the nature of the FWA's work led to competition rather than cooperation between the two agencies during 1948 as they vied for the advantage in their representations to the Harris Committee. At base the argument revolved around the emerging ideas as to the proper basis for marital work. These were to remain a focus of controversy. Mace reported to his executive that he had been forced to submit his evidence to the Harris Committee quickly because the FWA was maintaining that only casework could provide a satisfactory basis for marriage guidance.[58]

His concern was not without foundation. At the end of 1947 Astbury, the secretary of the FWA, told Home Office officials that he felt very uneasy about the quality of marriage guidance work in the provinces and that he felt there was no chance that voluntary workers of the right quality would be found in sufficient numbers.[59] In a lengthy memorandum prepared at the request of the Home Office in June 1948, A. T. M. Wilson stressed the importance of the revolution in casework practice that was occurring.[60] Social work was becoming increasingly aware of the need to move away from the middle class idea of personal services to families in economic distress to the psychoanalytically inspired concern with relationships within the family. He argued that voluntary casework must 'dissociate itself from overt attempts to deal with material need' if it were to tackle new problems and appeal to more than the working class. This was one of the first explicit appeals for family casework to shift its ground to the psychodynamic in the context of the welfare legislation of the 1945–9 period and the much heralded end of the poor law, and indeed of poverty. In the 1947 Younghusband report, social work was already depicted as concerned with individual and social needs rather than with material needs, but there was no mention of psychodynamics, which by the 1950s was central (Yelloly 1980). Up until World War II, the influence of psychodynamic theory on British social work had been restricted to the fields of psychiatric social work and child guidance. A. T. M. Wilson held up the idea of new family casework methods to the FWA as an approach designed to bridge past aims to achieve individual self-maintenance in a material sense, and the new preoccupations with self-support on the basis of normative adjustment. Post-war casework stressed a psychosocial concern with emotional and social well-being, and the constructive possibility of a warm, supportive and yet disciplined dynamic relationship between professional worker and client. During the 1950s, the relationship between casework and psychotherapy was to become a burning issue and the intensification of social workers' search for causality in personality, for example in the case of 'problem families', prompted the searing criticism of Baroness Wootton (Wootton 1959; Lewis 1986b).

Wilson's memorandum for the Home Office contended that marital problems were complex and not susceptible to amateur intervention. While he confessed to 'little or no direct experience of the work of special agencies concerned with marital problems', he felt that it did 'not seem unfair to say that the approach of most of these agencies is based on a mixture of what is called "common sense", ethical teaching, which may be overt or implicit, and crude biological instruction'.[61] He warned that common sense was particularly inappropriate and even dangerous to the client. In respect of ethics, there was, he argued, no correlation between marital difficulties and inadequate or intolerant social values. Therefore agencies such as the NMGC, which he discreetly omitted to mention, could have little role in treatment, although he allowed that they may have a part to play in preventive educational work in schools or ante-natal clinics. Other medical doctors, including C.P. Blacker, who was a leading member of the Eugenics Society, from which the MGC had received a small grant in 1938, was also of the opinion that it might be better to let the voluntary organisations involved in marriage guidance die a natural death because of the danger that unsuitable eccentrics might get involved.[62] Lay counselling in marriage guidance could be but an 'unfortunate stop gap' in Wilson's view. The way forward was to be found in experiments like the Family Discussion Bureaux (FDBx) where caseworkers would receive a more thorough psychodynamically informed training (by Wilson). Small wonder that at the end of the year the Marriage Welfare Sub-Committee fulsomely acknowledged the support of the Tavistock doctors in securing a Home Office grant.[63]

In October of 1948 a meeting between the Marriage Welfare Sub-Committee of the FWA and Mace appeared to reach a measure of agreement that marital problems required a range of experiments; that the FWA casework approach represented continuity in its work with the family and that, while the FDBx would do development work with a small number of cases, the NMGC would see a large number of 'emergency' cases.[64] However, Mace asked the Harris Committee to consider casework as a 'necessary auxiliary' to marriage guidance work and questioned whether the FWA should receive direct funding at all.[65]

However, the Home Office favoured the FDBx approach. A departmental minute of December 1949 recorded that 'they appear to be more aware of the complexity of the social need marriage guidance aims at meeting than one of the other two societies, and their approach is scientific and flexible with a desire to adjust their methods as their theories are proved or disproved'.[66] To the Home Office, the work of the Family Discussion Bureaux set up by the FWA represented more of a genuine experiment than that of either the NMGC or the CMAC, and the Harris Committee had called for the funding of experimental work in the marriage guidance field.

The Home Office was not entirely happy with the competence of the CMAC either, but felt it impolitic to deny it grant,[67] although the Church of England's Moral Welfare Council put in its own claim for monies in respect of its counselling work and the Archbishop of Canterbury was reported to be 'irked' by the grant given to the CMAC.[68] Many other agencies laid claim to government grant for marital work, including the Soldiers, Sailors and Airmen's Families Association and the Family Planning Association.[69] There was indeed often little to distinguish the counselling work of the marital agencies from that of less specialised organisations.

In fact, the Home Office would probably have preferred to fund the work of the Family Planning Association in dealing with marital sexual problems: 'The Departmental Committee were very favourably impressed by the witnesses from the FPA and were of the opinion that the Association's attitudes to the sexual problems of married couples was sounder than that of some other witnesses, including certain of those connected with the NMGC'.[70] But funding the leading birth control organisation was not politically feasible. Birth control was still not respectable and it was to take another twenty years for the FPA to receive financial support from government.

Marriage guidance also posed some problems for the Home Office in regard to respectability. While its purpose was conservative, its subject matter and the views of its leaders on issues such as birth control and divorce were often much more radical. All the founders of marriage guidance were united in their support of the use of artificial contraception, although this was sufficiently controversial an issue for there to be considerable dissent among the rank and file supporters of marriage guidance. Mace and his successor, A. J. Brayshaw, favoured cooperation with the Family Planning Association, but, as Margery Pyke shrewdly predicted after attending an MGC public meeting late in 1943[71], this proved unpopular with a large section of marriage guidance volunteers, despite the attention the movement paid to the eugenic arguments for birth control. Nevertheless, support for birth control was enshrined in the principles of the Marriage Guidance Council and actively promoted in the writings of its leaders. Similarly, while marriage guidance was devoted to saving marriages, this did not prevent Griffith especially advocating divorce law reform. Marriage guidance wanted to prevent divorce, but this did not mean that all its leaders necessarily defended the structure of the divorce laws, although there is evidence to suggest that by the late 1940s the views of the NMGC were hardening on this issue, in line with the organisation's eagerness to attach itself to those anxious to prevent further disintegration of the family. Certainly in the mid 1950s the NMGC threw its support behind the highly conservative recommendations of the Royal Commission on Marriage and Divorce (PP. 1956, Cmd 1678).

From the Home Office point of view, the crucial issue was the public image of marriage guidance. The marriage guidance organisations were operating in the highly sensitive area of private personal relationships and government officials expected that they should behave with extreme discretion. In his 1948 book on counselling, David Mace stressed the importance of local marriage guidance councils selecting neutral premises and putting up only a small sign to indicate their presence. Confidentiality and secretiveness were essential. Yet Mace was also a supreme populist and it was his journalism above all that gave the Home Office pause. In March 1948, a critical time in the negotiations over government funding, Mace wrote an article for *John Bull*, which appeared to endorse marriage bureaux and which prompted the bureaux concerned to say in their turn that they had received the endorsement of the General Secretary of the NMGC.[72] At the insistence of its membership the NMGC mounted its own investigation, under Brayshaw's leadership, into the procedures of marriage bureaux, which concluded that in future there must be no links between the NMGC and such organisations. The affair was a source of embarassment to the Home Office. While its officials concluded that there was no evidence of marriage bureaux being used for immoral purposes (the underlying fear), it deplored Mace's indiscretion: 'Dr Mace was ill-advised enough to write an article for *John Bull* in March 1948, commending the work of various marital agencies. He has been much too addicted to writing ill-advised articles for publication, partly because of his need of the money (he is paid for them) to enable the precarious finances of the NMGC to be kept going at all' [The articles had indeed served partially to pay Mace's salary].[73]

By the time of this Minute, the Home Office had made the decision to implement the Harris Report and provide the NMGC with funds for specified parts of its work for an experimental period. Education work was excluded, to NMGC's horror, for in a very real sense counselling was only one means to the greater end of promoting sound, stable family life.[74] The Home Office officials made it clear that they felt that educational activities could be self-supporting through the income earned from lectures and publications.[75] Nor were local centres given any direct grants. The Home Office grant was given initially for a five year period and provided the NMGC, the FWA and the CMAC with money for the training of marriage counsellors and for actual administrative costs. Notwithstanding the Home Office's doubts, the NMGC received the lion's share of £5000 compared to £1500 for each of the other two organisations. This decision was probably a function of both the much greater volume of work being done by the NMGC and the publicly expressed enthusiasm for it. The Harris Committee had felt that the remedial work of counselling was at the experimental stage and required both the development of training programmes and close supervision (PP. 1949, Cmd 7566, para. 14). One of the provisions of the Home Office grant was that a Joint Training Board be established with representatives from all three organisations and the Home Office, which was undoubtedly regarded as a way of safeguarding standards of practice. At the end of 1949, the Home Office again warned the NMGC, which had rushed to put in place a superannuation scheme for its staff, that it considered its work to be experimental rather than proven.[76] Home Office suspicion of both the NMGC's competence and publicity was slow to dissipate. It was one thing for marriage guidance to capture newspaper headlines and the attention of cartoonists, which it did regularly in the late 1940s, but another to advertise itself in what the Department deemed inappropriate ways. In particular the Home Office agreed with the Harris Report that 'any attempt at popularisation with a view to raising funds [such as Mace's journalism] may have undesirable consequences'.[77] The view of the Department was to change dramatically some forty years later.

For its part, the NMGC was delighted to receive government money, although Mace was reported by the Home Office officials to be 'antagonistic' towards government support of the FWA.[78] By the end of 1949, the NMGC was in buoyant mood. Its immediate future secured, Mace was optimistic that it would soon be able to become self-supporting, assuring the Home Office that 'it is our desire and intention not to allow this work to become parasitical on the public purse'.[79] The NMGC was as determined as participants in the House of Lords debate on the Denning Committee Report had been that the nature of its work demanded that it remain a voluntary organisation (*Marriage Guidance*, Oct. 1947: 2 and Jan. 1948: 3).

By 1949, the NMGC was an established organisation, both financially and in terms of its principles and aims. Marriage guidance in its first decade capitalised on contemporary anxieties about marriage and family life and also insisted on addressing the taboo topic of sex in marriage, which gave it a radical edge.

Marriage guidance characterised itself as a popular movement and was composed for the most part of committed volunteers, dedicated to promoting marriage. This image of a growing band of concerned citizens throughout the country, working for a cause acknowledged to be in the national interest, also made it possible for the organisation to develop a public discourse about private matters. However, when the NMGC was established as a formal organisation, its stated principles and aims reflected only its overarching desire to promote marriage and the family. During the 1950s, these principles were to define the organisation more closely. As Margery Pyke observed later in the 1950s, a list of principles 'looks so innocent but is such a drag'.[80] Having couched its work as part of the post-war desire to 'safeguard' the traditional family unit in the belief that its existence was crucial to the national welfare, those active in marriage guidance showed relatively little interest after 1950 in discussing the wider issues to do with either sexual morality and marriage, or male/female relationships. In this sense the organisation was more narrow and more conservative than it had been in the 1930s. It also meant that the marriage guidance movement was caught unawares by the radical shifts in attitudes towards sexual behaviour and in the changes in the law governing divorce during the late 1960s.

In its early years, marriage guidance was committed above all to the promotion of marriage and family life. Counselling was but a means to this larger end. Indeed, in the early years, education of the public through lectures and through the media was the organisation's primary activity. The terms of the Home Office grant inevitably meant that much more attention would be given to the work of counselling after 1949. Thus far, those involved in marriage guidance had taken pride in their voluntary and amateur status, but in the next phase of its existence the greater concentration on delivering a counselling service was to begin to produce tensions about the perceived need to become 'more professional'.

NOTES

1 A. P. Herbert introduced the 1936 Act which extended the grounds for divorce from simple adultery to desertion, cruelty and insanity. The term 'hotel divorces' was derived from the often carefully staged hotel scenes designed to provide the evidence needed for a divorce on the grounds of adultery. Herbert (1934) condemned the hypocrisy of these and was influential in creating the momentum for reform.
2 Beatrice Webb's Diary, 10/7/22, f. 3903, TS, BLPES.
3 Susan Kingsley Kent (1990) has suggested that the model of marital

accord built on the frank acknowledgement of the importance of sexual enjoyment in marriage was a response to the sexual disorder of war and was part of the post-war reconstruction of sexual relationships. But moderate churchmen and doctors were also responding to the sexual radicals of the 1920s.

4 *Men, Women and God* went through 16 editions between 1923 and 1946.

5 For example, this was the position of Mary Ward, a leading member of the National League for Opposing Women's Suffrage (Lewis 1991).

6 Griffith's introduction to his 1933–40 correspondence, 27/6/41, Griffith Papers A2, CMAC Wellcome Institute, London.

7 See Griffith Papers A14.

8 Minutes BSHC meeting, 20/4/37, Griffith papers A2.

9 'Suburban neurosis' was the forerunner of Betty Friedan's (1963) 'problem that has no name'. It was identified in the 1930s by doctors as a problem of young wives living isolated lives on the new suburban housing estates. As a solution they tended to recommend 'another baby' (see Taylor 1938).

10 Griffith to Popenhoe, 28/9/37, Griffith Papers A8.

11 'To Those Thinking of Marriage' and 'To Those about to Marry', 1938 draft leaflets, Griffith papers A2. See also Griffith (1981), p. 75 for a reference to the 'Birmingham Advisory Council on the Marriage Relationship'.

12 The other members were: Dr Blackett Jefferies, Dr Mary Collis, Dr Israel Feldman, Dr Doris Odlam, Dr Mona Rawlins, Mrs Pelling, Mrs Marjorie Hume (Secretary), R. Laydon Down MB and J. Burnett Race MB.

13 Minutes of the MGC Executive Committee, 25/5/38, Relate: NMG Archives, Herbert Gray College, Rugby.

14 MGC Exec. Minutes, 29/3/39.

15 'Memorandum on the Work of the Marriage Guidance Committee, 1938', Griffith Papers A2.

16 Griffith to Buzzard, 12/7/38, Griffith Papers A2 and Griffith to Ryle, 15/2/43, A11.

17 Griffith to Canon Pym, Bath, 9/12/38, and Gray to Griffith, nd, but circa Dec. 1938, Griffith Papers, A2.

18 'Sheffield Branch of Marriage Guidance Formed', *Sheffield Telegraph*, 24/3/39, Griffith Papers A2.

19 *Evening News*, 27/10/38; *News Chronicle*, 20/5/38; *Daily Mirror*, 20/5/38, Griffith Papers A42.

20 Dr Basil Yeaxlee to Horder, 29/3/43, Griffith Papers A11.

21 Mace to Committee, 8/4/43, Griffith Papers A11.

22 Gray to Griffith, 25/7/41, Griffith Papers A9.

23 Griffith to Harris, 9/9/41, Griffith Papers A9.

24 'Proposed Institute', 1941, Griffith Papers A9.

25 Gray to Griffith, 20/9/41, Griffith Papers A9.

26 Paul S. Cadbury to Gray, 17/10/41, Griffith Papers A9.

27 Mace to Griffith, 30/5/42, Griffith Papers A10.

28 Griffith to Mace, 5/6/42, Griffith Papers A10.

29 'Suggested Plan for the Establishment of a Marriage Guidance Centre', 1942, Griffith Papers A10.

30 MGC Executive Minutes, 1/9/43.

31 Bishop of London to Gray, 2/1/43, Griffith Papers A11.
32 MGC Draft Appeal Leaflet, 1942, Griffith Papers A10.
33 'Memo on the Need for a National Council for Family Welfare', MGC nd (circa 1944), FPA Archives, A13/69.1, CMAC Wellcome Institute, London.
34 'Lectures in the 1940s', Griffith Papers A15.
35 Report of a meeting with the FWA, 3/7/48, Documents relating to NMGC Executive Minutes. Personal Social Service Associations were established during the early twentieth century often as a counter to the local Charity Organisation Society.
36 NMGC Executive Minutes, 2/2/44.
37 *Ibid.*, 6/2/46.
38 *Ibid.*, 4/12/46.
39 *Ibid.*, 5/6/46.
40 *Ibid.*, 27/2/47.
41 JMEC AGM, 4/5/72, Chairman's Review, TS, JMEC Archives.
42 The Denning Committee was not the first to show an interest in the work of reconciliation. In the debate over the reform of the divorce laws in 1936, Lord Merrivale had argued for compulsory conciliation (a term used interchangeably with reconciliation before World War II) by probation officers for persons seeking divorce or separation in magistrate's courts (Hansard, H of L, 29/1/35; Merrivale 1936). The 1936 Harris Committee's Report (PP. 1936, Cmd 5122) on the operation of social services in magistrate's courts rejected the idea of routine conciliation, but nevertheless came out strongly in favour of the work probation officers were doing in this field.
43 'CMAC Memorandum for the Home Office', 21/10/46, PRO HO45/25202.
44 'Suggested Medical Case Sheet', 1943', Griffith Papers A11.
45 Mace to Griffith, 6/3/43, Griffith Papers A11.
46 Mace to Griffith, 21/10/42, Griffith Papers A10.
47 Griffith to Gray, 3/11/43, Griffith Papers A11.
48 Gray to Griffith, 11/11/43, Griffith Papers A11.
49 MGC Executive Minutes, 5/12/45 and 6/2/46.
50 NMGC Executive Minutes, 27/2/47. See also Mace (1948b, p. 107).
51 Miss Goode, Memorandum, 3/11/47, PRO HO45/25202.
52 Evidence to the Denning Committee by Ross Morton and Hutchinson, p. 13, PRO HO45/25202.
53 Mace to Miss Goode, 17/22/47, PRO HO45/25202.
54 Miss Goode, Memorandum, 5/9/47, *Ibid.*
55 Jowitt to J. Chuter Ede, 3/2/49, *Ibid.*
56 Mrs Eicholz, Memorandum on the work of the Marriage Welfare Sub-Committee of the FWA, October 1948, Minutes of the Administrative Committee, 14/10/48, FWA Records at the GLC Record Office A/FWA/C/A3/66. See also FWA Memo. to the Harris Committee, March 1948, PRO HO45/25203.
57 Report of the Marriage Welfare Sub-Committee of the FWA to the end of Nov. 1948, PRO HO45/25203.
58 NMGC Exec. Minutes, 17/3/48.
59 Miss Goode, Memorandum on the marriage guidance work of the FWA, 22/10/47, PRO HO45/25202.

60 A.T.M. Wilson, Memorandum prepared at the request of the Home Office, June 1948, PRO HO45/25203.

61 *Ibid*.

62 Minutes of the Departmental Committee on Grants for the Development of Marriage Guidance, June 1948, *Ibid*.

63 Minutes of the Admin. Cttee., FWA, 25/11/48, GLC A/FWA/C/A3/66.

64 Summary of a meeting between Mace and the FWA Marriage Welfare Cttee, Minutes of the Admin. Cttee, 26/10/48, *ibid*.

65 NMGC Exec. Mins, 20/10/48.

66 P. Boys Smith, Minute on the FWA, 6/12/49, PRO HO45/25203.

67 Miss Hornsby, Minute, 18/7/50, PRO HO45/25203.

68 Minute, 19/2/49, *ibid*.

69 Miss Goode, Minute, 9/2/49, *ibid*.

70 Miss Goode, Minute, 22/1/49, *ibid*.

71 M. Pyke to C. P. Blacker, 30/11/43, FPA Archives A13/69.1.

72 P. Boys Smith, Minute of a meeting with A. J. Brayshaw, 12/6/49, PRO HO45/25203.

73 Miss Goode, Minute, 27/7/49, PRO HO45/24688.

74 NMGC Exec. Mins. 15/12/48.

75 Miss Goode, Memorandum, 3/11/47, PRO HO45/25202.

76 P. Boys Smith, Minute, 6/12/49, PRO HO45/25203.

77 Goode to Taylor 28/5/51, *ibid*.

78 Minute, 19/2/49, *ibid*.

79 'NMGC Estimate of Annual Income Necessary to Provide the Effective Direction of a Marriage Guidance Service', nd, circa 1947, PRO HO45/25202.

80 M. Pyke to (?) 27/5/58, FPA Archives A13/69.2.

3 Private counselling versus public voice, 1948–68

In an address delivered by A. J. Brayshaw, general secretary of the NMGC, to its Annual Conference in 1960 (which had decided to exclude the press and engage in a frank discussion on the future) marriage guidance counsellors were congratulated on providing 'an expert service'.[1] It was only some twelve years since Mace had cheerfully admitted to 'learning by doing' and only five years since the NMGC had appointed a training officer, J. H. Wallis, with the task of developing its selection and training methods. The claim was obviously a large one. NMGC's training methods had been sharply criticised by the Home Office in the early 1950s and compared unfavourably to those of the Tavistock-influenced Family Discussion Bureaux. Wallis introduced new 'non-directive' counselling methods based on those of the American, Carl Rogers, and was beginning to elaborate a tutor system of supervision and support for counsellors, but understanding of his ideas was slow to diffuse throughout the organisation and the standards achieved by local marriage guidance councils varied enormously. Nevertheless, in terms of offering a widely available service, the NMGC remained virtually alone in the field, a position it guarded with increasing jealousy. The main competition at the end of the 1950s emanated not from the CMAC, which remained a small and rather closed organisation, nor from the Jewish Marriage Education Council, which still did no counselling, but from the Family Planning Association. By 1960 this challenge had been largely withdrawn, due to the strength of protest from within marriage guidance rather than any weakness on the part of the FPA, and in the work of counselling, A. J. Brayshaw could assure the movement that he was confident that all that was needed was further 'refinement' rather than any substantial change of direction.[2]

But as he also reminded his listeners in 1960, marriage guidance was not solely about counselling. Under Mace's direction, marriage counselling had been but one way – albeit the most original and the one attracting most attention and requiring most energy – of furthering the welfare of marriage and the family. Through his onslaughts via the media, Mace had also maintained the work of public education about the threats posed to the family in the wake of World War II and he had attached great importance to what he referred to as mass education. After Mace's departure to the USA at the end of 1949, marriage guidance continued to bask in the authority conferred on it by virtue of shared anxieties about the family, but there was no leader to continue to hold together the organisation's twin purposes of public education and marital counselling. Furthermore, by the early 1960s, significant strains developed, in regard to confidence in the mission of marriage guidance to promote marriage and the family, in other words in its public voice. Marriage guidance in the late 1940s had managed to be both conservative and radical: conservative in its view of sexual morality and radical in the importance it attached to sex in marriage. But when it formulated its ten principles (see Appendix 2), of necessity the conservatism showed. In particular, principle 5, which excluded the possibility of sex outside marriage, was to cause many members of the organisation increasing discomfort during the 1960s. But during the 1950s, marriage guidance appeared solidly to reflect the majority view on questions of sexual morality and the vote of confidence it received from the Royal Commission on Marriage and Divorce in 1956 confirmed its standing. However, just as the Royal Commission took its stand against changing the law on divorce, public attitudes began to change rapidly and marriage guidance was soon to appear out of date in its views on sex and marriage and divorce. No longer was it in the vanguard of debate on these subjects as in the earlier period, but rather found itself on the defensive.

As the public voice of marriage guidance faltered, counselling assumed a larger role within the organisation, becoming its *raison d'être* rather than merely a chosen method of fulfilling particular ambitions for marriage and family life. After Brayshaw's resignation in 1964, the officers of the NMGC heightened the attention they paid to developing counselling, which as a private, client-centred activity permitted practitioners to adopt a neutral stance on difficult questions of marital problems and sexual morality. By definition, the non-directive counsellor did not seek to impose his/her views on the client. It was no coincidence that in 1968 the vexing principle

5 was quietly abandoned. But the issue of whether the NMGC as an organisation was best placed to concentrate its energies on delivering a marital counselling service was not properly addressed.

PUBLIC CERTAINTY: INTERNAL DOUBTS, 1948–58

During the 1950s, the divorce rate fell back from the levels it reached in the wake of post-war dislocation (the number of dissolutions peaked in 1947 at 47,041, falling back to 29,096 in 1950). Marriage guidance was not afraid to claim its share of the credit[3] and most commentators agreed as to the value of marriage guidance despite the absence of any thorough attempt to evaluate its work. In 1952, the NMGC in common with many organisations and government departments received a cut in its grant from the Home Office. However, politicians reacted unfavourably and the cut was restored in full the following year. The House of Lords' debate on the subject of the NMGC's grant, initiated by Lord Merthyr (Chairman of NMGC's Council from 1951–58), rehearsed all the current anxieties about the family – particularly the perceived correlation between broken homes and juvenile delinquency – and extolled marriage guidance as an organisation holding the line on standards of morality and behaviour. The participants in the debate admitted their ignorance as to what marriage guidance actually did, but expressed their undiluted enthusiasm for what it set out to do (e.g. the Earl of Halifax, col. 1180). Viscount St Davids was not untypical in his exaggerated praise for its work: 'I would put this kind of work as almost more valuable than food. In this country we are a little short of food, but we are not dangerously starving. Personally I should be prepared to support a decrease in our food or an increase in its cost, rather than support a cut in this direction' (col. 1183–4). The unanimity was by any standards impressive. Only the government spokesman sounded a warning note: 'I believe we should deceive ourselves if we were to imagine that this terrible problem [divorce] can be overcome merely by an expansion of marriage guidance councils, because I do not think that it can' (Ld. Lloyd, col. 1189). Nevertheless the hope was invested in marriage guidance that it would prevent all sorts of social problems, principally by preventing divorce. In fact this was not wholly in accord with the NMGC's own position. Mace and Gray had been clear from the beginning that their main intention was to improve the welfare of marriages and, while deploring the increase in the divorce rate, at the level of the individual case their position was considerably more ambiguous. But while opinion – in the form of politicians, churchmen and lawyers – remained solidly in favour of holding the line on matters of sexual morality, this potential conflict between the organisation's public voice and its private practice did not become problematic.

During the 1950s marriage guidance was happy to affirm that the sum total of its work might be considered preventive in respect of divorce, while privately referring to counselling work as remedial, and even to present counselling as broadly in tune with the work of conciliation. In its Memorandum of Evidence to the Royal Commission on Marriage and Divorce, presented in 1952, it advocated the extension of conciliation work and urged that it be a voluntary service, evolving from existing (marriage guidance) organisations (NMGC 1952). At this stage, there was no clear dividing line in the thought or practice of marriage guidance between preventive and remedial work, conciliation and reconciliation. Counselling had not developed its own distinctive philosophy and vocabulary that in the end would eschew the idea of both conciliation and reconciliation as appropriate goals. In the meantime, counselling was there to be harnessed to marriage guidance's wider mission to safeguard and promote marriage and family life.

The Royal Commission on Marriage and Divorce, which included in its membership Alice Bragg (who was to become the President of the NMGC in 1958), devoted a whole section of its report to the importance of marriage guidance and conciliation. This was particularly significant in view of the conservatism of the report. The Royal Commission had been asked to inquire into the law on divorce 'having in mind the need to promote and maintain healthy and happy married life and to safeguard the interest and well-being of children' (PP. 1956, Cmnd 9678: terms of reference). The members of the Commission took this injunction extremely seriously, justifying their opposition to any relaxation in the divorce laws on the grounds that

> it is obvious that life-long marriage is the basis of a secure family life, and that to ensure their well-being children must have that background. We have therefore had in mind throughout our inquiry the importance of seeking ways and means of strengthening the resolution of husbands and wives to realise the ideal of a partnership for life.

(para. 37)[4]

The Commission viewed with great suspicion both the effects of women's 'emancipation', suggesting that some women did not realise that 'new rights do not release them from the obligations arising out of marriage' (para. 45), and modern psychology which, in their view, emphasised self-expression rather than self-discipline and overemphasised the importance of sex in marriage (para. 46). Above all, the Commissioners believed that it was the 'tendency to take the duties and responsibilities of marriage less seriously' (para. 47) that had resulted in the rise in the divorce rate. Their report repeatedly stressed the 'insidious' nature of this tendency (paras 47, 49, 50). Furthermore, their diagnosis meant that a harsher divorce law would not provide a remedy. Rather, the solution had to lie in education, which was why marriage guidance assumed such importance: 'It is our hope that a really marked extension in the work of education, pre-marital instruction, marriage guidance and conciliation would check the tendency . . . to resort too readily and too lightly to divorce' (para. 54). If this strategy failed, then, the Commissioners warned, it might indeed be better to abandon divorce altogether than risk the disastrous effects of large-scale marriage breakdown on society.

The position adopted by the Commission was considerably more conservative in many respects than that of Mace and the marriage guidance movement in the 1940s. While Mace viewed the rise in divorce with considerable alarm, and certainly shared the Commission's views on the position and behaviour of women, he did not condemn psychology, or indeed take so rigid a position on divorce itself. Marriage guidance had always endeavoured to avoid absolute pronouncements on divorce, preferring to make its target 'mediocre marriage' (Mace 1947b; 1952: 117) and to set forth its aim as a positive one of fostering 'successful marriage' (Brayshaw, 1952a: 7). For as Brayshaw admitted in 1952, marriage guidance workers were far from united in their position *vis-à-vis* the divorce laws, although he felt that they would agree that divorce represented failure. The first booklet issued by the NMGC to advise new local marriage guidance councils told workers that divorce was 'outside' the purview of marriage guidance in that it never fell to the lot of the counsellor to advise people on whether to divorce (NMGC 1949a: 12). Mace insisted in the late 1940s that what marriage guidance offered through its counselling was not a last minute rescue service, but rather 'a constant maintenance service' (Mace 1947b).

Nevertheless, the NMGC was happy to accept the Royal Commission's report uncritically in terms of both its diagnosis and its remedy. The recognition accorded education certainly represented something of a victory for marriage guidance, which had submitted a second Memorandum of Evidence on the subject which, strictly speaking, fell outside the Commission's terms of reference. As for 'conciliation', the report did not distinguish clearly between conciliation and reconciliation, suggesting only that the process of conciliation should start early enough for there to be a good prospect of reconciliation. At this stage, there was nothing in the thinking behind marriage counselling, other than the kind of desire expressed by Mace to foster a positive image, that prevented counsellors undertaking conciliation. But as the idea of counselling was elaborated in the late 1950s and early 1960s, it became much more difficult to contemplate this kind of work (see below pp. 103–11).

At the NMGC's Annual Conference in 1956, the report of the Royal Commission was welcomed as 'a milestone in our history' and delegates basked in the endorsement it provided for their work, which was reinforced in a special article in *The Times* (7/12/56). But marriage guidance also became associated with a conservative doctrine that in turn reflected the views of traditionally minded sections of the Establishment, particularly the Anglican Church (Church of England 1954). While in the wake of the Commission's report the Church of England's Moral Welfare Council asked its study groups to consider whether their local areas had adequate marriage guidance facilities (Church of England 1956), the reception of the Commission's report in other quarters was less favourable and this inevitably rebounded on the NMGC. In an ITV debate on the report, Brayshaw and Mrs Rose Hacker (a member of the NMGC's executive committee) found themselves facing criticism from Robert Pollard, of the Marriage Law Reform Council, and Frank Dawtry, secretary to the National Association of Probation Officers (*Marriage Guidance*, May 1956). While the latter merely stressed that the probation service was doing a lot more than the NMGC in the field of conciliation (probation officers saw some 25,892 clients in 1960, compared to the 13,000 couples seen by marriage guidance) (PP. 1962, Cmnd 1650: para. 123), the former accused marriage guidance of being overly religious and overly middle class. A similar charge had been levied by the Labour Women's Conference some three years earlier, when opposition to the reinstatement of the NMGC's full Home Office grant had been strongly voiced (*Marriage Guidance*, July 1953).

After the mid 1950s, the radical aspect of marriage guidance which insisted on discussing taboo subjects became much less visible to the population at large and instead cartoonists and press reports tended to portray the marriage counsellors as 'lumpy women in tweeds'. In its turn, marriage guidance became increasingly suspicious of contact with the popular press. In part this was a response to what marriage guidance viewed as press distortion of the nature of their membership and of their work, and in part it was the product of a desire to receive the respectful attention worthy of those doing a professional job of work. When Rose Hacker serialised parts of her sex education book, *Telling the Teenagers*, in the *Sunday Pictorial* in 1956, the executive of the NMGC objected, ostensibly because one of the articles gave details of a case, which broke the cardinal rule of confidentiality.[5] Articles in the quality newspapers were declared welcome, but for the rest it was decided that the organisation had best be 'careful'. Marriage guidance had travelled a long way down the road of respectability and away from a commitment to popularise its message on marriage and the family since Mace's weekly articles for *The Star* in the late 1940s. Opening NMGC's new headquarters in 1960, R. A. Butler, the Home Secretary, congratulated the organisation on its 'fine sense of publicity', but said that some of Mace's early articles had given him pause.[6] The most successful venture into the popular media during the 1950s was indirect, taking the form of press lunches which included the professional agony aunts who provided considerable publicity for marriage guidance in their columns.[7] But in 1959 Mace wrote critically from the USA of marriage guidance's failure to do enough for mass education (Mace 1959).

To a great extent marriage guidance's message about the importance of marriage and family – its public voice – was carried not so much by the popular press as by its education programmes in the early and mid 1950s. Its journal, *Marriage Guidance*,[8] reflected the larger concerns of its members and devoted a considerable amount of space to the social anxieties of the 1950s about family life: neglected children, 'problem families', juvenile delinquency and married women's employment. At the local level, marriage guidance councils often drew their chairmen from people concerned with one or other of these issues. Thus, notwithstanding the Probation Department of the Home Office's initial suspicion of marriage guidance and the rivalry sometimes expressed by the National Association of Probation Officers, probation officers were often closely involved with local marriage guidance work. In Liverpool, the medical officer of health, Dr Stallybrass, who started a marriage guidance committee within the Personal Service Society in 1947, was a leading writer on problem families at a time when the medical research on the subject was often carried out in conjunction with the Eugenics Society and emphasised mental deficiency as the major causal factor, casting doubt on whether such families were capable of living a 'normal life'. The NMGC also began to publish its own literature on marital problems. The first (1930s) pamphlet, *How to Treat a Young Wife* (reprinted in 1945 and subsequently, as *Sex in Marriage*), sold in excess of 35,000 copies. The period of Brayshaw's leadership of the organisation (1949–64) was the heyday of such 'information' literature. From the mid 1960s, as many pamphlets were produced on counselling techniques as on marriage and during the 1970s the publications department ceased to produce mass education literature.

In 1951, 52 of the 68 local marriage guidance councils reported having education programmes, which were estimated to reach 20,000 people in all.[9] Doubtless the volume of activity was spotty, but in the early 1950s the marriage guidance movement was small enough for the group of people interested in going out to spread the marriage guidance gospel both to know each other and to organise a solid programme of 'outreach' work that also served to project the public image of marriage guidance, whether through summer schools for teachers or lecturing to the WRAF at RAF stations. Lecturers in the early and mid 1950s were enthusiastic carriers of what one described as a message akin to that of preventive medicine: teach domestic budgeting and sex roles and people would be better able to survive marital stress and tension. Despite the enthusiasm for teaching social skills among a group of people who were all well educated but who had no specific training in such work, the public appetite for 'talks' was found, as ever, to be limited. By the late 1950s, marriage guidance was forced to rethink this part of its education work, but by this time its workers were no longer so confident of their message.

During the early 1950s the work of marriage counselling was more patchy than that of education. After a two day selection conference the trainee counsellor received six days training spread over a period of two years. At the end he or she (usually she) was visited by the field officer, Reg Pestell (later Lord Wells Pestell) and assessed. No further support was offered. Furthermore, the new counsellor was likely to find herself working for a small marriage guidance council with little support readily available. In 1954, 21 councils were reported not to have the one female and one male counsellor that was the minimum standard officially permitted by the NMGC.[10] Early in the 1950s, Pestell reported grimly that many local councils had but a 'dim understanding' of the principles and aims of marriage guidance and queried whether the extremely weak ones should be allowed to continue.[11] However, very few were shut down and most of those that did so closed on their own initiative. If a weak local council possessed a powerful local organiser or chairman it would usually survive.

In 1949, in its anxiety about the quality of marriage guidance training and work, the Home Office had recommended that training be provided by the universities on the social work model.[12] But the NMGC was already running its own training courses which included a substantial number of lectures, often given by academic staff. Indeed, the training in the early 1950s tended to be didactic, just as the counselling delivered to clients was described in terms much closer to reconciliation than psychotherapy. In an unpublished paper, Mace listed three aspects of the role of a counsellor in an interview with a client, which he reiterated in *Marriage Guidance* in 1952 (Mace 1952): catharsis, offering the client the opportunity 'to get it off his/her chest'; elucidation, helping people to see the nature of the problem; and finally mediation of their difficulties.[13]

The importance of 'hearing both sides' was reiterated by others during the early 1950s, despite the fact that in practice counsellors saw many more individuals than couples. To Brayshaw (1952a) it was this element of marriage guidance that enabled the counsellor to treat the marriage rather than the individual and thus fulfil the aims of the movement. During this early period, considerable suspicion and even hostility was expressed in the organisation's journal to any more theoretical approach to marital difficulties and especially to psychology. In large measure, marriage guidance workers were merely reflecting broader societal views. When Dr Alfred Torrie (1953) spoke to the Annual Conference on the subject of psychology, *Marriage Guidance* reported that because 'any word beginning with the suspect syllable "Psych" seems to be exceptionally open to misconstruction', he began by arguing that psychology had proved 'to be useful to productivity'. Even so the press reported his speech in terms of the psychiatrist trying again to do the work of the parson. At this stage marriage guidance attached most importance to the 'spiritual principles' informing its work. The difference between the selection process for marriage guidance and that of other organisations, readers of *Marriage Guidance* (May 1951: 3–4) were assured, was that everyone offered themselves 'humbly'. According to the Reverend J. Crowlesmith (who ran the Cambridge Marriage Guidance Council virtually single-handed for many years), marriage counsellors were united in their belief that marriage was God-given, love was spiritual, sex was a part and parcel of love rather than a sin, and marriage should result in parenthood if it were not to be selfish. The counsellor worked according to these principles, constantly guarding his 'inner life' to do so (Crowlesmith 1951). The secular insistence on self-awareness rather than 'inner life' and 'non-directiveness' rather than 'God-given principles' was not a part of the counselling of the early 1950s.

The Home Office representatives on the Marriage Guidance Training Board set up under the terms of the government grant to oversee training in all three marital agencies – the FDBx, the CMAC and the NMGC – remained unconvinced by the quality of NMGC's training. A report made in 1953 by the two government officials, one from the Probation Department of the Home Office and one from the Ministry of Education's Inspectorate, was extremely critical. The leaderless discussion element in the two day selection conferences, of which NMGC was so proud, was condemned as 'tense and not very revealing' and the training was criticised above all for its insularity. The officials felt also that the two day blocks of training were too intensive, while the content was too superficial and too didactic. They complained of too little liaison with other agencies and too little post-training support and supervision.[14] The position was nevertheless probably better than that prevailing in the CMAC, which refused to allow the Home Office officials entry on the grounds that their work was predominantly religious, which the Home Office apparently accepted (Brayshaw 1952b). As previously, the officials were most impressed by the 'calibre and professional competence' of the work of the FDB (the original two Family Discussion Bureaux became one in 1951), which was held up as an example to the other organisations: 'Although it would not be possible to train volunteer workers in a similar way, the MGC (sic) and the CMAC would do well to take cognizance of the approach and methods of the Bureau in considering their own training courses'.[15] The NMGC responded by sending four counsellors to do further training with the FDB, commenting sourly that even if it did not prove successful 'we would at least have shown that we are not unwilling to learn from other people'.[16]

While the Marriage Guidance Training Board inspectors admired the FDB for the professional approach that came from its close ties with the Tavistock trainers, the FWA itself had experienced some 'anxiety about adopting a Tavistock Institute outlook'.[17] The FWA's secretary, Astbury, told them that they must face the shift in focus from the material to personal relationships that was taking place in the field of casework (see above p. 80), but the adjustment was not made without considerable difficulty and soul-searching. In 1953, the Association managed to reach an accommodation between its past focus on the collection of full information about the family in order to promote economic independence and the post-war emphasis on family relationships and personal adjustment.[18] Drawing heavily on Una Cormack's definition of social casework, the FWA produced the following statement:

> The Association . . . sets out to help those who have found it impossible to adjust themselves satisfactorily to the society in which they live, or to deal adequately with personal and material problems while at the same time attempting to ease external and environmental pressures . . . The caseworker's task is to reinforce the client's inner capacity by releasing the feeling and anxieties that have hindered his adjustment, by helping him to appreciate the situation as it really is, and if necessary, by assisting him through direct intervention or encouragement to bring about an improvement in his environment.[19]

Nevertheless, the FWA admitted that the Bureau had found the medical/non-medical line increasingly hard to draw in their work.[20] From the first, the aim of the Tavistock doctors had been to see how much psychoanalytical training could be 'safely shared' with social workers working with marital problems (Bannister 1955: x–xi). Caseworkers were integrated with the medical services of the Tavistock's psychiatric clinic, and psychiatrists took the weekly case conferences. The training offered by the Bureau was described in terms that were to become commonplace in the NMGC by the early 1960s. Training was by case conference in which no case papers were used, rather: 'Throughout the whole supervision period the worker learns to develop the kind of *feeling* which is a firmly reliable guide to action' (Bannister 1955: 13 and 19, our itals). The FDB clearly insisted that there should be no pressure towards reconciliation.[21] By the late 1950s the FDB had been transferred to the Tavistock Institute of Human Relations and the claim of the FWA that, despite medical influence, it offered a distinctive, specialised, non-medical form of social work, became increasingly difficult to sustain (Woodhouse 1990: 79–80).

Despite the pressure exerted by the government representatives on the Marriage Guidance Training Board, the NMGC resisted moves to professionalise its training in line with the more medical approach taken by the FDB, although the issue of professional standards became increasingly difficult. Marriage guidance set out to use the volunteer labour of professional married women – Mace talked of using women doctors and social workers who had quit the workforce to have children – and rapidly came to the conclusion that the vast pool of married middle class female labour more generally could be called upon for part-time counselling work. Feminist writing of the 1950s, which was exceedingly moderate in tone, urged that women's skills be used in the national interest, but that it should be acceptable for a long break to be taken for childrearing. Such a 'bimodal' work pattern became characteristic for married women during the 1950s and 60s (Hakim 1979). Most writers agreed that such a pattern was preferable even to part-time employment of women with young children (Myrdal and Klein 1952; Hubback 1957).[22] But the three hours counselling a week for 40 weeks in the year required by marriage guidance of its volunteers was not so difficult to accommodate. Marriage counselling offered educated women interesting and possibly somewhat higher status voluntary work (there was after all training involved), as well as the opportunity for personal growth. Nevertheless, there were limitations imposed on the development of a training programme by the use of such a workforce, which were recognised in the 1953 report of the government inspectors. By the mid 1950s, the Home Office seemed to have accepted that the NMGC would continue to develop its own form of training suited to the kind of volunteer it used and the kind of service it offered. Indeed, the statistical analysis of marriage guidance work during 1952 and 1953 by Wallis and Booker (1958) revealed the average number of interviews per case to be only two and one half, information that was not included in the published text.[23] This smacked more of an emergency service than the 'constant maintenance service' referred to by Mace.

The relative weakness of the NMGC's training and practice in the early 1950s made it vulnerable to competition from other agencies. This came not so much from the FDB, which saw very few clients and was secure in developing an identity based on expertise in the psychodynamics of marital relationships, but from the expansion of the Family Planning Association. Both Mace and Brayshaw were eager to cooperate with the FPA and were firmly committed to the use of artificial contraception, but the membership of marriage guidance was split on the issue of birth control.[24] Marriage guidance's ninth principle, which acknowledged the use of birth control in 'assisting married couples to regulate the spacing of their children', also stressed that it became 'a danger when misused to enable selfish and irresponsible people to escape the duties and disciplines of marriage and parenthood' (NMGC 1949a). As Brayshaw acknowledged, it had been expressly framed to embrace all views on the subject.[25]

Because early marriage guidance put so much emphasis on sexual difficulties in marriage, correspondence between the two organisations was not unusual. As early as 1944, Mace urged the FPA to condemn a particular contraceptive that many marriage guidance clients had found unsatisfactory, but the FPA replied carefully that they did not condemn appliances, they only approved them and the one Mace complained about was not on their approved list.[26] The behaviour of the FPA proved time and again to be altogether more pragmatic and shrewd than the much more amateur zeal of marriage guidance. By 1951, the NMGC was worried that the FPA might extend the work of their clinic doctors into marriage counselling and sought a memorandum of agreement specifying the differences in function between the two organisations. Brayshaw hoped that this would dispel the 'coolness' that was beginning to exist between them: 'some of our people perhaps regarding your outlook as materialistic and some of your people perhaps regarding us as guilty of "uplift"'.[27] However, the FPA refused to set a limit on their future activities and the NMGC's suspicions were fuelled in 1954 by reports that FPA doctors were seeking training from the Tavistock doctors attached to the FDB.[28] The territorial nature of the dispute masked deeper fears in the NMGC about the fragility of its professional standing in the field. If the FPA doctors added marriage guidance to their repertoire, local marriage guidance councils might experience considerable difficulties in securing grant aid from their local authorities.

The news that the FPA was beginning to set up 'marriage welfare centres', thanks to a grant from Captain Oliver Bird[29] (who had also supported marriage guidance), prompted Brayshaw to propose amalgamating the two organisations in 1958. The suggestion was a 'bit startling' to the FPA in view of the past tenor of relations between the two organisations, and Brayshaw himself apparently admitted that he had his doubts about whether he could secure the agreement of his executive,[30] but the idea was not out of line with the priority the early marriage guidance movement had accorded mass education.

Brayshaw told his own executive that he did not think the Tavistock's 'perfectionist' approach to training and counselling would sit well with the FPA's 'mass productionist' approach in the long term, but that if marriage guidance did not try for greater cooperation with the FPA it risked falling 'between two stools'.[31] The FPA affirmed its willingness to cooperate, but marriage guidance continued to express anxiety that FPA doctors might begin to use the title 'marriage counsellor' when they had not received NMGC training.

Brayshaw's anxiety turned to outrage when at a meeting of 50 FPA doctors interested in doing marriage guidance work one, Helena Wright, whose 1930s views on the importance of sex in marriage had met with Herbert Gray's approval, spoke in favour of premarital sex. As Brayshaw wrote to Mrs Pyke: 'I know that pre-marital chastity is often treated as if it were a stuffy convention and nothing more, we do not take this view'.[32] In rather intemperate fashion he also complained to Sir Russell Brain, the vice-president of the NMGC and president of the FPA, which did little to heal the breach with the FPA, especially when Helena Wright had confined her comments to personal experience and had been in no way prescriptive, although by the late 1960s she was setting forth extremely radical views in favour of extramarital sex (Wright 1968). The FPA responded crisply: 'This sort of action [writing to Sir Russell Brain] can only have a bad effect on cooperation since it creates an impression that the MGC is so determined to make the FPA either to toe its line [on sexual morality] or to keep out of the field of marriage welfare, that it seizes any opportunity to force this issue'.[33] This perception of the NMGC's strategy was broadly correct. Marriage guidance might have wanted the protection that greater cooperation with the FPA could provide, but it was also hoisted on the petard of its firmly stated aims and principles. For while these served to mark out marriage guidance's message, they also, as Margery Pyke had perceived from the first, proved a barrier both to cooperation with other societies and to changing the NMGC's own ways of working, especially as social attitudes towards sexual morality began to change.

Nevertheless the FPA also recognised the NMGC's real difficulties, especially vis-à-vis the establishment of marriage welfare centres. Some local FPAs were guilty of trying to persuade local marriage guidance councils to become marriage welfare centres and the FPA as a whole was unwilling to accede to the NMGC's request that a marriage counsellor be in attendance at all marriage welfare councils. Finally, in 1960, the FPA promised not to extend the number of marriage welfare centres beyond twenty.[34]

Thus, while the public voice of marriage guidance received endorsement from the establishment and while the organisation felt confident and secure about its message, there was evidence, first, of lack of enthusiasm for its education programmes, second, of profound weakness in its counselling arm and, third, of vulnerability to perceived competition; marriage guidance also worried that the

Citizens Advice Bureaux were not referring clients to them.[35] The most obvious weakness was that of counselling. The combination of the NMGC's strongly stated principles and the lack of any clear distinction between counselling and guidance served to project a rather rigid image. In 1955, NMGC hired a new training officer, John Wallis, who was to struggle to give marriage counselling a new and more professional identity and to give it priority status within the organisation.

THE ELABORATION OF A COUNSELLING PHILOSOPHY, 1955–65

John Wallis was largely self-taught in terms of the principles and practice of counselling. His background was in teaching and business, with some knowledge of Adlerian analysis. He had chaired the early Marriage Guidance Committee's counselling sub-committee between 1943 and 1945 and worked as (an untrained) voluntary counsellor with a social centre in Slough for some years during the 1940s. Even this limited experience gave him the edge on his fellow NMGC officers when he arrived in 1955; at least he knew what it was like to deal with a hostile or anxious client in the counselling room. He is credited with pushing the principles and practice of marriage guidance work towards 'non-directive' counselling and with creating a system of support and supervision for counsellors beyond the stage of basic training.

However, ideas about alternative methods of counselling, mainly imported from the US, had been raised within marriage guidance before Wallis's arrival in 1955. David Mace was the first to ask in a more rigorous way what counselling consisted of, using his American vantage point. He informed readers of *Marriage Guidance* in 1951 about the debate in the US between directive and non-directive counselling and introduced the name of Carl Rogers to British readers. He explained that the non-directive school conceived of counselling as a professional relationship and that the most advanced considered that the counsellor should act solely as a sounding board (Mace 1951). For his part, Brayshaw (1951) confessed to being less than convinced by the American literature, which he viewed as ill-suited to the NMGC's clear statement of guiding principles. Apparently, many counsellors agreed with him. While the importance of being non-judgemental was readily conceded, one counsellor felt that the proponents of non-directive counselling were in danger of being much too passive:

I wonder whether non directive theories are not being pressed to such an extreme that we are in danger of 'falling over backwards'. The high priests of the new cult decree that at all costs the Counsellor must avoid the heinous crime of stating an opinion. The 'client' must just talk and talk until he has worked out his problems in his own way . . . I have heard it seriously argued (though not in MGC circles) that the interviewer should never ask any questions.

(Alfred 1953)

A psychiatrist, working as a consultant with marriage guidance, T. A. Ratcliffe (1953), tried to explain that 'non-directive' did not mean passive. But it was some years before the idea gained broad acceptance (see below, p. 233–7). Even after the practice of counselling became overwhelmingly non-directive, this particular anxiety was merely forced underground rather than disappearing altogether. As late as 1961, Wallis referred to the fact that he still heard 'jokes about the term non-directive and what it is (usually erroneously) taken to mean. It has become a term of good natured abuse, perhaps as a counter measure to the naughty word that advice has become' (Wallis 1961: 43). Non-directive counselling represented a substantial change in the counselling practice of marriage guidance; it was Wallis's strength that he managed to present the new idea in a manner that built on, rather than denigrated, the organisation's traditions.

When Wallis arrived, he set about the task of explaining the new principles of non-directive counselling in earnest. He summed up his main points in a talk he gave in 1955, contrasting the counsellor who demanded reasons and chased causes with one who listened to the way his client felt about the marriage. Wallis stressed that counselling was not just a matter of technique or psychology, but rather rested on the counsellor's own sensitive and intelligent understanding of life, in other words on the depth of insight into his or her own experience (Wallis 1955).[36] The emphasis on listening and on self-awareness in both counsellor and client, and the idea that what was needed was sensitivity rather than 'book learning', were to become the main tenets of marriage guidance counselling and Wallis's legacy to the organisation.

Wallis wrote copiously on marital counselling and addressed first the fear of many counsellors that failure to give advice involved abnegating responsibility. On the contrary, he argued, advice removed the responsibility for self from the client. The key was for the counsellor to establish a rapport with the client, to 'befriend'

him. This ideal differed little from the aim of caseworkers from
the 1870s onwards, but traditional caseworkers had then used their
position of trust to impose new behaviours on their clients. This was
forbidden the late 1950s marriage counsellor. Authoritarian attitudes,
Wallis contended, were fundamentally a response to threat and made
for dependency, obedience and discipline, but not for self-discipline.
In this he was supported by an influential study of the matrimonial
work of probation officers in the late 1950s, which concluded that
permissive approaches to the work were correlated with more
successful outcomes (Pollard 1962).

By listening, the counsellor could work out the elements of conflict
in the relationship. The task was then one of clarification. It was
pointless merely to articulate the problems for the client; he had
rather to be brought to the stage where he could see them for
himself (Wallis No. 13).[37] Nor was it necessary, Wallis argued, to
'hear both sides'. This might be common sense, 'but marital conflict
cannot be solved by common sense' (Wallis 1968: 125). Such a view
introduced the further fear on the part of some counsellors that a
more psychological approach to marriage guidance would result in
a focus on the individual rather than on the couple, a fear which
was not unfounded during the 1960s when marriage guidance
counsellors moved some distance away from the hitherto explicit
aim of treating the marital relationship. Above all, Wallis suggested
that the counsellor had to be able to see the client's behaviour as
an expression of feeling rather than thought. Crucially, the training
he developed came to reflect the counselling interview itself. Given
that the object of non-directive counselling was for the client to gain
insight, the goal for the trainee counsellor became self-awareness,
the assumption being that this would enable her to see what the
problem represented subjectively to the client. But this connection,
on which so much hinged, remained unproven. During the 1970s it
was to become subject to further mystification and counsellors and
trainers alike began to refer to the 'magic' of basic marriage guidance
residential training.

In some measure, the emphasis on listening and sensitivity training
was dictated by the need to train volunteers quickly and make sure
they did no damage to clients. But Wallis definitely saw non-directive
counselling as a 'practical skill' in its own right and took some
pains to distinguish it from psychotherapy on the one hand and
social work on the other: 'Counselling is the happy mean between
theorizing at the expense of daily reality and the tendency to see
these pressures as all important' (Wallis 1960a: 127). Here he was

associating psychotherapy with the former and social work with the latter. When Wallis acknowledged the more usual distinction between counselling and therapy – that the counsellor did not deal with the unconscious – he added that in practice the distinction was not so rigid (Wallis 1968a: 137). In his view, counselling undoubtedly tended to the therapy end of the spectrum. But marriage guidance generally remained extremely suspicious of theory. Counsellors were told that their work lay with the emotions and their success would depend on developing those aspects of their personality that would enable them to offer friendship and empathy to their clients.

It was this emphasis that allowed Wallis to build on the existing traditions of marriage guidance. In his books and pamphlets, he used the word 'love' rather than 'empathy'. Time and again he portrayed the marriage counsellor fulfilling the role usually played by the spouse in a happy marriage (e.g. Wallis No. 2). Accepting the client, understanding him as he was and helping him to understand himself amounted 'to another way of saying that all things are possible through love' (Wallis No. 8: 7). This harked back to the language of Gray and, while Wallis did not say so explicitly, Christian qualities of love and charity were good proxies for what selectors looked for in potential counsellors. In his study of counselling, published in the mid 1960s, Halmos (1965) listed, as his first element in the counsellor's faith, belief in the triumph of love over hatred and observed the way in which what he called 'vitalistic psychology' had reinforced 'traditional ethical regimens of love, sympathy, and reverential notions of spirituality' (*ibid*. 192), although Halmos was concerned chiefly to demonstrate the triumph of counselling in the context of the 'end of ideology' rather than to point to continuities in its philosophy. It was in large part these continuities that made marriage counselling so resistant to other methods, for example those based on behavioural theories. While disclaiming any knowledge of the latter, Wallis contended that they could play no role in marriage counselling because there was no 'correct' behaviour in marriage (Wallis 1963a). Certainly it was the connections Wallis made between non-directive counselling and the older marriage guidance traditions that evoked a positive response from counsellors. Nancy Holt (1958) stressed the importance of 'lovingly accepting' the client and Esther Adams (1958) linked non-directive counselling to the work of Martin Buber, who proved enormously influential within marriage guidance on the I/Thou relationship: love being the responsibility of an I for a Thou.

Counsellors using non-directive methods did struggle to 'accept' their clients and to help them understand the nature of their difficulties. But this did not necessarily mean that they had no views of their own about how marriage *should* work, and it necessarily remains a moot point as to how far these affected the way in which they pushed clients towards a particular interpretation of their problems. However much Wallis warned of the dangers of the counsellor having a clear idea of what constituted a 'normal' marital relationship,[38] he himself clearly operated with assumptions as to how marriages worked best and restated these at length in his work, without seemingly perceiving the extent to which they were socially contructed rather than 'natural'. Not surprisingly, the most striking of these assumptions concerned the appropriate roles of husband and wife. If anything, Wallis was more conservative and more rigid than Mace in his thinking on this subject. His insistence on reversing the usual convention of using the pronoun 'she' for the counsellor and 'he' for the client signalled a certain insensitivity on this score, while his self-confessed embarrassment (in 1968) at the title of the NMGC's first publication – *How to Treat a Young Wife* – seemed to turn more on what he perceived as its 'feminist title' than anything else (Wallis 1968a: 164). In a book published in 1963 on marriage, Wallis took as his main theme the importance of whether the wife felt it was a good or bad thing to be born a woman. If she tried to play the role of the man and 'wear the trousers' or was resentful about her domestic responsibilities trouble would surely follow. Husbands' expectations would be affected by the extent to which their mothers had adjusted to the role of wife and mother (Wallis 1963b: 23 and 79). While Wallis went on to say that, in an age of female emancipation, sex roles were not fixed, the emphasis of the book was nevertheless on the need for the *wife* to adjust to what were considered to be her proper responsibilities. There was very little discussion of the husband's role, the assumption being that the responsibility of breadwinning was clear and accepted. Only women were showing signs of behaving problematically: 'normal' women would like being women and want to be mothers, and would therefore be happy to stop work on marriage (*ibid*. 87).

The contributions in *Marriage Guidance* (April 1955) on this issue (mostly from women) broadly agreed with Wallis. Writers describing themselves as feminists also stressed the importance of mothers staying at home to look after their children, albeit emphasising that societal adjustments were needed to enable women either to take career breaks or work part-time. Wallis's emphasis on the need for each wife to settle down to her job of wife and motherhood could not but result in blaming the individual woman if she failed to succeed. Like many commentators on marriage and the family,

Wallis remained attached to the idea of innate sexual difference (see also Walker 1957: 163). As late as 1970, he recalled that the Adlerians had used the term 'masculine protest' for women whose attitude towards men was one of envy or hostility. While he confessed to finding little evidence of 'basic differences' in personality, he felt it impossible to 'neglect' such ideas and concepts entirely (Wallis 1970: 146). In another passage in the same book, he exhibited less caution, asserting that men were probably less inherently promiscuous than women, wishing only that their wives should play many roles and resorting to 'other women' only out of desperation (the implicit accusation being when their wives 'failed' them).

This emphasis on female failings was common to many other analyses of social problems centring on the family during the 1950s and 1960s. Work by psychologists on children deprived of their parents during the war, either by death or as a result of evacuation, helped to bring home to a wider audience the idea that the mother was crucial to the child's normal development. Influential child development theorists, many of whom, like Winnicott, acted as their own popularisers, saw the mother/child relationship as the key to healthy child development and the 'adequacy' of the mother as the most important variable (Riley 1983). Winnicott (1958: 88) told his radio listeners in the 1950s: 'Talk about women not wanting to be housewives seems to me just nonsense, because nowhere else but in her own home is a woman in such command'. The importance of continuous mothering received its most influential support from the work of Bowlby (1946, 1951), who made a direct connection between 'affectionlessness', or 'maternal deprivation', and delinquency. Women's work outside the home therefore stood condemned as likely to produce juvenile delinquency, something that marriage guidance was both perceived as, and advertised itself as, preventing. Basil Henriques (1955), an influential East London magistrate, was convinced of the importance of bolstering traditional family life as a means to ending child neglect and delinquency and was also a firm supporter of marriage guidance. Earlier in the century, women had been perceived as ignorant and in need of education (Lewis 1980), but in the post-war period child neglect became interpreted as a sign of maternal inadequacy while, as Linda Gordon (1989) has observed, marital violence also became a sign of wifely dysfunction. The focus on women's need to adjust to their proper tasks of wife and motherhood was all-pervasive.

In many respects the parallels that existed between the approach of the NMGC to intimate relationships and those of professionals can only have enhanced the image of the organisation. Similarly, the greater correspondence between non-directive counselling and the work of the FDB, which was considered by the Home Office to be so much more advanced (even though its standing within the Tavistock world of psychiatry was relatively low), helped to provide marriage guidance with a somewhat more professional standing. Professionalism, or lack of it, was a source of continuing concern to the organisation. The emphasis it placed on the importance of selection was often invoked as a way of playing down amateurism and of stressing that marriage guidance was a 'sophisticated modern movement' (Parr 1962). However, the wide disparities between the quality of work done by different local councils and the evidence of lack of understanding and, in some cases, opposition to Wallis's ideas about counselling made these claims shaky. Reg Pestell, the field officer, provided a graphic description in 1960 of a counsellor who gave little thought to disappearing for weeks at a time and urged that 'counsellors must stand in relation to the client as something more than a passive bucket into which the client is encouraged to be emotionally sick'.[39] All too often it seemed that in practice non-directive counselling did become passive listening. In addition, the standards of the training itself remained somewhat doubtful. At the closed Annual Conference of 1960, Wallis pointed out forcefully that while marriage guidance talked of training its counsellors over a year they in fact received eight days of training interspersed with practical experience with clients, with virtually no supervision or support.[40] Certainly, one officer of the NMGC in the 1970s remembered that when he trained in the early 1960s the day-long sessions compared poorly to those he had participated in as a probation officer with the FDB, consisting mainly of members of the group reading paragraphs from a manual in turn. Only the case discussion groups (taken at that time by either a psychiatrist or the sole regional officer, Eric Parr) proved rewarding. Possibly it was this worst kind of didactic teaching that made Wallis encourage trainers in the 1960s not to use any written material at all.

Despite the movement towards developing a more consciously non-directive method, marriage guidance continued to lag far behind training developments in the FDB, which by the early 1960s had become more consciously theoretical. At a conference held at the FDB in 1961, Lily Pincus (who had been employed from the first at one of the two early Bureaux) explained that the central theoretical idea underlying the Bureau's work was that 'each marriage must be conceived of as a psychodynamic entity'; the dynamic of the marital interaction provided the focus for the caseworker (Pincus 1962: 8). She stressed that this did not simply mean working with both partners or trying to effect reconciliation, but rather looking at the individual and trying to understand what he was doing in the marriage, what was being unconsciously expressed for him by the other, and which of his own internal conflicts he was unconsciously trying to solve in what was going on. The idea of the marital relationship as a 'container' in which the most powerful feelings, good and bad, were expressed came to be one of the FDB's most powerful conceptual tools. When the FDB changed its name in 1968 to the Institute of Marital Studies (IMS) it did so in order to reflect more effectively its investment in training and research based on therapeutic practice. The contrast with the debates in marriage guidance over non-directive counselling was extreme. Erika Stapleton, one of the first tutors to be appointed by the NMGC, puzzled in the April 1964 issue of *Marriage Guidance* about the hostility to 'that bugbear psychology' and the barriers it imposed on the development of skill, insight and understanding. On the occasion of the NMGC's 30th anniversary in 1977, John Wallis recalled that in the 1960s it had been decided to drop the name of a potential speaker for the Annual Conference when it was found that he had been psychoanalysed (Wallis 1977). As the FPA revealed to Brayshaw early in the 1960s, the FDB trainers, particularly Dr Enid Balint, had a singularly poor opinion of marriage guidance's methods.[41] In his history of the Tavistock Clinic, published in 1970, H.V. Dicks saw fit to put his reference to marriage guidance counsellors in quotation marks (Dicks 1970: 215). But marriage guidance was committed to training relatively raw volunteers quickly and to helping large numbers of people.

The CMAC was similarly committed, although the number of its clients was but a small fraction of that of the NMGC. Its training and counselling practice was probably less well developed than that of the NMGC, but in 1967 the debate about the approach to counselling moved ahead of that in the NMGC. On the occasion of the setting up of a counselling committee, Dr John Marshall, a psychiatrist and sometime editor of the CMAC *Bulletin*, propounded the principles of non-directive counselling in terms akin to those used by Wallis. But Jack Dominian (1967), a leading member of the CMAC and Director of the Marriage Research Centre at the Central Middlesex Hospital, raised a crucial question: 'having with skill, and perhaps a bit of luck, reached the point of dialogue [with a client], where do we go from there?' Dominian believed counsellors could do more than just listen and clarify, but they needed to be taught new skills. In fact, the CMAC was to be the first in the 1970s to pioneer a more 'skills' oriented training for marriage counsellors.

Between 1955 and 1960, Wallis succeeded in doubling the numbers of counsellors who were selected and trained.[42] He was convinced that the kind of non-directive training he advocated could work for clients and that volunteers could deliver it, but he also believed that the credibility of marriage guidance required that counsellors be given more support and supervision. In the mid 1950s he recruited regional tutors who helped counsellors with case discussion groups, but did no assessment. Most case discussion groups were run by psychiatrists until the early 1970s. The case discussion group and an assessment on the basis of about 20 cases, which candidates either passed or were deferred for a year, remained the only elements of post-residential supervision until the 1960s. By the mid 1960s, Wallis had decided that marriage guidance needed a team of paid tutors and he proceeded to contact likely candidates. The national network of tutorial support, which became the bedrock of marriage guidance's claim to excellence in counselling in the 1970s, was set up with little consultation and many local councils were aggrieved to find their best counsellors going to work for the national body. The NMGC's control of training and its technical elaboration of counselling was firm, and contrasted strongly with its lack of capacity to control the way local councils were managed and worked. Protests from local councils that the NMGC would never divulge why many of the candidates they sponsored failed to be selected (NMGC claimed for reasons of confidentiality) were frequent. The professional quality of marriage guidance training and work remained suspect. Although Wallis created the preconditions for the tutorial system which emerged later, his work also served to lay the foundations of a therapeutic culture within marriage guidance which derived its power from a mystique born in large measure of secretiveness and which was in turn linked to the heavy emphasis on confidentiality and the lack of either a theoretical or skills component to the training.

PUBLIC VERSUS PRIVATE VOICES, 1960–68

Wallis's determination to enlarge the counselling enterprise of marriage guidance and to make it more professional created profound tensions for the organisation. A. J. Brayshaw first raised what he began to perceive as the dilemma between the public and private voice of marriage guidance in 1957: 'There is a dilemma at the heart of our work. How are we to be the infinitely kindly, receptive, uncensorious people we want to be, who never presume to pass judgement on one another, while at the same time we uphold standards of kindness and honesty, honour, loyalty and love?' (Brayshaw 1957: 154) How was, in other words, the public face of marriage guidance presented to bodies such as the Royal Commission on Marriage and Divorce and its stated mission to promote marriage and reconciliation to be squared with what went on in the non-directive counselling room, where the emphasis was placed on acceptance of the client's frailties? Indeed, an executive member, Lady Venables (1964), felt that 'permissive' would be a better term to use than non-directive.[43] But nothing could be further removed from permissiveness than the NMGC's original set of principles. Brayshaw elaborated this theme in 1960. While he said that he was resigned to the inevitability of the dilemma, he made a strong plea for marriage guidance to stand firm for 'responsible standards' and 'the highest ideals' in marriage and family life.[44]

Tensions arising from the dilemma identified by Brayshaw were expressed at a number of levels. First, the view of marriage identified and defended by Brayshaw became increasingly out of step with public attitudes towards sexual morality. Soon marriage guidance was on the defensive even with regard to elements within the churches, and this produced considerable uncertainty as to the organisation's public voice, which had found expression during the 1950s primarily through its education programme. Second, when this uncertainty was taken together with the boost that Wallis had given to the counselling work of marriage guidance, severe tension developed between the two arms of the organisation's work, education and counselling. In 1964, the training for education and counselling work was integrated, but this manoeuvre merely masked the extent to which counselling had replaced education as the organisation's main activity. Third, at the same time, the counselling culture permeated the structure of the organisation itself and in the mid 1960s Wallis, together with the training and field officers, questioned the need for any hierarchical management structure. By 1968, counselling had become the effective *raison d'être* of the organisation and this in turn begs some consideration as to how far marriage guidance was in a position to turn itself from a 'movement' promoting marriage into an 'agency' delivering a service. With the primacy achieved by counselling, marriage guidance tended to turn inwards, becoming more of a private world. This tendency together with the suspicion the counselling department harboured about administrators, especially when these were not trained counsellors, boded ill for the development of a service agency.

One of the NMGC's principles more than any other caused the organisation heart-searching during the 1960s. Principle 5 stated its opposition to both premarital and extramarital sexual relationships. In 1947, such a commitment had seemed unproblematic and as late as 1956 it received the approbation of the Royal Commission on Marriage and Divorce, but writers on sex and marriage were shifting their ground on this issue during the 1950s and by the early 1960s even the position of some churchmen was equivocal.

It is, however, difficult to be definitive as to the climate of opinion about sex, marriage and divorce. In 1963 John Profumo resigned his portfolio because of his extramarital relationship with the call girl, Christine Keeler (*The Times* 6/6/63). The political outcry in the case centred on Profumo's lie to the House of Commons about the affair (Wayland Young 1963). But the public outcry in the popular press (if not *The Times*) centred on the sex scandal, involving as it did 'high life' in the form of the Cliveden set, and 'low life' in the form of one of Keeler's boyfriends, a black salesman, as well as the hint of a spy scandal for good measure. Some twenty-two years later Cecil Parkinson experienced only a slight hiccough in his ministerial career because of an extramarital affair that resulted in an illegitimate pregnancy for Sarah Keays. Given the great changes in measurable sexual behaviour over that period (the number of one parent families and cohabitees had more than doubled) as well as the increasing acceptability of such behaviour, even a modest punishment might seem hard to explain. But again, the response to even such a public and minutely documented affair is hard to assess. The circumstances of the Parkinson case were very different from those of Profumo, involving an eminently respectable woman secretary and fellow member of the Conservative party. In part, the strength of her personal outrage (in contrast to Keeler's more shrewd manipulation of the situation) seems to have provoked a public backlash that served to soften Parkinson's fall, perhaps indicating that the costs of complicated personal relationships must be allowed to lie where they fall, which will usually be on the women involved. In this respect, little has changed from the late Victorian period, when the marital relationship was defended because of the way in which it represented in microcosm the order and stability of the polis, with divorcees and unmarried mothers suffering accordingly. What changed in post-World War II society was the extent to which the costs included stigma. In the case of divorcees, this had lessened substantially by the early 1960s and the same became true of illegitimacy in the 1980s.[45]

During the 1950s, marriage guidance was determined to stand up for marriage as a public institution as well as a private relationship. But the trend among writers about marriage and the family was to focus on the analysis of personal life to the exclusion of the external world. This in turn, even when the writer was intent on exploring the theology of sexual love, provided the space for rethinking the ordering of personal relationships on their own terms, without the constraint of societal sanctions. Kenneth Walker and Peter Fletcher, who had begun in the late 1930s to formulate the idea of 'spiritual reconstruction' through the development of the personality in marriage (see above, p. 65), encouraged their readers to escape from a world saturated with utilitarianism into the higher life of personal relationships. They contended that neuroses were the result of a particular form of ignorance of personal life and that what personal life had to offer was, above all, love. A couple's love life should be understood, they argued, as 'discourse', or a form of conversation. This was a not dissimilar analysis to the much more famous work of Berger and Kellner (1964), which talked about each partner writing and rewriting the marital script. Like Walker and Fletcher, Berger and Kellner wrote of such 'scripts' as if they were composed in isolation from the world outside (Burgoyne and Clark 1984; Morgan 1985).

The emphasis on love as the moral cement of personal relationships was not new. Gray had also emphasised this in the 1930s, but had then faced the problem of the relationship between love and marriage. If love were not present in a marriage, then was it not immoral, and could love not exist outside marriage? As personal life was increasingly divorced from public regulation, which manual writers came to condemn as having impeded rather than promoted the development of personality, then the tie between marriage as an institution and sex as the expression of love became increasingly harder to sustain. By the early 1960s, MacMurray's argument that sex was the expression of personality and would only be regulated from within, rather than by social institutions (see above, p. 52), was more broadly accepted. In 1957, Walker endorsed premarital sex between lovers, while continuing to deplore promiscuity, while Fletcher continued to blame societal pressures for commercialising marriage and turning it into a purely economic and sexual, rather than a truly personal, relationship (Walker 1957).[46]

Perhaps more influential in the long run was the work of those who commanded the ear of the church. Particularly important was the writing of Dr Derrick Sherwin Bailey (of the Church of England

Moral Welfare Council), who in his book *The Mystery of Love and Marriage* (1952) thanked his 'great friend' David Mace. Bailey urged the church (of England) to reorient its attitude towards sex and marriage and in particular to develop a theology of sexual love. He condemned the way in which marriage had been viewed as an institution rather than ontologically. In many respects Bailey merely developed the views of both Gray and Mace that sex was not an expression of sinful desire, but rather of love, and that non-procreative sex could not therefore be condemned. In particular, he argued that the use of birth control in no way conflicted with the idea of 'one flesh', and could assist the development of the personal relationship between husband and wife (Bailey 1957). He also urged that love be 'considered in terms of personal relation (sic)' and invoked Martin Buber's categories of I and Thou, marriage being built up by two people who recognised the Thou (Bailey 1952: 10). Like Gray and Mace, Bailey argued strongly that the I/Thou relationship and one flesh were sustained by fidelity. He therefore strongly opposed extramarital sex, but also had to admit that a marriage was over when love failed. Thus while cessation of love would be too difficult to verify, it was nonetheless the fundamental ground for divorce. Bailey expressed his honest doubt as to what constituted 'good' and 'bad' marriages to an annual marriage guidance conference in 1958, deploring the fall in 'moral standards', but also urging tolerance.

Writers like Bailey had problems when the argument was taken a stage further by the manual writers and the link between sex and marriage broken. In 1959, Eustace Chesser, also a friend of Brayshaw, joined Walker in questioning premarital chastity (Chesser 1960).[47] The outcry was enormous. Published under the auspices of the BMA, his book was withdrawn from sale and Chesser resigned from the BMA. Bailey also publicly condemned it. By-passing the more philosophical preoccupations of people like Gray, MacMurray and Bailey as to the nature of the relationship between love, sex and marriage, Chesser, more in the manner of a Griffith, asked bluntly why there was a premium on marital virginity and whether a girl could remain a virgin and yet lose chastity – a reference to the concern about 'heavy petting' which absorbed American, and to a lesser extent British, writers on sex in the 1950s (Weeks 1981). Chesser was not advocating promiscuous sexual relationships among the young, nor extramarital sex, but his matter-of-fact presentation of his position, without any real attempt at a moral defence, caused grave concern. The reaction to the third of G. M. Carstairs's (a professor of psychological medicine) Reith lectures in 1962, which also asked whether chastity was the supreme moral virtue, provoked a similar fuss. In Carstairs's view: 'our young people are rapidly turning our own society into one in which sexual experience, with precautions against conception, is being accepted as a sensible preliminary to marriage, making marriage itself more mutually considerate and satisfying' (Carstairs 1962: 51). Yet those wishing to defend a more traditional position also had soon to cite scientific evidence. Most, including officers of the NMGC, relied on selective quotation from Kinsey's American research, and in particular the finding that extramarital sex was twice as common among women who had had premarital sex, which seemed neatly to indicate the dangers of Chesser's position.

While Bailey's position did not signal any fundamental change in attitude towards sex outside marriage, his stress on the importance of the quality of the marital relationship, rather than on sex as a means to generation and marriage as a means of avoiding sin, did succeed in changing the framework within which the church began to think about marriage and family life. In 1958, a group convened by the Archbishop of Canterbury to report on the family in contemporary society (including Bailey and Gordon Dunstan, an active supporter of marriage guidance and a signatory to *Putting Asunder*, which gave its approval to the idea of 'no fault' divorce in 1966) concluded that 'one flesh' was now commonly accepted to be not just a means to procreation, but a two-in-one relationship which had value in itself and glorified God (Church of England 1958: 122). By the early 1960s, a considerably more radical view was emanating from some churchmen. The Bishop of Woolwich rejected the traditional Christian thinking on marriage and divorce and advocated a position 'based on love', pursuing it to its logical conclusion where nothing could be labelled as 'wrong' – not divorce, nor premarital sex – unless it lacked love (Robinson 1963: 118). Echoing MacMurray about thirty years earlier, he rejected the idea that there could be packaged moral judgements for Christians.

More radical still were the views expressed by a group of Quakers, published in the same year, 1963 (a marriage counsellor was a member of the group). The origins of the essay, *Towards a Quaker View of Sex* (Heron 1963), lay in the group's wish to address the question of homosexuality. Recording their appreciation of Bailey in his refutation of sex as sin, they nevertheless explicitly parted company from him on the tie between 'I love you' and marriage. Sexual morality could only come from within and could only be based on the avoidance of exploitation of another human being. Such a morality would, they argued, prove 'deeper' and more 'creative' and would release love, warmth and generosity into the world: 'The life of society desperately needs this warmth of contact and intimacy. Everywhere we see sociability without commitment or intimacy . . . the emphasis on morality has so often gone with a cold and inhibitive attitude' (*ibid.* 10). It may be argued with the benefit of hindsight that such ideals failed to perceive how a commitment to self-generated morality could feed into, rather than replace, the kind of emotional and material selfishness that was being condemned; and also underestimated the power relations in society, particularly between the sexes, that would exert pressure on women especially to conform to the new morality, without any resort to more direct forms of exploitation. But the writing in the essay was powerful in its commitment, openness and invitation to a brighter world. It delivered a particular warning to counsellors not to 'tread with heavy feet' (*ibid.* 43) and above all to be non-judgemental and to preserve confidentiality.

It was to this book that Brayshaw, himself a Quaker, responded most forcefully. He could accept that the spirit of love was more important than physical fidelity and that it was therefore possible to forgive unfaithfulness – this was something marriage guidance had always accepted as making reconciliation possible – but it was nevertheless important to hold onto the moral rule and to encourage people to live up to it, helping them if they failed. He acknowledged that maintaining standards without at the same time censuring those who fell short of them had special relevance in the marriage guidance movement, and agreed that marriage counsellors had to accept people as they were. But Brayshaw continued to believe passionately that the values marriage guidance stood for could inform marriage counselling without necessarily being imposed on clients and that marriage guidance should be prepared to stand up and be counted on issues to do with sexual morality (Brayshaw 1963). But at the 1963 annual marriage guidance conference this position came under heavy attack, when guest-speaker Ronald Fletcher (1963) denounced as immoral the idea of marriage as a legitimation of sex.

The evolving theology of love and marriage posed even greater problems for Catholics. CMAC members also acknowledged that if sex were the expression of love then sex without procreation was not denuded of meaning and human value (O'Callaghan 1966). But if they hoped for any shift in the position of the Roman Catholic hierarchy, they hoped in vain. Vatican II consigned the question of birth control to a special committee and in 1968 *Humanae Vitae* reiterated the church's opposition to artificial contraception. The Director of the CMAC thus found himself, not unlike Brayshaw, with the task of reconciling the private work of counselling with a rigid set of moral principles, albeit not of his own choosing (O'Leary 1969). Counsellors were advised in terms akin to those of Wallis, that they were not to be the expositors or interpreters of church teaching, nor the providers of solutions, but were rather to aid the client to reach his own responsible decision.

Within the NMGC, Brayshaw found himself increasingly isolated in his robust defence of the NMGC's founding principles. Writing in *Marriage Guidance*, the Reverend Charles F. Davey (1964), an executive member of the NMGC, firmly dissociated himself from Fletcher's remarks, but admitted that marriage guidance needed urgently to address both the idea that sex should not necessarily be confined to marriage and the reform of the divorce law, adding that, of the two, the former posed the more fundamental challenge. Furthermore, other officials paid and unpaid within marriage guidance failed to take as robust a stand as Brayshaw. In 1961, the executive agreed that if a potential counsellor had only a 'theoretical objection' to principle 5, it could be countenanced.[48] In particular, Wallis refused to adopt a stand against sex outside marriage as a matter of marriage guidance's public policy. He declared that he was not in favour of premarital sex, but that it was a personal view (albeit shared by most authorities). However, premarital sex did not inevitably bring disaster and was in the end a matter for private decision (Wallis 1963). Wallis was impatient with the endless discussions within the organisation over principle 5 and tended to avoid any discussion of what the NMGC's position should be on moral issues, which was irrelevant to the enterprise of counselling. Alfred Torrie, Fellow of the British Psychological Society, who wrote the Foreword to Wallis's 1964 book, *Sexual Harmony in Marriage*, said that it was a relief to read a book about sex without coming across the word 'chastity' (Wallis 1964a). Wallis himself argued that sex could not be thought of solely in moral terms. It was a language of feeling and attention should focus on feelings rather than morals.

It would be wrong to see the position defended by Brayshaw as totally overthrown by the mid 1960s. In 1967 the psychologist, James Hemming, asked in *Marriage Guidance* whether there was a future for marriage and argued, first, against the moral loading on marriage as the only respectable way of having a sex life and, second, in favour of the trend he perceived towards a humanised and secularised marriage that was entered into only as a matter of personal choice after a period of cohabitation (Hemming 1967). The response from readers was largely negative, although one respondent acknowledged that the marriage guidance movement was very divided on the issue (Brown 1967). Most significant was that marriage guidance lost its confidence in its public mission to promote marriage and family life. Doubt in this regard assisted the process by which delivering counselling became the real work of the organisation and with it a tendency to become increasingly inward looking, something Brayshaw deplored and Wallis approved of, believing that private troubles were too easy 'to vulgarise'. After Brayshaw resigned in 1964, the organisation was led by a like-minded triumvirate, Wallis, Gerald Sanctuary (formerly the field secretary) and, for a short time, Owen Whitney, education officer between 1963 and 1965. Sanctuary took the title of national secretary and, in his own view, completed the transition from a religiously inspired movement to a secular social service agency (even though in 1968 the Annual Conference still started with prayers). Unlike Wallis he was prepared to give the press quotable quotes on subjects from wife swapping to chastity belts – 'more will be made than worn' – but more important still the NMGC's principles were quietly revised and in 1968, a year before the stand taken by the 1956 Royal Commission on Marriage and Divorce was also reversed and the divorce law reformed, marriage guidance abandoned its principle 5. By the late 1960s, it was also possible, although very rare, for a divorced counsellor to continue in practice.

In terms of the work of the NMGC, the loss of confidence in its public voice had direct repercussions for the organisation's education programme. Throughout the 1950s, the commitment of marriage guidance to the promotion of marriage and family life had remained firm and with it a commitment to mass education, chiefly through the production of information literature. But as faith in the organisation's founding principles faltered, so too did its education work, and while Wallis was elaborating the philosophy and practice of non-directive counselling, education lacked coherence. Marriage preparation groups, summer schools for teachers, selective work in schools and the NMGC's own publications were all included under the heading of 'education'. While most people in marriage guidance agreed on the importance of education there was violent disagreement as to the best way of doing it. Alan Ingleby, appointed education officer in 1949, had come to the issue of education for marriage and family life via counselling and tended to regard the most important aspect of education as that concerned with emotional development. In 1956, Ingleby decided to prioritise 'groupwork' as the best means of achieving this end. Together with Wallis, he deplored anything that might smack of 'educational indoctrination'. However, the role of group leader proved hard to define and training remained weak, as Ingleby admitted.[49] As it developed, groupwork was not intended to be therapeutic, rather the idea was to explore how the marital relationship might change, with the arrival of a baby, for example. However, theoretical foundations for this work were even shakier than those for non-directive counselling, and in the beginning the work was all too easily confused with group counselling. Ingleby himself described it as 'partly educational and partly therapeutic'.[50] Local marriage guidance councils certainly had little appreciation of the task expected of them and Ingleby complained that few had either understood the objectives of groupwork, assuming it had something to do with sex education, or grasped the way in which to organise such work. Furthermore, the annual returns from local councils showed large numbers of group leaders he had never heard of, while others whom he did know were omitted altogether.[51]

In keeping with his commitment to the NMGC's original principles, Brayshaw promoted the NMGC's publications department and the more didactic forms of its education programme. In 1960 he suggested that working class youth might not feel comfortable in the small discussion groups favoured by the education secretary, Alan Ingleby, and might prefer the anonymity of the big lecture hall.[52] Two years later, in a submission to an *ad hoc* internal committee on the future of education, Brayshaw was more forthright still in his views: 'The very fact that we call our educational workers "group leaders" (which sounds like Boy Scouts or Civil Defence) indicates our preoccupation with this method'.[53] He complained further that the good lecturer was sometimes turned down at selection if he or she did not have the makings of a good group leader.

This position brought him into direct conflict with Ingleby and, as both recognised, the underlying issue was that of values and their relationship to the work done by counsellors and group leaders. And as Ingleby pointed out, the issue was if anything starker in respect to education than to counselling;[54] Brayshaw urged that marriage guidance stand up for moral values, but were they to reject or harangue young people attending a lecture or a group who did not hold to them? In his submission to the *ad hoc* committee on education, Ingleby summed up his differences with Brayshaw:

There has always been a fundamental difference in approach between the general secretary and the education secretary in regard to education work. This is difficult to define roughly without injustice to both. Very rightly it could be said that the former is primarily interested in propagating ideas about marriage, in mass influences, public impact and a quantitative approach. The latter [himself], while recognising the need for publicity, is more concerned with the processes by which people learn, thus feeling as well as facts; he believes it more consistent with the spirit of the movement that its education role is an essentially personal one, and that mass influence can safely be left to the BBC and the press "aunties" [agony aunts]'.[55]

In his view, therefore, the development of education work literally paralleled that of counselling and during the late 1950s and early 1960s he was constantly seeking 'parity of esteem' with Wallis's growing counselling workforce. This was doomed to disappointment in view of both the inevitably limited scale of operations that marriage guidance as an organisation could achieve in the education field, and the greater coherence of the task of marriage counselling.

Just as Brayshaw's defence of the NMGC's principles was losing ground, so also was his position on education. He tried particularly hard to protect the NMGC's publications department, but written materials found little place in the ideas of either Wallis or Ingleby as to what constituted the proper training and practice of counselling. In the 1960s, the NMGC was handing out the FPA's reading list to engaged couples in its marriage preparation classes because, according to Brayshaw, the prevalent opinion within marriage guidance was that the personal relationship with the client was all important and this should not be diluted by the written word.[56] The field was dominated by Wallis and Ingleby who fought a battle with each other not over principle, but prestige. In keeping with his determination to elaborate an education programme on the same lines as that of counselling, Ingleby favoured integrating the training for education and marriage counsellors, which he viewed as an important step towards parity of esteem. In 1960, this was clearly rejected by Wallis[57] but, when Ingleby resigned in 1963, Wallis agreed with his young successor, Whitney, to 'integrate' education and counselling. In their proposal, Wallis and Whitney stressed their intention to integrate the *work*; in other words, by integrating training every new counsellor would be able to undertake marriage counselling, and youth and group counselling, which would make marriage guidance workers more flexible and efficient.[58] While Wallis and Whitney presented their proposal to the executive committee as having nothing to do with the rivalry between the two departments,[59] the hope of education was clearly for parity of esteem and education workers pronounced themselves content to take on the name 'counsellor' – no one was happy with the term 'group leader'.

Wallis's motivation was more complicated. Marriage counselling was securely based and Wallis did not like much of the education work done by marriage guidance. But he also disliked the way the organisation expressed its commitment to education in terms of a commitment to 'prevention', while marriage counselling had historically been labelled 'remedial'. In 1968, he described his main reason for agreeing to integration as a 'subtle' one, viewing it as an opportunity to bring those 'who enthusiastically believed that groupwork with young people was a more normal, constructive and healthy contribution than concerning oneself with marriage breakdown and pathological conditions' into the counselling fold (Wallis 1968a: 177). In this context and together with the priority accorded counselling within the integrated training, the adoption of the common term 'counsellor' assumed much greater significance. Once education was placed under the counselling umbrella, the conflict in principle between the two sides of the work disappeared: education ceased to be the main vehicle for the expression of marriage guidance's mission to promote marriage and family life and came to play second fiddle to marital counselling.

When Brayshaw announced his resignation in 1964, Wallis suggested that in the light of the integration of counselling and education work all the job descriptions of the officers employed by the NMGC might be reviewed.[60] Wallis, together with Whitney and Sanctuary, proceeded to send a memorandum to selected honorary officers, which argued that the organisation was about counselling, education and fieldwork (the development of local councils) and that these officers were capable of getting on with their allotted tasks without the further supervision of an administrative general secretary.[61] Behind this lay many years of struggle between Brayshaw and Wallis, over Brayshaw's right to exert administrative control over counselling and over the organisation's purpose and principles. Brayshaw regarded Wallis as the orchestrator of the manœuvre and denounced his regard for 'counselling as a kind of religion of which he is the high priest, and counsellors as radically different from other people'.[62] He perceived the whole matter as an attempt by Wallis to build a counselling empire. Certainly Wallis had made no secret of the fact that he wanted to develop marriage guidance training further and to undertake training for other organisations.[63] More fundamentally still, as Brayshaw reflected in an account of his work for marriage guidance written in 1986, he felt 'rather out of tune with the way in which – as it seems to me – absorption with the psychodynamics of personal fulfilment had eclipsed concern for the welfare of marriage and the family'.[64] It is significant that whereas both Wallis and Sanctuary had experienced a conversion to the world of counselling from the male dominated pursuits of business and law respectively, Brayshaw had not. Both Wallis and Sanctuary (in common with many counsellors) undoubtedly experienced a profound sense of personal liberation in exploring the world of feelings, but Brayshaw's depiction of their zeal was also correct.

On the advice of an internal commission of inquiry, the executive committee of the NMGC decided to appoint Sanctuary as national secretary, but for the four years from 1964 until he resigned in 1968 he operated very much as a *primus inter pares* in the manner set out in the Memorandum that he had written with Wallis and Whitney. Representatives of local marriage guidance councils who were invited to put their views to the commission of inquiry raised much larger issues for consideration: for example, the proper relationship between the NMGC and the local councils, whether the executive committee was sufficiently representative and, as the Seebohm Committee began to look into the whole position of social work, the relationship between the work of marriage guidance and the statutory social services.[65] But these critical issues were shelved and were not debated within the organisation for the rest of the decade.

After 1964, Wallis turned to developing a tutorial system. Terry John, who replaced Whitney, continued to work with local education authorities – the idea of tutor groups was becoming popular in the new, large comprehensive secondary schools and marriage guidance advised on these, but education work remained extremely patchy. In Brayshaw's perception, the ethos of non-directive counselling had penetrated the very structure of marriage guidance. Certainly the organisation became more inward looking and there was little attempt at strategic policy review; the counselling, education and field work officers got on with developing the work of their departments. But as Wallis began to perceive, if marriage guidance was to complete the transition from a 'movement' to an 'agency' delivering a professional service, further changes were urgently needed.

In particular, Wallis (1968a) saw the need for continuous in-service training and also recognised that this would only be possible if marriage guidance reduced the number of its counsellors and extracted more work from those who remained. To this end he was perfectly prepared to encourage the use of paid counsellors. Even in the late 1960s, it was apparent that marriage guidance was caught on a treadmill in which virtually as many counsellors resigned each year as were trained. Furthermore Wallis, as well as Sanctuary's predecessor, Pestell, were well aware that an efficient and effective counselling service required a much more even set of standards between local councils, which in turn would require the weaker councils to band together.[66] Some recognition of the importance of these two issues was also evident in the NMGC's *Newsletter*, which started publication in 1966.[67]

Having succeeded in turning marriage guidance away from its publicly stated role as a 'value guardian'[68] of marriage and the family, the necessary steps were not taken to make the organisation capable of becoming entirely service centred. Wallis had pinpointed two crucial areas which required fundamental change: the terms of employment of counsellors, involving a shift from voluntary to paid labour, and the relationship between local councils and the national body. But if local councils were to be *required* by the NMGC to raise their standards, this would threaten the autonomous, federal structure of the organisation. But not even Wallis, let alone marriage guidance as an organisation, clearly appreciated the nature of the decisions that would have to be faced. In 1967, Wallis publicly defended the professionalism of marriage counsellors in the face of the accusation of amateurism and with it their volunteer status (Wallis 1967, Clark 1966). The desire to claim that marriage guidance had achieved expert status in counselling served to thwart any move towards fundamental change. At the same time, the executive committee, aware of the questionable standing of many weaker local councils, decided nevertheless that the number of councils should be dictated by local need and local decision-making rather than NMGC fiat. The executive declared that they had been encouraged in their decision by Paul Cadbury's conviction that where there was need, money would be found.[69] Indeed, this had by and large proved to be the organisation's experience thus far. Despite odd hiccoughs, the Home Office grant had increased substantially and marriage guidance enjoyed the full support of R. A. Butler as Home Secretary, whose father-in-law, Samuel Courtauld, had been a major benefactor of the organisation. Furthermore, building on a generous donation by Captain Bird, the NMGC was able to raise enough money to open a large new headquarters in London in 1960. There were therefore no major financial problems to provide an incentive to major structural reform.

There is no doubt but that the principles which marriage guidance had been so eager to assert in the late 1940s and which gave the whole organisation credibility, in the eyes of government especially, were a source of major tension by the 1960s. It is difficult to see how the organisation could have avoided changing them substantially; whether it was also wise to make marriage counselling its *raison d'être* is another matter, but having done so it was inevitable that the organisation's structure would also have to undergo fundamental change. However, marriage guidance was very slow to perceive this. In the late 1960s, its officers were immersed in their departments and its executive also failed to see beyond the demands of the administrative moment. The resignations of Sanctuary and Wallis in 1968 had more to do with the inability of a triumvirate to provide adequate day-to-day administration than with issues concerning the organisation's direction and purpose. As we saw in Part I, it was not until 1985 that Robert Chester, an academic and member of the executive, pointed out what he perceived as a shift from 'movement to agency', which he characterised in terms of a series of contrasts between a commitment to values and unpaid, amateur work on the part of a movement, and an emphasis on objectives and paid and professional work in an agency (Chester 1985). This formulation captured two of the basic issues – the fate of the organisation's 'public voice' in relation to the shift in focus from 'values' to 'objectives', and the nature of its workforce – but missed the importance of the relationship between local councils and the national body. As to the cause of the shift, Chester stressed the importance of both internal organisational processes and changes in the external environment of marriage guidance, particularly in relation to the professionalisation of the caring services and the changes in the traditional concept of marriage itself. Chester's discussion focused on illuminating the nature of these changes during the 1970s, but key shifts had already taken place in the 1960s, particularly in attitudes towards sexual morality, which were instrumental in determining the outcome of internal tensions within the organisation between education and counselling. Evidence as to the extent of professionalisation in the caring service had long been visible in the probation service (McWilliams 1985) and was just beginning to become a major issue in regard to other forms of social work with the report of the Seebohm Committee (PP. 1968, Cmnd 3703), which was to result in the separation of social work from public health services. Indeed, it was sufficiently evident for Paul Cadbury to hold out the spectre of a statutory takeover in 1968 if marriage guidance could not resolve its differences over the leadership of the organisation.[70]

While all the possible elements involved in a shift from 'movement' to 'agency' are difficult to identify and date, in the case of marriage guidance one factor seems to have been of overwhelming importance and that was its loss of a public voice. In a very real sense, once it had effectively adopted counselling rather than the promotion of marriage and family as its mission, it had become an agency. To be sure, marriage guidance continued to call itself a 'movement' in the 1970s, which became the source of much confusion, for the sense in which it did so was quite different: members of the organisation in the 1970s identified with an inward-looking counselling culture, rather than with publicly stated principles on marriage and the family. Crucially, the shift from movement to agency was not fully understood by either the paid or unpaid workers within marriage guidance during the late 1960s and 1970s; Chester was the first to perceive it and then his diagnosis was partial. The issues raised by Wallis as to the changes needed – in terms of training, the output of counsellors, and local standards of work – for marriage guidance to deliver a professional service persisted during the 1970s, but without any accompanying debate about either the large issue of the organisation's direction and purpose or the equally pressing concern of the quality of management within it. During the 1970s, marriage guidance clearly perceived only the need to elaborate its training. The other issues raised by the shift from movement to agency were mentioned on more than one occasion, but were never systematically addressed.

NOTES

All material located in Relate – NMG archives unless otherwise stated.

1 'Looking Ahead'. Addresses Given at the Annual Conference of the NMGC 1960, p. 24.
2 *Ibid.*, p. 4.
3 *Ibid.*, pp. 3–4.
4 Smart (1984) has also examined the work of the Royal Commission in relation to the case law of the period.
5 NMGC Executive Minutes 21/11/56.
6 Speech made by R. A. Butler on the occasion of the official opening of the new headquarters of the NMGC, 4/10/60, TS, p. 1.
7 A. J. Brayshaw, 'Years with the NMGC 1948–1964', Sept. 1986, TS, A. J. Brayshaw's Private Papers.
8 The circulation of *Marriage Guidance* is unknown. It was primarily an in-house journal, but is also to be found in specialist and academic libraries.
9 NMGC Executive Minutes, 19/5/51.

10 Documents relating to NMGC Exec. Mins, 13/5/54.
11 NMGC Exec. Mins, 20/6/51.
12 *Ibid.*, 21/9/49.
13 David Mace, 'Talk on the Technique of Marital Conciliation', nd (circa 1947), PRO HO45/25146.
14 Report to the Marriage Guidance Training Board by Mr S. Barrett and Mr W. R. Elliot, Documents relating to NMGC Exec. Mins, 1953, TS. This was the first and the last thorough investigation of the work (as opposed to the finances) of marriage guidance by the Home Office.
15 *Ibid.*, p. 16.
16 NMGC Exec. Mins, 15/9/54.
17 FWA Administrative Cttee Minutes, 27/1/49, GLC Record Office, A/FWA/C/A3/66.
18 Halmos (1965: 29) stresses the continuities in personal service during the twentieth century.
19 Draft Report from the Central Committee on Aims and Policy, FWA Aims and Policy Cttee Mins, March 1953, GLC A/FWA/C/A19/1.
20 FWA Administrative Council Mins, Nov. 1953, GLC A/FWA/C/A7/2.
21 *Ibid.*, 4/12/52, GLC A/FWA/C/A7/1.
22 Judith Hubback also contributed an article on her research to *Marriage Guidance* (April 1955), pp. 10–12.
23 'Looking Ahead', p. 22.
24 Note of a meeting between the FPA and A. J. Brayshaw, 13/10/49, FPA Archives A13/69.2, Wellcome Institute, London.
25 *Ibid.*
26 Mace to Pyke, 24/3/44 and Pyke to Mace, 28/3/44, FPA A13/69.1.
27 Brayshaw to Miss James, 6/2/51, FPA A13/69.2.
28 NMGC Exec. Mins, 21/4/54.
29 *Ibid.*, 18/5/57.
30 Internal Memorandum, 28/2/58, FPA A13/69.2.
31 Documents relating to NMGC Exec. Mins, 14/2/58.
32 Brayshaw to Pyke, 20/5/58, FPA A13/69.3.
33 Pyke to Brayshaw, 28/5/58, FPA A13/69.3.
34 Report of a meeting between NMGC and the FPA, 7/6/60, FPA A13/69.4.
35 Memorandum of cooperation between the CAB and NMGC, No. 1950, FPA A13/69.2.
36 It has been the usual convention to call counsellors 'she' and clients 'he' (in fact 'she' would have been more accurate in both cases in respect of marriage guidance). Wallis, however, reversed this customary usage, which was in keeping with his attitudes on gender roles (see below p. 107).
37 These counselling booklets were put out by the NMGC during the mid and late 1960s. Most are undated and all have therefore been listed in the bibliography in number order.
38 The importance of the emergence of the concept of 'normality' in medical measurement has been noted by Miller and Rose (1988) and by Armstrong (1983).
39 'Looking Ahead', p. 25.
40 *Ibid.*, p. 20.
41 Elstone to Brayshaw, 19/1/61, FPA A13/69.4.

42 'Looking Ahead', p. 4.
43 The term 'permissive' was not yet pejorative. John Selwyn Gummer (1971) fired the first sustained blast at 'the permissive society'.
44 'Looking Ahead', p. 10.
45 On Keays' view of the scandal, see Keays (1985). The public acceptance of illegitimacy is signalled not only by the Parkinson affair, but by TV 'soaps', for example ITV's 'Gentlemen and Players', 28/4/89.
46 Fletcher contributed the last chapter to the book.
47 The BMA published this book in 1959 as the fourth in a series of popular books on sex and marriage under the title *Getting Married*; 200,000 copies were sold before it was withdrawn.
48 NMGC Exec. Mins, 20/9/61.
49 'Looking Ahead', p. 14.
50 *Ibid.*, p. 11.
51 *Ibid.*, p. 15.
52 *Ibid.*, p. 8.
53 Documents relating to NMGC Mins, 9/12/62, views of Ingleby.
54 'Looking Ahead', p. 16.
55 Documents relating to NMGC Mins, 9/12/62.
56 Note on Public Policy, 25/2/60, FPA A13/69.4.
57 'Looking Ahead', p. 19.
58 Documents relating to NMGC Mins, 18/9/63.
59 NMGC Exec. Mins, 18/9/63.
60 Wallis to Brayshaw, 29/6/64, Brayshaw Papers.
61 Sanctuary, Wallis and Whitney, Memo on Implementing the Integration Scheme, 10/7/64, Brayshaw Papers.
62 Brayshaw Memo to the Commission of Inquiry into the Structure and Organization of the Marriage Guidance Movement, 18/9/64, Brayshaw Papers.
63 NMGC Exec. Mins, 16/10/63.
64 Brayshaw, 'Years with the NMGC', pp. 6–7.
65 NMGC Exec. Mins, 17/10/64.
66 'Looking Ahead', pp. 23, 25–6.
67 This *Newsletter* (during the 1950s there had been two Newsletters, one for education and one for counselling) remained confidential to marriage guidance workers until July 1973; references before this date are therefore in the form of footnotes. Since *Marriage Guidance* ceased publication in 1987, it has been the sole organ of the organisation.
68 The term is Kramer's (1981).
69 Documents relating to NMGC Mins, Jan. 1960.
70 NMGC Exec. Mins, 11/5/68.

4 'Rugby magic': the flowering of a therapeutic culture, 1968–85

In 1968, the NMGC executive, and in particular Paul Cadbury, looked for a 'strong man', capable of sorting out the administrative difficulties caused by the period when the national secretary had been but a *primus inter pares*. Cadbury approached the Home Office to seek the help of Nicholas Tyndall, a marriage counsellor and member of the prison service who in the late 1960s was working at the staff college in Wakefield where he taught management studies. As an investigator he therefore represented a compromise figure at two levels: standing between an 'outsider' and an 'insider', and between the 'technical' (counselling) and 'administration' sides of marriage guidance. Tyndall produced a report which set out a new administrative structure for the NMGC, including a firm recommendation that a chief officer be appointed. The executive failed to appoint at the first round of interviews and Cadbury then went to the Home Office to ask for Tyndall himself to be seconded for a year to the post. Not until the Home Office agreed was Tyndall consulted. The atmosphere at the 1969 Annual General Meeting was a marked improvement on the angry occasion the year before. The executive committee breathed a collective sigh of relief at finding a new messiah. Only the President, Lady Bragg, uttered a cautionary note:

> Pausing on the word Tyndall, she said that the Executive had taken three steps recently (a) they had called in a detached, outside consultant, (b) they had appointed an acting Chief Officer and (c) they had appointed a permanent Chief Officer. All these appointments were the same man, and she thought we must guard against pushing him into the impossible position of being the

panacea for all ills which would be bad for him, the Executive Committee and all of us.[1]

Tyndall might have had good cause to agree when sixteen years later he faced another tumultuous AGM and another call for an external review of the NMGC's affairs.

In and of itself, a new administrative structure could do little to address the underlying issues regarding the organisation's work as a service agency, which Wallis and others had begun to articulate during the late 1960s. From the beginning Tyndall made clear that he understood marriage guidance to be an organisation whose chief concern was counselling, and he also demonstrated awareness of the increasing urgency of issues to do with professionalisation in the context of the dramatic changes in social work following the Seebohm Report and the setting up of the new social services departments. In addition, a series of internal *ad hoc* working parties, which were a feature of the way marriage guidance conducted its affairs during the 1970s and early 1980s, highlighted, and often rediscovered, a number of fundamental concerns: the wide variation in the standards of local councils and the paucity of management capacity in the weaker ones; the tension between the technical and administrative workers in the organisation and the lack of clear role prescriptions especially at local and regional levels; the continued decline of educational work despite a reiterated commitment to it; and the problems marriage guidance faced in overcoming the 'treadmill' aspects of its existence, whereby it continued to lose as many counsellors as it trained each year and failed significantly to reduce its waiting lists. These problems begged further consideration of the organisation's financial structure, the possible benefits to be gained from paid rather than voluntary counselling, and ways of easing the pressure on appointments secretaries, for example, by introducing reception interviewing or even moving towards short-term 'crisis' counselling.

All these major issues were inter-related to an extent that made it extremely difficult to build a development strategy to tackle them. As it was, the connections between them were but dimly perceived and there was no clear idea as to where to intervene first. Most of the reports from internal working parties effectively disappeared into some kind of black hole. Furthermore, the NMGC was additionally constrained in its endeavours by the autonomy enjoyed by local councils and by its own continued uncertainty about its mission. To all intents and purposes, counselling had become the organisation's *raison d'être*, but the kind of counselling marriage guidance delivered was increasingly called into question, both in terms of its narrow focus, and, by the end of the 1970s, in terms of its content. However, during the 1970s, marriage guidance remained convinced that its claims to professional expertise rested on the quality of its training and on the specialist nature of the counselling it provided. Much of the energy of the organisation went into further elaborating the system of counsellor supervision, through tutors and later tutor consultants, whose appointment actually served to exacerbate the split between technical and administrative staff. The whole content and organisation of counselling became increasingly unassailable, with the result that *ad hoc* working parties tended to pick up particular issues in isolation, producing reports which the executive invariably accepted as advisory documents, thereby effectively burying them. But at the same time, marriage guidance was expanding rapidly in terms of the numbers of active counsellors (from 1257 in 1970 to 1690 in 1982), local councils (from 129 in 1970 to 162 in 1982), and clients (from 20,000 new cases a year in the early 1970s to over 30,000 by the early 1980s). This rapid expansion in the level of activity, which was not matched by a comparable rise in the Home Office grant and which took place during a period of high inflation, made the failure to consider the whole nature of the agency's work more serious. By the early 1980s, financial crisis loomed.

As marriage guidance expanded along the pattern set in the late 1960s, so it also became a more inward looking organisation. Senior technical and administrative staff were usually drawn from within the organisation, and the move out of London to the residential training college in Rugby, while well justified in terms of lowering the costs of the residential component of basic training, also served to cocoon the senior officers and the organisation more broadly from the outside world. 'Rugby magic' was the phrase used by counsellors and tutors to describe the awareness training counsellors received in residential training courses. The mystique conveyed by the phrase was additionally unassailable for being unarticulable. 'MG', as those involved came to call it, became increasingly a world of its own, at one level more and more sure as to its identity and its purpose, but at the same time unable to communicate what it believed in – the power and importance of counselling – to the outside world. Opportunities to expand the organisation's horizons, most importantly in connection with the discussion of conciliation services following the provisions for conciliation in the 1969 Divorce Act, were not pursued, in part because it was eventually felt that counselling and conciliation were not compatible activities, in part because of lack of financial resources, and in part because marriage guidance did not seem to envisage itself playing the leading role that such a decision would have required. Similarly, when the leading marital agencies came together with government to produce the document *Marriage Matters* in 1979 (Home Office and DHSS 1979), which Tyndall hoped would put marital counselling and the NMGC on the map, the organisation showed no capacity to take the project further when government leadership failed to materialise. In many respects, marriage guidance was doing the things it was doing in the late 1960s – education apart – much better by the early 1980s, but lack of vision beyond the delivery of the counselling hour and lack of appreciation of the increasing and interlocking difficulties surrounding the delivery of that service boded ill for the future. Particularly significant were to be the costs of training the many counsellors who either dropped out or did little counselling, whether the needs of clients were being adequately met, and how effective management could be achieved in an organisation in which there was much rivalry and mutual suspicion between technical and administrative staff.

SETTING THE PARAMETERS, 1968–71

On entering the organisation, Tyndall clearly perceived the need to define what he believed it to be about. In many respects, his definition followed that of John Wallis: the organisation was there to provide marital counselling. But in contrast to Wallis, Tyndall employed the language of 1960s organisational theory to argue his case. He was concerned above all to provide marriage guidance with a clearly defined space within the expanding world of statutory social services, which in turn gave rise to much debate over the future role of voluntary organisations. He sought to accomplish this by clarifying marriage guidance's 'primary task' as marital counselling, effectively subordinating both its education work and campaigning stance *vis-à-vis* the family and marriage to a secondary position. While the transition to a service agency had been largely made during the 1960s, Tyndall's firm statement as to the organisation's purpose was important not least because it was made with a consciousness of the changing context of social services. In many respects Tyndall's concept of the primary task was framed as a survival strategy for an organisation which had lost confidence in its original role as the defender of marriage and the family and hence in its educational work, and which was being invited, like all voluntary organisations, to reassess its position in relation to the statutory services. However, in and of itself the concept of primary task provided but a limited guide to developing the content and organisation of the work of marriage guidance.

In the report he prepared for the agency in 1968, Tyndall stressed the need to look at marriage guidance in the context of social work and the new-found power of self-governance within the new social service departments.[2] Certainly in *Marriage Guidance* there was a greater preoccupation with the implications of the Seebohm Report for the organisation's professional position than with the Divorce Law Reform. Marriage guidance feared government takeover of voluntary organisations and hoped that it would be able to fulfil Seebohm's expectations of the voluntary sector as 'vigorous and outward looking', with a flair for innovation and free of 'the condescension and social exclusivity of the past'.[3] Tyndall (1970a) drew attention to the three roles Seebohm saw for voluntary organisations: as service pioneers, as the providers of alternative services, or as the providers of specialist services, and stated his belief in the capacity of marriage guidance to undertake any or all of these roles. But in his report he warned that the increasingly professional approach that would be demanded of voluntary organisations would require the setting of more rigorous standards by the national body. He thus justified the emphasis he was to place on the appointment of a chief officer, a more representative executive body and a stronger regional structure, with clear communication structures between them and the local marriage guidance councils.

The Aves Report on voluntary organisations published in 1969 spelled out more clearly the roles envisaged for the voluntary sector and, in its remarks on marriage guidance, urged greater cooperation with the new social service departments. Tyndall took this as his starting place in elaborating through 1970 and 1971 his ideas as to how marriage guidance should develop its work. In particular he began to apply the concept of the 'primary task' as a way of carving out a clear niche for the organisation within the rapidly changing fabric of social services. He suggested that the strength of marriage guidance lay in its capacity to deliver a specialist national marital counselling service. The only other specialist organisation in the field with the same aim was the IMS, but this served only some 150 London clients a year and was as much involved in research as counselling. Neither the much smaller CMAC nor the JMEC provided a national service. Marriage guidance's pioneering role would be more limited. He cited education work in general and youth and group work in particular as areas where marriage guidance might play the pioneering role suggested by Seebohm, passing successful initiatives onto the statutory authorities for further development. He urged marriage guidance to aim for clarity as to its role:

MGC must acknowledge that it is an established institution with all the strengths but all the drawbacks of institutionalisation. As MGC claims the right increasingly to a cooperative working relationship with other professions, so it must accept the responsibility of providing a full service of a professional standard. This means that the provision of an efficient service must take primacy over other factors, such as the preservation of the voluntary principle, parity among counsellors or local loyalties . . . The strength of a voluntary organisation lies in its sensitivity to the changing world outside. It fails if it clings onto methods appropriate for the pioneering phase after it has become a specialist agency.

(Tyndall 1970a)

It was during the 1970s that the organisation became known to one and all as 'MG', symbolised by the introduction of a new logo in 1979. The acronym captured the sense of a cohesive, tightly knit organisation, as well as helping to circumvent the frequent doubts raised about both 'marriage' and 'guidance' as appropriate names.

The concept of 'primary task' was developed by the Tavistock Institute of Human Relations with which Tyndall had been closely connected in his work with the Home Office before going to MG. A. K. Rice (1963) defined 'primary task' as the task an organisation had to perform to survive. In the Tavistock's development of the theory of organisations during the 1960s, the definition of the primary task became an essential component in reconciling task performance and human need – the formal and informal elements within an organisation (Miller and Rice 1967). Securing agreement about the primary task from all members of the organisation (in MG's case from those committed primarily to education as well as from those involved only in marital counselling), together with clearly defining the roles of individuals, were viewed as crucial components in the management of an organisation.

In an address to the CMAC's Annual Conference in 1971, Tyndall followed Miller and Rice in stressing the importance of differentiating between the rational and sentient sides within organisations. Any voluntary organisation was, he suggested, inevitably a collection of '"our sort of people"', meeting the needs of its members to belong to a corporate entity, to contribute at a personal level and to bolster self-esteem. There was nothing wrong in this, he added, as long as these human needs did not conflict with the task of the organisation, and as long as the means did not become more important than the end. As Tyndall pointed out, and as was to be forcefully reiterated by an outside critic at the end of the decade, such a danger was particularly acute in an organisation dealing with the deeply personal and emotional subjects of marriage and sex. An agreement as to the primary task of MG would serve to focus attention on the goal of the organisation to deliver a service, rather than on the human needs of its members. He emphasised that the 'primary' label was a statement about the relationship of the particular work to the organisation and was not 'a judgmental comment on the value of particular aspects of the work'. No slight on educational workers was intended, but MG was not primarily either an educational organisation or a pressure group. Nor was its purpose to be an organisation employing volunteers, but rather to provide an efficient service. He argued, therefore, that its goal should be development of its expertise in terms of its training in order to meet the demand for its service more effectively.[4] A first crucial step would be to move to a new headquarters in Rugby that would provide a residential training centre. If MG was not primarily a campaigning organisation, it did not need to be in London. Indeed, as early as 1969, Tyndall had declared himself to be in something of a dilemma over MG's response to the Divorce Law Reform Bill, because, in his view: 'The traditional position of the NMGC is that it is not a pressure group and does not have an official or concerted viewpoint on matters of social legislation which are not directly concerned with counselling'.[5] While this was consistent with Tyndall's clear concept of MG's primary task and indeed with Wallis's view of the organisation, it was very far from Brayshaw's idea of MG's role.

At the 1970 Annual Conference, Tyndall spoke to the theme 'Looking Ahead' and recalled the 1960 Conference which had adopted the same theme. He offered a selective summary of the recommendations put forward on that closed and often angry occasion, noting that the tutorial system favoured by Wallis, the regional structures advocated by Pestell and the integration of training for education and counselling work demanded by Ingleby had all taken place (Tyndall 1970b). Only Brayshaw's prediction as to a continuing decline in the divorce rate had not come to pass. The demand for MG's service was rising and was likely to rise further as a result of the reconciliation clause in the new divorce Act, which obliged solicitors to offer 'the names and addresses of persons qualified to help a reconciliation' to their clients (clause 3(i), Divorce Reform Act 1969). There was therefore a strong case, Tyndall felt, for focusing scarce resources on the primary task of marital counselling. In view of this, he felt that any change of name for the organisation would not be a good idea, chiefly because it would shift attention away from marriage when this was the clearest focus for the agency's work.[6] He also listed, in a rather unstructured way, some of the implications of providing a professional service. A target, such as assuring clients of an interview within a week might have to be agreed (many local councils already had waiting lists running to months). This would necessarily involve new ways of staffing, using more paid counsellors and providing incentives for counsellors to stay in the organisation longer (Tyndall 1970a)). The development of MG's own research centre would be, he felt, a logical outcome of the clear focus on the primary task of marital counselling.

When Tyndall looked back in mid 1975, on the occasion of the announcement of the Home Office Working Party on the marital agencies (which was to bring out *Marriage Matters* in 1979), to his 'Looking Ahead' speech of 1970, he reflected on the insularity of its preoccupations. He was referring to his lack of reference to cooperation with other agencies, but the insularity went deeper than this. Tyndall's concern, which was legitimate in the context of the Seebohm reforms, was to secure a defensible niche for MG. The definition of MG's primary task was therefore predominantly reactive and smacked of retrenchment. In his early work on the concept of primary task, Rice (1963) had warned that it should not be confused with 'mission'. The mission of an organisation was its overall objective; the concept of a primary task was necessary for organisational model building. In its early phase, MG's mission had been clearly stated as the promotion of marriage and family life. Mass education was by implication the primary task of the organisation. But, in part as a result of the terms of the Home Office grant, counselling rapidly became more prominent, and by the late 1960s was defined by Wallis in particular as the organisation's primary task. In the meantime, MG was experiencing increasing doubt as to its mission (see below, pp. 157–63), with the result that during the 1970s counselling came to serve as *both* mission and primary task, without the problems this raised in terms of MG thus becoming a fully-fledged professional service agency being addressed.

Nor did the assertion of counselling as the primary task of MG in and of itself solve the problem of MG's historical commitment to education. In 1971, the AGM passed a resolution in favour of more groupwork and set up a sub-committee to consider educational work. Its report demanded as large a place for 'preventive' as for 'remedial' work and urged that MG aim to do 'marriage and family education work'. It was not happy about the fact that MG had effectively forsaken all education work other than 'groupwork', which had tended to become more group counselling than education in groups. Educational work occupied only one eighth of the organisation's time; in order to bring it to equal status the report advocated recruiting 1300 education counsellors, a 'startling but not ridiculously high' number.[7] As Miller and Rice (1967) had pointed out, different parts of an organisation would define the primary task differently. Within MG there was a vocal minority who forever resisted the idea of education playing second fiddle to marital counselling. However, during the 1970s, local councils failed to take up the challenge to increase their education work and activity in this area was reduced by a further 25 per cent between 1973 and 1978 (Tyndall 1980). But education never disappeared from MG's collective consciousness, which in view of the organisation's original aims and objectives was hardly surprising, and at the end of the 1970s, the chief officer and the executive agreed to another attempt at an experiment in education work. Education remains something that the agency has never been able adequately to develop or to relinquish.

Tyndall's concept of primary task served effectively to narrow the vision of MG. It invited the organisation to focus on the delivery of marital counselling without necessarily also inviting reflection on the nature of that work. In addition, while at this stage Tyndall clearly perceived the kind of changes that would have to be made in order to secure a more efficient and cost effective workforce, there was little sense of an accompanying strategy to achieve this. It was as if it was believed that the mere articulation of a clearer focus for the agency's work would in and of itself produce the necessary changes. This was unlikely to happen given the widely differing views and priorities at the local level. For example, the large London Marriage Guidance Council had instituted a paid counselling scheme in 1968, by which nine experienced women counsellors undertook eight additional paid hours of work (on top of the three voluntary hours that were expected) for which they received £1 an hour. This resulted in a 37 per cent increase in the number of interviews for a 10 per cent increase in costs (Watts 1969). However, paid counselling spread extremely slowly throughout the organisation and in 1969 considerable opposition was expressed to the increasing reference to the need to 'professionalise'[8] and in particular to the perceived opposition between voluntary and unpaid, and professional and paid workers. At the end of the decade Tyndall (1979a) was still reiterating the need for experiments in paid counselling.

RUNNING TO STAND STILL 1971–80

Internal developments

In many respects all the major problems facing MG as a marital counselling agency were laid out clearly in the early 1970s by Tyndall himself and by two reports – 'Spoors' and 'Gowler' – which were called for in response to changes in the local authority boundaries and the need for local marriage guidance councils to improve their capacity to seek local funding.[9] Marriage guidance's need to become more 'professional' in the delivery of a service was clearly perceived and the two reports on local councils were notable for the way in which they provided a relatively comprehensive picture of the organisation at the point of delivery of the service; subsequent investigations either focused on only one particular issue, or favoured a top down approach, which tended to ignore the limited effect that changes instigated by the NMGC or the regional offices could hope to have on autonomous local councils. However, the common assumption in the early 1970s was that clarification of the way in which MG did its work, particularly in terms of its management practices, would suffice. Thus both the Spoors and Gowler Reports on local councils followed Tyndall in conflating clarification of practical problems with the larger issue of the nature of the work itself. Neither report was acted upon. Instead, MG devoted its energies to further elaborating the framework of training and supervision of counsellors, and then to investigating the way in which this produced additional friction between technical and administrative staff (particularly between the new tutor consultants and regional officers), something that might have been anticipated if greater attention had been paid to the Gowler Report in particular.

Despite the relatively wholehearted focus on marital counselling during the 1970s and the commitment to delivering a professional service, the quality of the service had not been tested, a failing common to the statutory sector as well. Counselling remained predominantly non-directive and in 1980 a report compiled by an Australian, Peter O'Connor, working with MG on a temporary basis, was scathing in its denunciation of the organisation's failure to move with the times, both in terms of the theoretical and the skills content of the training it offered its counsellors.[10] Nor was there much sign of any widespread attempts to offer different kinds of counselling, even within the marital framework, while the problems of counsellor wastage and output remained as large as they had been in the early 1970s. Success in terms of meeting clients' needs remained hard to assess. Research was another aspect of work that MG acknowledged to be important but made little thorough attempt to perform. In particular, the emphasis on the importance of confidentiality served to inhibit any evaluation of the service.

Problems identified and shelved

In 1972, MG obtained a Carnegie grant to investigate the position of local councils. The impetus for the Spoors' working party was twofold. First, government had signalled that local authority boundaries were to change. Local authorities were the main source of funds for local councils and the NMGC was therefore anxious that councils should be helped to achieve standards of efficiency that would enable them to attract grants from the new bodies. Second, the NMGC had sold its London headquarters preparatory to moving to Rugby and in so doing had made a substantial profit. It was therefore for the first time in a position to provide some financial assistance to local councils if they could be encouraged to adopt a development strategy.[11] [It was at this point that local councils began to perceive the national body as something of a gold mine, a view that was slow to fade as inflation began to bite and the NMGC's assets to dwindle.]

To aid its work, the Spoors working party asked two members of the Manchester Business School, Dan Gowler and Karen Legge, to conduct a detailed investigation of one provincial council. The chief officer clearly viewed their work as an opportunity for clarifying roles and relationships within MG, a necessary second step after the formulation of the organisation's primary task. As he observed, power and authority within the organisation were often confused because of its federal structure. For example, a counsellor might feel answerable to the tutor and thence to the NMGC, but in fact was accountable to his or her local council (Tyndall 1973). Nevertheless, the chairman of the working party, Mary Spoors, was also anxious to reassure the technical staff of MG that the review could in no way be construed as threatening, because its focus was to be the structure of local councils and their external relationships, not counselling.[12] In fact, Gowler and Legge provided more than sufficient evidence that any effective overhaul of MG's organisational structure would have to centre around the issue of whether counselling was meeting client needs, which in turn had much to do with the 'hidden structures' pertaining in a therapeutic culture. But, not surprisingly, this point was not made in the Spoors Report nor discussed by the organisation.

The Gowler Report pointed out the extent to which small councils especially developed something of a 'cosy equilibrium' which served the interests of the counsellors above all and which did not encourage communication within the organisation or with the outside world.[13] Some ten years later Professor Charles Handy, a management consultant who prepared a report on improving effectiveness in voluntary organisations for the National Council of Voluntary Organisations (Handy 1981), remarked on the same phenomenon, referring to local marriage guidance councils as 'artists' colonies', harbouring small groups of professionals who worked for the most part individualistically with little by way of formal management (*Newsletter* no. 73, Nov. 1982). Gowler and Legge advocated that local councils adopt a 'management by objectives' approach which would, they believed, encourage more 'corporate' effort. Inevitably they hesitated as to how such an approach was to be actively promoted. In their Interim Report, they passed the responsibility to the national body. But in their Final Report, they stressed that objective setting would have to remain a local matter: 'Bluntly, we believe that any attempt by 'National' to set objectives for local marriage guidance councils would, given the current climate of opinion, result in dysfunctional conflicts and misunderstandings'.[14] Local councils' jealous defence of their autonomy made any move to standardise objectives or practices difficult, and this in large measure explains why, ten years later, Handy observed very similar phenomena to Gowler and Legge. In addition, the Gowler Report identified the operation of a 'highly developed, non-directive, anti-management' culture among the counselling workforce, which they suggested created a situation in which 'the expression of concern about a bureaucracy that does not exist is no more than a defence for the autocracy and 'adhocracy' that most certainly does!'[15] Gowler and Legge's recognition of a non-directive counselling culture was rediscovered at the end of the decade by Peter O'Connor, who compiled a yet more critical report, emphasising not so much the implications for management, but the way in which the culture served to promote the personal growth of counsellors rather than clients (see below, p. 150).

In line with the trend in the management literature of the day, the Gowler Report recommended an unrealistically elaborate matrix organisational structure for local marriage guidance councils, which emphasised the need to pay greater attention to issues of role definition within MG. Small local councils were unlikely to have the resources to implement the full Gowler structure, which meant that the force of their recommendations regarding the appointment of local managers was diluted. But their observations as to the importance of maximising the power and authority of those appointed to management positions were of considerable importance in the elaboration of regional structures. As they perceived, legitimacy within MG stemmed from technical competence, that is from counselling, and in turn carried power. It was therefore important to combine technical and administrative expertise in the person appointed to the position of regional officer. They also perceived that the post of regional officer was the only point within the organisation's structure at which technical and administrative roles could effectively be united, and they urged for the sake of the future welfare of the organisation that 'at some point the technical and administrative structures of the movement *must* be integrated'.[16] Their warnings were prescient, for the concept of tutor consultants, who were soon to be appointed in parallel with the regional officers at regional level, was still under discussion. Had the Gowler and Legge warnings been heeded, the conflict between the regional officers and tutor consultants, which proved to be a running sore throughout the 1970s, might have been avoided.

The most significant and damaging aspect of the Gowler Report was the way in which it traced the effects of the individualistic, non-directive, anti-management culture they described on the service MG aimed to deliver. In particular they called attention to the interview/counsellor ratio. In the councils they looked at, the waiting list remained long in spite of a considerable increase in the total amount of work done, because, while the number of interviews increased, the number of new clients increased hardly at all. In other words, the number of interviews per client was increasing. The Gowler Report emphasised the extent to which the counsellor's own measure of success focused on the length of her relationship with clients and pointed out that, in the absence of other means of valuing their work (for example by payment, or the existence of a career structure), long cases became the main source of job satisfaction for counsellors. They also warned that the introduction of paid counselling in the London Marriage Guidance Council in 1968 had resulted in a 'worsening' of the interview/counsellor ratio from an average of 4.6 interviews per case in 1967 to 6.1 in 1968 and 7.3 in 1971. Because of their voluntary status and low number of working hours, counsellors were not always available to see clients at times that suited the latter and tended to give priority to meeting obligations to existing clients. Gowler and Legge concluded that 'sooner or later, marriage guidance councils will be required to answer difficult questions about performance and accountability'.[17] However, their analysis proved only partially correct. In fact the number of clients seen by MG increased substantially during the 1970s and while the average number of interviews per case also increased significantly (from 4.4 in 1970 to 5.5 in 1980) this was not sufficient to result in the kind of stasis forecast in the Gowler Report. But even if the emphasis the Report placed on the interview/counsellor ratio was misplaced, it was right to stress the importance of analysing the dimensions of client need and the capacity of counsellors to respond. With regard to the latter, issues of payment and other forms of reward, and ways of securing more work from counsellors were crucial. Furthermore, Gowler and Legge had raised an important and uncomfortable issue which refused to go away: the extent to which counsellors' satisfaction took precedence over client need.

Very few of Gowler and Legge's findings found their way into the report of the Spoors' Working Party for which they were prepared. The status of counselling and counsellors, the type of counselling offered, and financial forecasting were all deemed to lie outside the terms of reference of the working party. Instead, it focused on the internal organisation of marriage guidance councils and urged local councils, first, to amalgamate and form effective units and, second, to take seriously the idea of 'management by objectives' (MBO) and the appointment of a paid 'director'. Only 'managerial drive and competence' would secure local funds. The Spoors Working Party laid greatest stress on their belief that a firm MBO strategy would encourage 'aim not drift'.[18] In many respects this was but a gloss on Tyndall's hope that solutions would flow from the definition of the organisation's primary task. The Gowler Report agreed that MG should focus on marital counselling rather than on education work, for which small councils had few resources. But it cautioned against a tendency to overspecialise in terms of one particular form of marital counselling to the exclusion both of other types of counselling and of external activities; in particular, it recommended that the national body take responsibility for developing an outward looking education programme.[19]

But in regard to the provision of a marital counselling service, neither the concept of primary task nor the strategy of MBO provided the agency with a tool with which to examine the fundamental aspects of its work and structure. Having established marital counselling as the primary task, objectives, where they were adopted at all, were developed within the existing framework of MG and the hard questions and choices were avoided. In any case, the organisation had already been assured that the issue in question was administrative rather than technical competence, thereby delimiting the arena in which change could be expected. In the event, the Spoors Report was accepted by the executive as an advisory document. The national body had no authority to direct local councils to amalgamate, appoint paid administrative staff or revise their ways of working. Local reactions to the report were described as very mixed, ranging from 'strongly anti' to 'guardedly for' (Allen 1973). While the importance of paid staff (albeit usually in the form of an appointments secretary or organising secretary rather than a manager at this stage) began to increase more rapidly in the late 1970s and some local councils federated, the number of local councils actually increased (from 129 in 1970 to 162 in 1980). The national executive showed no inclination to refuse applications by small and relatively weak local councils for constituent status. After a visit to two medium sized provincial marriage guidance councils in 1976, Rugby staff reported that in neither place had the Spoors Report been a matter for discussion and that an essential 'cosiness' prevailed.[20]

Instead: further refinement of training and supervisory structures

The major focus of MG in the 1970s was the further refinement of the training and supervision it offered its counsellors. The more single-minded attention that the new chief officer brought to the development of marital counselling was signalled early on by the reorganisation of the Queen Ann Street office. The officers moved upstairs to take over the large committee rooms that had been used during Brayshaw's period of office for publicity events. Soon thereafter the move to Rugby's Herbert Gray College facilitated the focus on counselling and the development of an inward looking therapeutic culture. The paid staff of the NMGC took over one floor in the residential college. The move to Rugby also facilitated the development of a much more standardised basic training and the formation of the tutor training team. Terry John, the education officer, instigated the formation of the training team, but it was Joan Sullivan, appointed in 1969, who built up the supervisory – 'in-service' – work of the tutors in the regions and who introduced the tutor consultants to work alongside the regional officers. The manner of Joan Sullivan's appointment set the tone for what was to become a powerful, tightly knit and inward looking technical staffing structure. She was hand-picked by the chief officer from the probation service. No interviews were held and no job description drawn up. Her title, head of counselling, was decided after she was appointed.[21]

The broad essentials of MG's training remained fixed throughout the 1970s: a day-long selection process (at which between 40 and 45 per cent were successful), followed by six residential courses of 48 hours each held over a period of two years, and tutorial and case discussion group support provided in the regions for counsellors (Tyndall 1971). The residential training continued to develop along experiential lines, emphasising personal insight and awareness. In the words of one officer who trained during the 1970s, successful counsellors were at that time 'caught but not taught'. As another put it, the first module of residential training at Rugby was 'all hugging each other'. Because very little was written down and didactic teaching was frowned upon, even in respect of human growth and development and the psychodynamic view of personality, the teaching at Rugby acquired a powerful mystique. Theories were discussed but labels were not attached; counsellors were therefore rarely able to identify exactly what they had learned. There was also the danger that too much significance would attach to the personality and capacity for growth of the individual counsellor, with the result that failure became personalised. In-service tutors in the regions inevitably spent a lot of time reassuring and counselling counsellors after periods of training at Rugby, rather than discussing cases. Nevertheless, the training was generally acknowledged to produce 'feeling' people, who for the most part, after a year of post-training experience, were able to offer a sensitive service to clients. There were also factors inherent in the phenomenon of 'Rugby magic' which had little to do with the much criticised non-directive culture. The counselling workforce remained predominantly female and, for a large number of those women, their training at Rugby represented their only experience of the often intensive fellowship that characterises the life of students who go away from home to study. Given that they were being invited at the same time to explore emotions and feelings, it was little wonder that the residential training at Rugby acquired a disproportionate and even mystical significance.

In retrospect, many MG staff have sought to distance themselves from the kind of training offered in the 1970s and in particular from the idea of 'Rugby magic', recalling instead early efforts (lost to the written record) that were made to introduce skills training to give counsellors more diagnostic capacity and to enable them to manage more effectively the whole process of interviewing. Certainly there was some discussion in MG, especially in the *Newsletter*, about new approaches to counselling and what they might offer. Those who attended courses at the Tavistock Centre, or who became fellows there for a year under a new scheme organised by Tyndall and Sullivan (both of whom had good contacts with the IMS), found that case discussion groups were much more structured and 'avoided the inconclusive situations that sometimes occur in our own groups'.[22]

It was not that MG was deliberately closed to new ideas, but rather that it failed to take its eclecticism seriously, preferring to have its counsellors concentrate on the development of intuitive processes during training, rather than on coming to an appreciation of the main theories on which they were drawing, or of the range of skills that they might need to perform their task in the counselling room. This was in spite of a decision to take up the behavioural therapy of Masters and Johnson in respect of sexual problems in marriage, which might have been expected to have had spin-off effects on MG's main counselling work, and in spite of moves within the CMAC towards greater recognition of the importance of skills training. In 1973, MG set up a marital sexual therapy (MST) programme broadly following the ideas of Masters and Johnson. David Mace brought details of his work in America in this area to MG in 1972 and at the same time two marriage counsellors started work on an experimental basis in their local council (see below pp. 249–50).[23] Again, in retrospect, several of those active in developing MG's training during the 1970s said that they had hoped that this initiative would help to 'break the mould' of MG's marital work, but MST remained a separate initiative in terms of both its training and the way in which it was administered.

In the CMAC, non-directive counselling developed strongly in the wake of *Humanae Vitae*. The idea of providing confidential support and the eschewing of judgement served counsellors well in balancing Catholic dogma and the realities of Catholic behaviour (Townsin 1970), even though the CMAC *Bulletin* carried periodic calls for greater 'theological stiffening' in the work of counselling (Nichols 1978). The administration of the organisation was overhauled in the mid 1970s and with it a working party on training established which included Joan Sullivan and Douglas Woodhouse from the IMS (Marshall 1978). Jack Dominian had signalled the importance of going beyond 'listening' as early as 1969 (see above p. 110) and shortly thereafter the CMAC invited one of the early proponents of skills training, Egan, to come and present his ideas.

That Joan Sullivan was involved in the working party whose report prefigured the introduction of skills training within the CMAC perhaps lends credence to the view that there was some effort made to instigate changes within MG. But it would seem that the weight of a home-grown training and supervisory structure militated against change. In the main, changes in the structure and substance of MG's training during the 1970s consisted of efforts to 'rejig' rather than radically to alter and were carried out on a very *ad hoc* basis. The only significant development came in response to renewed concern about the downward spiral in education work. In the mid 1970s, education work was made a separate option. Thus, after basic training, the counsellor could choose to opt either for two courses in education or two in further marital work. But this change, designed to give greater prominence to education, failed to increase the number of counsellors coming forward to do groupwork. In 1977, only 12 local councils attained a volume of education work regarded as minimal in 1973,[24] and the AGM of that year again called for more attention to be given to 'groupwork'. The resolution at the AGM implied that counsellors were not given any encouragement by their tutors to take the education option, something that was denied by the members of the training team,[25] but which was consistent with the bias in the tutors' own training experience and work preferences.

There remained considerable confusion as to the content of education work and hence training. Education work was still referred to by the title adopted in the late 1960s – groupwork – and some understood this only in terms of group counselling. But in 1977 the chief officer identified three forms of groupwork: group counselling with clients, 'focal' groups with, for example, young parents or children, and 'training' groups with other professionals. These were all characteristic of MG's work, but, he suggested, required different skills and considerable amounts of organisation, time and money.[26] Tyndall acknowledged that MG had not committed itself to education in a manner comparable to the CMAC or JMEC. Unlike the CMAC, MG had no audio-visual library, publications, or officer to advise on educational material for schools. Indeed, both the CMAC and the JMEC continued to train more people for education work than for marital counselling. In 1973, the Gowler Report had effectively recommended that local councils not try to develop parallel education and marital counselling services, but rather to focus education work, in the manner of the CMAC (and of MG in the 1950s), at national level. However, the impetus that had pushed many towards 'groupwork' in the late 1960s remained strong. It was felt to be desirable that both education and marital counsellors should receive the same training, but given the increasingly strong therapeutic culture of MG, together with the costs in terms of money and organisational energy inherent in organising a parallel 'groupwork' service (especially with focal groups), it was inevitable that education would remain a poor relation.

The move to Rugby made possible the blossoming of tutor training and during the 1970s the number of tutors steadily increased, the aim being to appoint one per twenty counsellors, and by the mid 1970s virtually all case discussion groups were taken by MG-trained tutors rather than, as had often been the case in the 1960s, by external psychologists or psychiatrists. Joan Sullivan clearly felt this to be a mark of MG's own professionalism and a significant move away from medical domination, but it also contributed to the closely knit, inward looking spirit that characterised MG by the end of the decade. Counsellors trained after 1971 were 'born' with a tutor and the influence exerted by the tutor workforce became correspondingly great. Self-employed, the tutors were nonetheless virtually the only contact the NMGC had with its counselling workforce. Tyndall (1975) referred to them as NMGC's 'agents' and the 1974 working party on the tutor system, which recommended a 7 per cent increase in their pay also recognised their potential influence over the counsellors.[27] The power of tutors derived from their technical competence and their role as guardians of national standards of work. They alone could force a counsellor to stop working and the local manager had to accept their decisions, sometimes without being told why.

The technical staffing structure was completed in 1973 with the appointment of the first tutor consultant at regional level. This effectively completed the elaboration of the therapeutic culture. Tutors resourced (the term 'nourished' was often used by respondents) counsellors and were in turn resourced by the tutor consultants, who met on a regular basis with Joan Sullivan. The 1975 job description for tutors actually specified the primary purpose of the case discussion group as a place for counsellors 'to share their anxieties',[28] rather than for the discussion of cases.

The tutor consultants were introduced without consultation and without any thorough discussion by the executive committee. In a planning paper submitted by the chief officer to the executive in mid 1972, he reported that while there was no great enthusiasm for regional training officers there was 'a need' for more 'technical officers' in the regions.[29] Joan Sullivan firmly believed that the regional officers did not possess the skills to manage the tutor group. This was probably true of some, but certainly not all. As it was, regional officers resented the introduction of tutor consultants, who were apparently introduced 'as a resource', when it was obvious that they would take away a large chunk of the regional officers' work. In consolidating MG's therapeutic culture the appointment of tutor consultants also served, as the Gowler Report had warned, to exacerbate the split between the technical and administrative staff, which found expression at every level in the organisation.

By 1975, discontent among the regional officers had grown to the point where they asked the executive to review their position. Their grievances were twofold: first, there was the issue of role definition *vis-à-vis* the tutor consultants and the allied question of salary differentials; and, second, they felt unsupported by Rugby staff and in particular by the chief officer, again in comparison to the tutor consultants whose need for support as members of the technical staff was recognised and met by regular meetings with Joan Sullivan. Given that most of the regional officers in the 1970s were also trained counsellors, they felt the lack of support provided to administrative staff more acutely than might otherwise have been the case. One who resigned from the job in 1978 described to the Wheeler working party (set up to investigate the position of senior staff in response to the complaint by the regional officers) the pressure of working in the absence of clear guidelines and without the power to exert control over autonomous, ill-managed local councils. In this regional officer's perception, meetings with officers from Rugby were more a matter of 'defending your corner' than occasions for constructive criticism and support. In many respects it would seem that the position of female regional officers was the hardest in this respect, although in his evidence to the working party the chief officer dismissed this idea and was reported as saying that 'there was much fantasy around' as to the kind of relationship that was needed between regional officers and Rugby staff.[30]

The Wheeler working party ended up endorsing what it termed the chief officer's 'open and consultative style of management', but admitted that his belief in leaving staff to get on with things might cause difficulties for some.[31] The working party did not report until 1978 and its proceedings provided a focus for bitterness and discontent between regional officers and tutor consultants, and between regional officers and the chief officer for the remainder of the decade. Initially excluded from the working party, the chief officer deplored the lack of trust engendered by the exercise.[32] In their evidence, the regional officers complained that administrators had become the Cinderellas of the organisation and stated their belief that the regional officer needed to be recognised as the 'boss' of the region.[33] Dan Gowler and Karen Legge, called back to produce an assessment of the problem, could not resist pointing out that they had predicted conflict between regional officers and tutor consultants in their 1973 report and they reiterated the need for the integration of the administrative and technical sides of the organisation in one person at regional level.[34] In the short term, they recommended that the regional officer be paid more, but in the long term the structure would have to change, because the introduction of the tutor consultants, together with the growing strength of the tutor group, had served to reinforce a situation whereby status, authority and legitimacy were inseparable from perceived 'technical' competence, and this had served additionally to undermine the managerial role.[35] The Wheeler Report agreed that regional officers should be paid more in recognition of the final responsibility for the region that they carried, but, feeling that it would be invidious to decide whether the regional officer or tutor consultant was more important, did not take up Gowler and Legge's idea of redefining roles at regional level.

A professional service?

As an organisation MG was very proud of the framework of training and supervision it had developed by the late 1970s. The chief officer had been determined to carve out a niche for MG on the basis of its specialist expertise. The solid training backbone of counsellors, tutors and tutor consultants built up by the organisation during the 1970s was felt to testify to that expertise. It therefore came as a considerable shock when a visitor produced a review of MG's training that was highly critical. Peter O'Connor worked as a tutor consultant in the north-east regional office for a year and compiled his report from interviews with tutors in the region. He represented the views he put forward as those of his respondents, although this was somewhat disingenuous, for O'Connor had strong ideas as to how the organisation should develop and imposed a tight interpretative framework on his data. He began with the assumption that the agency should be aiming to become more professional, which he construed as meaning that it should be more prepared both to engage in 'deeper' counselling and to move towards paying counsellors. Part of the negative reaction to the O'Connor Report was prompted by the feeling that he had little patience with MG as a voluntary organisation employing volunteers. However, in the first place, O'Connor was taking up issues that had emerged at the end of the 1960s and had been clearly identified during the early 1970s, and which any agency aiming to deliver an efficient and effective service needs must address. Second, while O'Connor certainly evinced little sympathy for MG's voluntary ethos, the organisation persisted in conflating the issue of voluntary status with the employment of volunteers, when in fact the former did not necessarily require the latter.

In particular, O'Connor deplored the theoretical limitations and the lack of introduction to counselling skills in MG's training. The emphasis on self-awareness and the idea that 'without looking in, you can't look out' meant that 'training runs the risk of being a conversion experience rather than an education experience'.[36] O'Connor took the view, first, that this emphasis benefited the counsellor in terms of personal growth rather than the prospective client – amounting to a 'mental health programme' for those fortunate enough to be selected – and, second, that it resulted in the training being effectively divorced from the counselling task, which in turn reflected the disastrous administrative/technical split within the organisation. The theoretical limitations of the training meant that counsellors were unable to recognise patterns of interaction. Theoretical knowledge was intrinsic to good diagnosis but, because it was deemed 'anti-empathetic', thinking was sacrificed to feeling. Lack of theory resulted in the mystification that became 'Rugby magic' and amounted to a failure to make sense of experience. 'Sticking with the pain' [of self-awareness] resulted in a naïve belief in osmosis; training became the mirror image of counselling with the result that clients were likely to get a second-hand version of training rather than good counselling.[37]

Nowhere, O'Connor charged, were counsellors taught how to conduct an interview, ask questions, get a history, listen, observe or record. The Rugby residential training emphasised self-awareness and the in-service tutors spent much of their time counselling counsellors after periods of residential training, with the result, first, that counselling skills were never taught and, second, that in any case a prejudice developed against skills training. According to O'Connor, many counsellors considered it 'obscene' to be asked in a tutorial what they thought was going on between a couple. Nor did counsellors want to use case discussion groups to discuss clients, preferring to turn them into Rugby self-awareness groups. One counsellor reported to O'Connor that her case discussion group discussed cases when there wasn't anything else to talk about.[38]

O'Connor found in-service tutors to be a demoralised and tired group, lacking the prestige of those associated with the residential training and endeavouring to face in two directions – towards the national body and towards their local councils. These tutors ended up colluding in the general failure to distinguish between counselling and supervision. O'Connor did not blame the tutors for his findings. Because MG was essentially a closed system with tutors and tutor consultants recruited from the ranks of counsellors, there was a lack of familiarity with any other models of working. In addition, he believed the tutors' own training to be inadequate. The O'Connor Report was not given general circulation, only tutors and tutor consultants were invited to respond, and they broadly agreed with his findings.[39] O'Connor had after all made it clear that he did not wish to blame the technical staff for the situation he described, rather it was the fault of the organisation which did not perceive the need to 'professionalise'.

As a result of the O'Connor Report, MG took steps to set up its own training review, but this was not intended to raise questions about the broader picture of counsellor recruitment and ways of working, which had been a necessary concomitant of O'Connor's consideration of training. For O'Connor had also raised the issue of the nature of MG's work, pointing to the large number of 'one interview cases', and had charged that it was but a 'fantasy' for MG to believe it was engaged in anything but emergency work when the average number of interviews per case was only 4.5.[40] On this, he was implicitly making a completely different set of assumptions to the Gowler Report, which had criticised the increase in the interview/counsellor ratio. Whereas O'Connor adopted a 'technical' perspective and assumed that longer counselling meant deeper and more professional counselling, the Gowler Report had taken a management perspective and made tackling the waiting lists a first priority. O'Connor also drew attention to the high rate of counsellor wastage – 28 per cent left in the course of basic training (as many as 40 per cent in the south region) – and to 'the sausage machine' aspects of MG's existence, whereby 250 counsellors were lost and 250 recruited each year.[41] In fact the average working life of a counsellor was something between five and six years.

Many of these larger and more fundamental aspects of MG's performance as an agency had also been raised by the Gowler Report in 1973, but had never been fully aired and discussed. Problems of the recruitment, retention and hours worked by counsellors, together with the questions that followed from O'Connor's findings about whether counsellors were capable of meeting client needs and whether MG as an organisation had enough innovative capacity to adapt to changes in those needs, were pressing, albeit suppressed, issues by the late 1970s.

MG appointed a research officer in 1972 with the express intention of finding out more about its clients and about the behaviour of its counsellors, but both the quality and the quantity of research carried out during the 1970s was poor. In a study of why a sample of 200 counsellors resigned, published in 1974, the research officer, Jill Heisler, concluded that MG had cause to congratulate itself, there being very little by way of complaint against the organisation. Yet the figures showed one quarter of those who resigned were 'dissatisfied' and those resigning within three years of being selected were more likely to have 'unmet expectations'. The precise content of their dissatisfaction and unmet expectations was not made clear, but 'some' were reported to have had problems liaising with their local councils and 'some' were reported as finding that they felt unable to help couples in trouble or to 'produce results', which accorded with O'Connor's estimation of their lack of counselling skills. Certainly Pat Hunt's (1985) later and much more sophisticated research on client responses to counselling again highlighted the problems counsellors experienced in structuring interviews. In 1983, a further study of why one third of the new intake of counsellors resigned blamed lack of support rather than inability to cope either with their local councils or in the counselling room (Gaunt 1983). In all likelihood the causes were multiple and complex, and reflected additionally on the effectiveness of selection procedures. MG still favoured selecting for training those on their first rather than subsequent marriages, and tended to reject applicants with a more social administrative or management bent (Heisler 1977a), which again may have reflected the importance MG attached to feeling rather than thinking.

The relatively short working life of counsellors must also have been related to the lack of any career structure, although this was not mentioned specifically in either the 1974 or 1983 studies of why counsellors resigned. Counsellors could go on to become tutors, but within the counselling workforce there was no recognition accorded to skill or years of experience. Indeed, O'Connor remarked on the determination of the organisation to treat workers at every level as equals. Perhaps because of dwindling job satisfaction, the longer a counsellor served the fewer hours he or she was likely to counsel (Usher 1982). Payment schemes might have served to raise the number of hours worked, but paid counselling schemes spread slowly (in 1982 only a quarter of councils had such schemes) and payment levels remained low. Some form of external accreditation was also discussed but rejected within MG during the 1970s. One regional officer felt that the creation of a two-tier counsellor structure by the introduction of a diploma would have provided 'somewhere for counsellors to go' (Mann 1974a). The London Marriage Guidance

Council called for accreditation at the 1975 AGM, but a subsequent report decided the time was not ripe.[42] The process of accreditation thus remained internal, which was very much in tune with the nature of MG's development during the 1970s.

Most important of all was whether MG's counsellors were delivering the kind of counselling that met clients' needs. O'Connor raised the question as to whether this was at all likely in one-interview cases, but in a sense his concern was with whether the organisation was meeting its own aim of being a professional counselling agency rather than with what the client wanted. MG's own research on its clients concentrated on the collection of descriptive information, recording the steady increase of interviews with couples rather than with either a husband or wife (from 19 to 27 per cent between 1975 and 1982); the major categories of presenting marital problems (over half were classified as 'personal traits' and almost a third as 'sexual problems' in 1975); patterns of referral (70 per cent were self-referred in 1982); whether the clients were representative in terms of their socio-economic status of the population as a whole; the number of interviews per case; and whether the counsellors felt there had been any change in the clients' situation for the better (Heisler and Whitehouse 1975, NMGC 1982). During the 1970s, MG's own research insisted that its client population was representative of the population at large. However, it was most certainly not representative of the divorcing population, which was and is heavily weighted towards the Registrar General's social classes 4 and 5. In view of the government's hope that MG would promote reconciliation, which originally inspired the Home Office grant, this was potentially problematic. In regard to the number of short-term cases, the NMGC's officers could never decide whether or not they were a problem. Professionally counsellors gained more satisfaction from long cases and in some indefinable way long cases also tended to be judged as professionally more sound.[43]

Beginning in the mid 1970s, Douglas Hooper (1976), chair of the counselling advisory board, and W.L. Parry-Jones, a psychiatrist consultant to MG, urged the organisation to take stock of what kinds of counselling might be needed in the 'market place' and to pay more attention to diversifying the forms of counselling it offered. Hooper pointed out that the same mould that created the counsellors and non-directive counselling in the second decade of MG's existence also created the tutors, and that little change had taken place in the organisation since in terms of what it prepared its counsellors to do. The divorce rate was increasing dramatically (from 4.7 per 1000 married population in 1970 to 12.0 in 1980) and yet, despite the reconciliation clause in the 1969 Divorce Act, studies on divorce and conciliation showed that only 13 per cent of those intending to divorce contacted MG.[44] Furthermore, studies showed that those clients who came to MG found the service to be of only limited help (Hart 1976). Hooper drew a comparison with Australia, where a more flexible pattern of service delivery had developed and where more people received marriage counselling than divorced. He reiterated his pleas for different approaches to counselling at regular intervals, urging MG to think more in terms of the kind of market that might exist for counselling and to shed the 'withdrawn sanctity' which he felt characterised MG's efforts; to take counselling outside the counselling centre itself – to drop-in centres, for example; and to recruit people from outside the organisation in order to bring in new ideas (Hooper 1976, 1978, 1982).

One tutor replied to Hooper, claiming that the research he cited failed to take account of MG's 'enabling to part' work with couples (Dodd 1978), but the response was muted, reflecting MG's uncertainty about how it should be addressing the issue of divorce or any other kind of specialised counselling. Virtually the only experiment attempted by local councils during the 1970s was with reception interviews: short interviews in which the nature and purpose of counselling was explained. These were instigated chiefly in response to the problem of lengthening waiting lists and only after considerable anxiety as to whether they might not prove too 'authoritarian' (Adams 1973; Monger 1973). In 1975 counsellors were reported to gain little job satisfaction from reception interviews (Heisler 1975). Similarly, a counsellor working out of premises on a local council estate reported a high incidence of one-interview cases and broken appointments and few of the long-term clients whom 'we all appear to find so satisfactory to have on our case lists' (Newton 1973). Rather more popular with counsellors was work in local health centres as part (albeit the only unpaid part) of the primary health care team. By the early 1980s some 74 GPs' surgeries used counsellors in this way (de Groot 1985) but, as their evidence to the Home Office working party on the marital agencies showed, the Royal College of General Practitioners remained equivocal about their usefulness and certainly showed no inclination to pay for their services (Home Office and DHSS 1979: 146). In the course of a correspondence with the Samaritans about the possibility of the two organisations exchanging representatives at conferences in 1979, Tyndall rejected the idea that MG might diversify along the lines of the emergency telephone counselling the Samaritans specialised in, reiterating the traditional MG view that the organisation focused on the marital relationship and risked 'being seduced' by one partner if it opened a telephone line.[45]

Other research conducted outside MG at the end of the decade pursued the theme as to whether MG's counselling met client needs. Both Brannen and Collard (1982) and Timms and Blampied (1985) stressed that MG's training did not invite counsellors to consider social contexts, including the gender-specific context, of clients approaching the agency, while Hart's (1976) research on couples divorcing concluded categorically that MG proved of little assistance because of the organisation's commitment to marriage. Brannen and Collard observed, probably more accurately, that counsellors varied in their assumptions about the desirability of 'marriage saving', but that these assumptions remained unarticulated. Some counsellors were determined to save the marriage if at all possible, others gave priority to the individual happiness of the partners. Hart too easily conflated the emphasis MG as an organisation continued to place on marriage in its formal aims and objectives and in its selection practices (which very much favoured those in their first marriages), with the personal views of counsellors, which were undoubtedly more diverse. From their research with CMAC counsellors and clients, Timms and Blampied reported that counsellors remained agnostic about the explicit requirements of the agency in respect of its views on the importance of preserving the marriage. Both Timms and Blampied's research on CMAC centres and Pat Hunt's (1985) research published by the NMGC identified a gap between clients' expectations and their experience of counselling. Both pieces of research reported clients' desire to 'make sense' of what had happened and both raised, as had O'Connor, the issue as to whose needs were really being met, those of the client or those of the counsellor. MG was disappointed that a television series on marriage counselling did not result in any significant increase in demand for its services, and acknowleged that in showing the 'extreme non-directive phase of counselling (counsellor sits impassive as warring couple slog it out and then languidly drawls, shall we make another appointment?)' (Tyndall 1976) it might have done more harm than good.

MG made little attempt to evaluate its service during the 1970s. As Keithley (1977) pointed out, little was known about what happened to clients and measures to assess the outcome of counselling were hard to devise. Wallis and Booker's (1958) attempt to get counsellors to record their view of the outcome of each case during the mid 1950s was repeated in the mid 1970s with remarkably similar results. In Wallis and Booker's sample 'improvement' was recorded in one third of the cases, no improvement in just over a quarter and in 38 per cent of the cases the counsellor was unable to give an opinion. In the mid 1970s, 25 per cent reported no improvement and 34 per cent still could not say whether or not the client had been helped (Keithley 1977). In a CMAC study of 1973, 50 per cent of counsellors were unable to give an opinion, although more thought they had helped the individuals concerned rather than the marriage (*ibid.*). Nevertheless, MG was delivering more counselling to more clients in more local councils during the 1970s. Whatever the criticism, the demand for the service appeared buoyant. This, together with the growth in MG's apparatus of supervision, provided every appearance of a thriving and dynamic agency, but it masked the failure to address fundamental issues and the extent to which recommendations of working parties appointed to look at specific problems were ignored.

Facing the outside world

MG was very inward looking during the 1970s. The chief officer himself acknowledged this when he announced the setting up of the Home Office working party on marital counselling (Tyndall 1975). Reflecting on the period, many respondents referred to MG as a 'family', drawing attention to the way in which each level of the organisation looked to the one above for support – counsellor to tutor to tutor consultant – with Tyndall and Joan Sullivan playing the roles of father and mother. MG's supervisory structure was closely knit and internally recruited, which meant that ways of working were learned by osmosis. There were few written guidelines and procedures. MG became a sheltered community, insulated from the outside world, with its own ways of doing things.

Throughout the decade, the organisation continued to experience considerable difficulty in defining its relationship to marriage and the family. To a large extent the focus on non-directive counselling, together with the tendency to become more inward looking after the move to Rugby, did not require it to do so. But MG was a national organisation and was expected to take a view on marriage and family issues in particular. In 1979 the editor of *Marriage Guidance* complained that 'hackles rose in Rugby, London and Liverpool whenever anyone got into print or talked on the radio as "a spokesman for the mgc"', but who should speak and did MG have a view? (Editorial 1979).

Even more pertinent to MG's work was the extent to which the shifts in thinking about marriage, particularly by sociologists, and the changes in sexual and marital behaviour failed to penetrate the organisation and hence also the way in which it trained its counsellors and delivered its service. This in turn became increasingly problematic as the divorce rate rose. It was ironic that, when after a long struggle MG had effectively renounced its aim of reconciliation (at least in its own view, if not in that of the public at large), the issue of working with divorcing clients, albeit to effect *conciliation* rather than reconciliation, should have become a major issue for debate.

Finally, MG's relative isolation was reflected in its lack of cooperation with other organisations, which was criticised by the Aves Report on voluntary organisations early in the decade and by *Marriage Matters* at the end of it. MG's objectives in approaching other organisations were very different from those of the early years. Whereas during Brayshaw's period as general secretary MG had sought alliances with other organisations that would strengthen its position as the leading voice on marriage and family life, Tyndall was more concerned to establish MG's position as a counselling agency in relation to the statutory social work service. From the early 1970s, Tyndall manœuvred to bring about the Home Office working party on marital work, whose report would, he hoped, put MG firmly on the map.

Public policy issues

In 1972, MG took 'marriage today and tomorrow' as the theme of its annual conference and Tyndall highlighted the difficulty MG had experienced a decade before in espousing non-directive counselling and at the same time 'stoutly maintaining that certain forms of behaviour constituted "the right basis". This was thought to give the impression that our counselling services were available to those with marital difficulties, but only if those difficulties had "the right basis"' (Tyndall 1972:164). Tyndall stated his belief that MG's revised position (as of 1968, see Appendix 2) – confirming its concern with marriage and family and its belief that the well-being of society was dependent on the stability of marriage – was broad enough to embrace 'those who have a strong feeling for a traditional pattern of marriage and those who look more objectively but nevertheless with equal concern at this relationship' (*ibid*. 165). He thus acknowledged MG's ambivalence about marriage and welcomed it, while asking what MG's response should be to critics of marriage and the family and cautioning that it must listen to its clients and understand their changing circumstances.

MG invited Eva Figes, a well-known feminist, Angela Willans (Mary Grant of *Women's Own* 'Problem Page' and later an executive member of NMGC) and Ronald Fletcher to speak at the 1972 conference. It was almost ten years since Fletcher had caused a furore by condemning as immoral the idea of marriage as a legitimation of sex (see above p. 117). In 1973 he sounded less radical than many commentators on the family. Feminists (Mitchell 1971, Greer 1971) and anti-psychiatrists (Cooper 1972, Laing and Esterson 1970) had already mounted swingeing attacks on the institution of marriage and the family as the source of women's oppression and of neuroses. In fact, as Ellen Ross (1980) has observed, the advice books of the 1970s were increasingly characterised by two conflicting trends, the one advocating more contractual relationships and cohabitation, and the other a return to traditional marriages. Fletcher (1972) did not line up with the abolitionists, suggesting merely that marriage in the future would be more a bonding of 'good friends', prefiguring what other sociologists (principally Young and Wilmott 1975) were to identify as the emergence of the 'symmetrical family', characterised by greater equality and mutuality between husband and wife. The response to his talk was much more muted than a decade before, although one counsellor confessed that while he agreed with Fletcher's values at a personal level, he nevertheless found the talk disturbing.[46] Angela Willans raised the idea that, in future, marriage might not last past the point when the children left home, a point also made by Robert Chester (1973) a year later. Eva Figes began to make the point that was to become central in feminist analysis of marriage – that there were two marriages, his and hers.[47]

In the same spirit in which he had accepted the ambivalence that existed in MG about marriage, Tyndall welcomed the views of all three speakers.[48] This tolerance of a variety of ideas about marriage and the family as they related to the individual marital relationship was characteristic of MG during the 1970s, although the 1972 Annual Conference marked one of the few occasions on which such views were publicly sought. In some respects there was a parallel with MG's attitude towards the burgeoning variety of approaches to marital problems, but in neither case was an attempt made actively to carve out a position for MG or to provide a clear direction for the future. Instead, local councils and counsellors were left to work out their own destinies. Such a *laissez faire* approach had much to recommend it given the contentious nature of marriage as an issue and MG's historical position on it, and the federal nature of MG's constitution. However, it failed to provide any clear principles by which to determine the organisation's future course in respect both to diversifying the service it provided and to changing its training. At the broadest level, MG as an organisation continued to experience difficulty in clearly articulating any position on marriage and the family, although locally some fundraising initiatives during the early 1980s were prepared to take up a 'Save the Family' theme. An Editorial in the December 1982 edition of *Marriage Guidance* bewailed the fact that while 'I'm OK you're OK' (a reference to a popular counselling text by T. A. Harris 1973) might be fine in the counselling room it would not do for MG's principal funder, the Home Office. At the national level, the only vestigial public commitment to marriage and the family was to be found in the Marriage and Family Trust, set up in 1979 as a means of raising funds for what was perceived as an unpopular cause.

During the 1970s, MG implicitly followed the view of many academics and policymakers in emphasising a trend away from male domination and towards companionate marriage. By the late 1970s, the Church had also come to the point where it believed that the institution of marriage 'now stands or falls on the quality of the interpersonal relationship between the couple' (Church of England General Synod 1978), which effectively gave official blessing to the kind of views expressed by Sherwin Bailey during the late 1950s and 1960s (see above, p. 115) and by sociologists and medical writers, who had stressed the importance of personal life rather than of marriage as an institution. The idea of marriage as a companionate and increasingly symmetrical relationship represented a development rather than a rejection of the ideas of functionalist sociologists of the 1950s, who had portrayed marriage as companionate, but with husband and wife playing complementary and different, rather than symmetrical, roles. Both interpretations ignored the relationship between the married couple and the wider social world and inequalities between husband and wife. MG increasingly adopted a psychoanalytical approach to marriage as an interpersonal relationship and, while emphasising the importance of conflict in marriage as a means to personal growth, paid little attention to institutionalised gender inequality. The NMGC's evidence to the government's Select Committee on Domestic Violence in 1975 revealed the organisation's weakness in addressing new critiques, especially from feminists, of marriage and the family, and its lack of capacity to come to terms with institutionalised conflict in marriage (NMGC, 1975a). Harking back to some of its oldest themes, the NMGC stated that it tried to see both sides; a wife might come, through counselling, to understand her 'provocative' role. Furthermore, within the particular relationship, violent conflict might play a positive role in bringing the partners to seek help.

Marriage Matters, the report of the Home Office working party on which all three marital agencies receiving Home Office grant were represented, also adopted the idea of marriage as a symmetrical relationship, citing as evidence Geoffrey Gorer's two studies of sex and marriage published in 1950 and 1971, in which he charted a shift from an emphasis on the complementary roles of breadwinner and housewife to an emphasis on the importance of mutual regard. The report also stressed the creative aspects of conflict and the possibility that couples might come for help in order to separate as well as to be reconciled. Thus the document accurately reflected the priority that MG accorded to what happened within the individual marital relationship, together with its ambivalence about marriage as an institution, in face of which the blandly optimistic formulation of marriage as an increasingly symmetrical relationship provided a useful escape. Brayshaw perceived this in his pamphlet on *Public Policy and Family Life*, written for the Policy Studies Institute in 1980, when he commented acidly on the 'progressive watering down' of MG's principles over the years and charged that *Marriage Matters* was committed to individual growth rather than to marriage saving. In 1983 MG decided that it could no longer subscribe to the idea that the 'well-being of society is dependent on the stability of marriage' and revised its aims and objectives to read: 'The NMGC is concerned with marriage and with the family and personal relationships and believes that the quality of these relationships is fundamental to the well-being of society'.[49] The distancing from marriage and from the aim of reconciliation, begun in the 1960s, was complete, but there was still a vagueness as to what to put in its place.

This vagueness proved problematic in terms of the difficulty MG experienced in making decisions about new directions in the 1970s. Education work was poorly conceptualised in terms of its aims and methods and Hooper's call for greater attention to client needs went unmet other than in respect of marital sexual therapy. In particular there was little attempt beyond reception counselling to do more short-term, crisis oriented work, which was in fact more what Hooper had in mind, and the opportunity to take the lead in conciliation was passed by. The latter provides a particularly interesting working out of the line of development followed by MG after the late 1960s, especially when compared to the enthusiasm MG showed for taking up marital sexual therapy (MST). Conciliation would have been welcomed by Brayshaw as fitting in with MG's broader commitment to issues involving marriage and the family. But the skills it used did not accord well with non-directive counselling. Yet, while MST used behavioural therapy that was also alien to the counselling methods practised by MG, it could be presented as a form of specialisation which linked well to the importance that the organisation had attached to sex in marriage. MST was also attractive in that sexual difficulties were much more amenable to solution than say, infidelity, and the success rate with MST clients was both measurable and high. In contrast, conciliation appeared to undermine the professionalisation MG was striving for in its counselling throughout the 1970s.

When the reconciliation clause was included in the 1969 Act, Tyndall at first envisaged a large increase in the number of clients coming to MG. This did not materialise,[50] in part because solicitors did not refer their clients in the manner that had been anticipated and perhaps because, as subsequent studies showed, those who were referred did not find MG very helpful (Hart 1976; Murch 1980). The sort of work marriage counsellors did was not suited to the structured negotations required to solve practical issues to do with custody and property. MG had moved away from its original object of 'reconciliation' and at the same time from its original aim of 'saving marriages', but this did not mean that the method of non-directive counselling that had evolved could easily be adapted to *conciliation* cases where the decision to part had often been reached, and where there was an element of conscious, mediated bargaining.

Significantly, when the Finer Report on one-parent families (PP. 1974, Cmnd 5629) was published, it effectively ignored the work of MG in its discussion of conciliation. Noting the Denning Committee's recommendation in favour of a 'marriage welfare service', it stated that nothing had been done. Finer was obviously thinking in terms of a state service, but its only reference to MG was to the Wallis and Booker findings of 1956, which it referred to as the only attempt to measure the effect of 'reconciliation work' and which it dismissed as doing little to clarify matters. In particular, Finer cited the conclusion that 'in about one third of the cases the counsellors thought they had done good, in about one third they saw no evidence of improvement, whilst in the other third they did not know what the result had been' (*ibid*: 185 fn.5). Finer thus continued to equate MG's work broadly with 'reconciliation' and, most damagingly, was sceptical as to what it could hope to achieve in this regard. In many respects MG would have agreed. In the counselling room the non-directive counsellor kept 'an open mind' and, if appropriate, couples were 'enabled to part'. But in the first place, as the Finer Report demonstrated, MG had not been wholly successful in communicating the nature of its work to the wider public and, furthermore, the work of non-directive counselling raised uncomfortable questions about what government thought MG had been doing when it gave the grant and what marriage counsellors were actually doing.

MG continued to discuss the issue of conciliation and what its contribution to it might be throughout the 1970s and early 1980s without ever reaching a firm decision.[51] MG proceeded cautiously, exploring with conciliation agencies at a local level how work might proceed when clients came saying 'we can't cope, do the necessary' which was perceived to run counter to MG's aim of helping people to find the confidence to cope themselves (*Newsletter*, March/April, 1972: 1). Some local experiments in conciliation work were set up but, in 1982, MG's own Legal and Social Policy Advisory Board (set up that same year in a largely unsuccessful effort to provide MG with a mechanism for responding to public policies) recommended that conciliation be a separate service (NMGC Social Policy Advisory Board 1982). But this did nothing to meet the criticisms from outside MG that charged that its counsellors had little to offer clients who could see no purpose in prolonging their marriages (Hart 1976).

Other public debates, for example over child abuse following the Maria Colwell Inquiry of 1974 (DHSS 1974), caused some counsellors to wonder whether MG should not diversify into family counselling (Crick 1974), but again no decision was reached and MG's initiatives remained small scale and local. Diversification into either conciliation or family counselling would have required considerable changes in the training MG offered to its counsellors. The argument was that MG could ill afford to get into new areas of work when its resources were slim (by the late 1970s the effect of inflation on the level of grant, decided once every three years until 1977, had begun to bite), and when there was a waiting list for the service it already provided (NMGC 1980). Nevertheless, an editorial in *Marriage Guidance* in 1982 referred to a growing feeling that MG had 'failed to grasp the nettle of change' (Editorial 1982).

MG's uncertainty regarding its purpose was reflected in the poverty of its publicity materials relative to other voluntary organisations in the 1970s. The Annual Report of 1975 took the rather complacent view that MG might be stuffy, but it was known 'to understand marriage' (NMGC 1975b). In fact, while MG was still asked for its views, for example by Sir Keith Joseph seeking information on education for parenthood in respect of the investigation he ordered into 'transmitted deprivation' (Tyndall 1972), the Finer Report showed that the work of MG could also be virtually ignored. The CAB continued to refer the bulk of its cases to solicitors; very few were sent to marriage guidance during the 1970s (Wallis 1973). In 1984, CAB clients were reported to want emergency help and therefore to be deterred by MG's long waiting list (Boucher 1984). Certainly the publicity methods employed by MG in the 1970s were very different from an organisation such as MIND, which played a far more explicitly campaigning role. One paid officer reported that during the 1970s he had been working in the voluntary sector outside MG and had never registered MG's presence as an organisation trying to raise funds. MG remained hesitant as to how far it wanted to invite publicity. Tyndall's 1968 report on the organisational structure of marriage guidance had doubted the need for a full-time publicity officer. A part-timer was appointed in 1973 and counsellors were assured that nothing 'gimmicky' was intended,[52] but many within the organisation continued to believe, despite the occasional question as to whether they might not be behaving paternalistically towards clients, that the business of counselling was too private and confidential to be exposed to public scrutiny.

Marriage Matters and relationships with other marital agencies and the state

The Aves Report (1969) on the voluntary sector criticised MG for not cooperating sufficiently with other organisations and particularly with statutory social workers. Tyndall responded to this criticism and the more fundamental issue of MG's purpose by seeking a more secure niche for the marital agencies. In 1973 the CMAC, the IMS and the NMGC made a joint approach to the Home Office seeking a review that aimed to clarify the roles of the respective agencies and to evolve a strategy that would ensure the maximum use of existing resources.[53] The resulting document, *Marriage Matters*, published in 1979, represented the culmination of Tyndall's efforts to obtain official recognition for MG while still retaining its voluntary status. However, the report proved but a pyrrhic victory. Government did not take the (costly) steps that were necessary for the work of the marital agencies to be strengthened and MG failed to step in to take the initiative.

In 1973 Douglas Woodhouse of the IMS made clear to Tyndall his wish to see a comprehensive review, including the way marital problems presented themselves and the outcome of counselling. He envisaged it 'as an epidemiological study' as well as serving to clarify roles and move the agencies towards a more secure pattern of finance.[54] In the event, *Marriage Matters* did not attempt to review the nature of marital problems, but its tendency to favour the medical model, particularly in its research recommendations (especially para. 8.8) where the analogy with epidemiological research was drawn most clearly, was probably inspired by the IMS approach. More critical from MG's point of view was the firm support *Marriage Matters* provided as to the impossibility of affording a solution to 'all problems of life' via statutory services (Home Office and DHSS 1979: para. 2.36); the need of the NMGC for more adequate financial support if it was to increase in confidence and standing and to develop cooperative programmes with other organisations; and the need of other professionals, particularly social workers and GPs, for training in marital work (*ibid.* paras. 2.36, 4.12, 6.4). Tyndall stressed that it was important that *Marriage Matters* had rejected the idea of a new generic counselling service and instead had given MG the task of training other professionals. But by 1979 there could have been little chance of government giving serious thought to another expansion of the social work services.

Thus *Marriage Matters* was perceived by MG as giving much needed recognition to its work. References to the report always spoke of the boost in confidence it had given the organisation. But government needed to adopt the idea of developing a Central Development Unit for marital work recommended in the report (*ibid.* para. 9.7) in order for the report to translate into the greater financial support that MG hoped for, and this did not happen. Two years after the publication of the document no progress had been made towards securing MG a place within, and yet independent of, government machinery. Nor was there much evidence of greater cooperation even between the marital agencies themselves.[55] Some eight local marriage guidance councils shared premises with the CMAC, but there were no plans to share counsellors because the NMGC considered the CMAC's standards to be lower than its own.[56] What was required, as Parry Jones (1979) perceived, was for the NMGC to take the lead in campaigning for the implementation of *Marriage Matters*. This it failed to do. Rather, the discussions in the wake of the report continued to focus on MG's dilemma as to whether substantially to diversify its service, an issue the report had not succeeded in laying to rest. For while it stated explicitly that no new services were required, it also observed that MG might need more flexibility to deal with less well-educated clients, that priority had been given to counselling at the expense of other activities such as marriage preparation and education for marriage and family life, and that MG faced particular problems in seeking to deliver a professional service with voluntary workers (paras 4.4–4.18). Despite the euphoria that greeted the report – Tyndall (1979) referred to it as the 'coming of age' of marriage guidance – in the end, *Marriage Matters* did not provide the professional recognition MG had sought; nor did it solve MG's internal problems, which deepened with the worsening financial crisis of the 1980s and the Thatcher government's very different attitude towards the financing of voluntary organisations. After 1979, there was little hope of a substantial increase in government funding for either a Central Development Unit, or for MG as an organisation.

REFORM AND CRISIS, 1980–85

Within MG, *Marriage Matters* appeared to provide a new impetus for new activities and for reform during the early 1980s. A series of social research seminars was started to promote more contact with academic and other researchers outside the organisation[57] and a number of proposals for structural and service reforms were tabled. In 1981, a consultative document was produced by an executive planning committee urging local councils to try paid counsellor schemes; only 60 of 162 had developed these during the 1970s. It was pointed out that *Marriage Matters* had raised this issue specifically and had noted the high cost of training in relation to the number of hours counsellors worked; the high proportion of counsellors in basic training; the loss of counsellors to other agencies and the short (five years on average) working life of counsellors. Paying counsellors, it was argued, would increase MG's professional standing, improve the availability of counselling and help to attract and retain counsellors.[58] The following year the executive planning committee produced another consultative document which set out ideal standards for the management of local councils.[59] Like the document on paid counsellors, it repeated arguments from the early 1970s, referring back to the Spoors Report of 1973 and pointing out than ten years later there were more local councils rather than fewer, that on average councils were not much larger than in 1973 and that consequently few had the full-time salaried staff Spoors had recommended. While the documents evinced a new energy, the evidence they provided of lack of real change in two areas highlighted in the early 1970s was depressing. When Professor Charles Handy (1982) addressed the Annual Conference in 1982, he deplored the lack of any managerial control over the work of local councils and also told the organisation that it must identify more clearly its goals and tasks. Nevertheless, the drive to reform and sense of renewal remained strong in the early 1980s with the introduction in 1983 of both a new training scheme in the wake of the O'Connor Report and a firm education initiative. The 1983 Annual Conference was therefore an occasion for congratulation. The failure fundamentally to reshape education and the decision to ignore the more contentious aspects of the O'Connor Report passed unnoticed. But a mere two years later the executive committee found itself facing a motion of no confidence and it was decided to call for a complete external review of the organisation.

Education reform

Six years after Tyndall had defined the primary task of MG as marital counselling and four years after the Collier Report had tried unsuccessfully to reinstate education work as an equal partner within the organisation, the 1977 Annual General Meeting passed a resolution in favour of more 'groupwork', which by the late 1970s constituted virtually the sum total of MG's efforts in the education field. In 1978 an educational projects officer was appointed to set up pilot schemes with a small number of local councils and to introduce training. But by the late 1970s education had become a part of its work that the organisation no longer had any idea how to conceptualise or organise, while remaining convinced of its importance.

The new education projects officer, Kate Torkington, pointed out in no uncertain terms the impossibility of using the same rationale for education work as for marital counselling. She advocated a programme of education and preparation for parenthood which she felt had the advantage of avoiding both the contested ground of marriage and the family and the huge category of personal relationships.[60] To do this effectively she believed that education workers should receive a separate training. Her philosophy of education bore no relation to the earlier didactic approach and emphasised instead the importance of encouraging people critically to examine their worlds. The response to her proposals was strong and for the most part negative. In particular, counsellors refused to contemplate the idea of going back to separate training for education workers and marriage counsellors and feared that MG would end up with two value systems, one for education and one for counselling. A 1980 report of the education review group chaired by Colin Fishwick, who became Chair of the Executive in 1980, addressed both these concerns. Training would not be separated and education work would seek to combine the counsellor's emphasis 'on affective learning with cognitive skills', which would enable education workers to go on to work out the effects of greater self-awareness.[61] This rather tortuous interweaving allowed the new education initiative to be seen as a development of, rather than a competitor for, counselling work, and linked the need of professional education workers for more skills to effect cognitive learning with counsellors' needs for skills training in their marital work. Kate Torkington was given a separate budget but it remained underspent, according to Torkington because of lack of interest at the local level, which in turn reflected counsellors' unease with work in groups that went beyond working with feelings.[62]

Two years later, Kate Torkington left and the NMGC's education advisory board produced an education strategy which clearly recognised the primacy of marital counselling within the agency. While endorsing the idea of helping people to 'understand' their position and to 'identify' their own values, it remained committed to a common training and contemplated no redirection of funds; new funding would be sought.[63] It was still envisaged that the initiative to develop an education programme would come from local councils staffed by specialised education workers, who would be in turn supervised by tutors. This document was enthusiastically received together with one elaborating the new training at the 1983 Annual Conference. However, the chances of developing what was effectively envisaged as a structure for delivering an education service parallel to that of marital counselling became increasingly remote when the Department of Education and Science turned down the application for a new education grant. By 1985 the education budget had nevertheless increased fourfold, but the new education development officer described her role as principally one of 'encouraging and enthusing'.[64] While the importance of educational work had been reiterated and its philosophy separated firmly from that of group counselling, it was doomed to remain but a pale imitation of the marital counselling service.

Training reform

The new counsellor training that was also introduced in 1983 was intended to meet O'Connor's specific criticisms as to the lack of theoretical content and skills training. It did not attempt to address O'Connor's assumptions as to what MG should be aiming for in its marital work, for example, his explicit condemnation of the one-interview case. One member of the training review working party, Bernard Davies, a lecturer in applied social studies, identified MG's non-directive counselling as being a product of a period during which it was believed that material poverty had been eliminated and the problems that remained were ones of personal adjustment.[65] He offered a reading of the O'Connor Report as saying that the training focused on the emotional exchange between husband and wife rather than on the social context of the marriage. This proved influential in making the case for change, but it probably misrepresented O'Connor's views in that his aim was to professionalise MG's training according to the most up-to-date literature in the counselling field, rather than to take on board the sociological critique of the psychoanalytic tradition which had so radically penetrated Davies's own field of community work during the late 1960s and 1970s.

The report of the working party, which included four people from outside MG, made use of the importance Davies attached to economic and social change, but also stressed 'professional change' in terms of, first, the way that the introduction of new theoretical material – systems theory, communications theory, behavioural theory and transactional analysis – in MG had been piecemeal and unsystematic and, second, the need for counsellors to be equipped with skills training to take responsibility for their behaviour as change agents.[66] The working party also urged that greater recognition be given to 'senior counsellors' whom they felt should be able to take over some case discussion work from tutors. Most significant perhaps in view of MG's tendency during the 1970s to look inwards was the importance the working party attached to the need for MG to become an 'open system', exchanging ideas with those beyond its boundaries, educating counsellors 'for scepticism' and recruiting supervisory staff from outside the organisation.

A document produced later in 1983 giving details of how the new training would be implemented acknowledged that Rogerian ideas had tended to the view that counsellors were 'born not made', with the result that 'the culture of NMGC became such that counsellors were encouraged through training to add to their basic 'counsellor qualities' some understanding of psychodynamic concepts and an ability to use these to interpret marital interaction'.[67] The content of the training was restructured to introduce skills training in stages one and three and more explicitly theoretical work in stage two.

A substantial increase in levels of supervision in terms of tutorials was also envisaged. The document also openly acknowledged the 'inevitable tension between the voluntary and professional elements in the organisation', but it did not recommend that senior counsellors do supervisory work, or that tutors be recruited externally. In the light of subsequent positions that were adopted, it seems likely that both omissions reflected fierce tutor opposition.

The new training was welcomed in large part because of the widespread feeling that MG's training had fallen behind other agencies. The CMAC for example had already introduced skills training, and those counsellors participating in IMS courses and case discussion groups had become aware of vagueness that often pervaded these within MG. However, some discussion continued within the organisation as to how much of the training actually changed. There was still no mechanism for integrating theory and practice and, given that no more time was devoted to the residential modules, the amount of skills training that could be offered was necessarily limited. Nor was supervision increased, because by 1985 the NMGC was facing a financial crisis. But the training was demystified. Members of the training team reported that counsellors in training still associated a certain 'magic' with the (reduced) self-awareness training, but the attaching of labels to ideas and methods meant that above all counsellors gained in confidence. They were no longer dependent on a mysterious process of training whose parameters were never made explicit. As a result it became additionally easier for them to move out of the organisation after a short period of time if they so wished. By the mid 1980s, the problem of counsellor retention was becoming more pressing with MG continuing to lose nearly as many counsellors as it trained.

Financial crisis

Throughout the early 1980s, MG continued to expand, and this was felt as a cause for optimism. The 29,000 cases dealt with in 1979 became 38,000 by 1983 (NMGC 1979, 1983). The implementation of the new training and the education initiative imposed additional financial burdens on the organisation and there is no evidence that these were ever discussed in depth. MG had faced a cost crunch before. In 1973 Tyndall had endeavoured to explain that training for marital counselling alone cost the NMGC £30 per counsellor, while local councils paid only £6 of this (Tyndall 1974a); the difference had to be met by the Home Office grant. In 1976 the fees charged to local councils (for constitutional status, sponsoring and training) were increased 150 per cent to cope with the effect of inflation. By the mid 1980s, the position was considerably more grave. Since the late 1960s, MG had followed a policy of permitting expansion according to the wishes of councils, then seeking an increase in grant from the Home Office, but the Home Office had never given any idea as to the size of service it was prepared to support and during the 1970s the increase in the grant it provided appeared to have more to do with the pay increases awarded to staff than the size of the service. After 1979, the Home Office grant increased only in line with inflation. Local marriage guidance councils had done somewhat better because, although local authority grants had also failed to increase much beyond the rate of inflation, client contributions increased threefold between 1979/80 and 1984/5 (Tyndall 1985a). This caused MG counsellors considerable soul searching and threw up complicated justifications of negotiated contributions as a therapeutic tool and 'a first step in the client's exploration of his motivation for change, self value, his difficulties in giving and receiving' (Shapiro 1982). In 1979 the chief officer, while affirming that the future lay with a 'mixed economy', advocated seeking more public money, a course that must have been reinforced by the legitimacy *Marriage Matters* was perceived to confer on the organisation. In 1985 MG sought a 70 per cent increase in its Home Office grant, which reflected both the increased costs of training and the renewed demands by tutors for their 1974 pay award to be met.[68] MG faced a £34,096 deficit for 1984/5 and a projected deficit of £96,842 for 1985/6. But after formally reviewing the basis of its grant to MG, the Home Office refused to increase it beyond three per cent. Moreover there was little cause to hope that the government view would relax. Whereas during the financial stringency of the 1960s the Home Office had commiserated with MG staff, acknowledging the disappointment the organisation must feel,[69] the government approach of the 1980s was explicitly to promote greater self-sufficiency on the part of voluntary organisations.

The chief officer was therefore forced to draw up a number of cost saving proposals. He listed a number of choices, some short-term and some long-term: increasing the fees charged to local councils, cutting the number of counsellors trained, charging counsellors initially for board and lodging during residential training and later for part of their training costs, developing contracts with counsellors to ensure their retention and appointing a fundraiser. In the event, MG decided only on an immediate course of action and presented the 1985 AGM with a call for a 20 per cent increase in the fees charged to local councils and cuts in the number of case discussion groups and tutorials. The AGM was a stormy affair. Representatives from local councils criticised the way in which the crisis had been allowed to develop and the lack of any information as to the seriousness of the financial position. But the increase in the fees paid by local councils was passed. A firmer stand was taken on the proposed cuts in supervisory support, which involved the introduction of shared tutorials and the reduction of case discussion groups from 18 to 15 a year.[70] While it is not clear that more tutors attended the AGM than usual, most observers believed this to be the case because they chose to sit together as a group and gave their solid support to a resolution from Barnet Marriage Guidance Council deploring the cuts in supervision.[71] During the 1970s the tutors had become the backbone of MG's training structure, the guardians of its counselling standards and the keepers of its therapeutic culture. When attempts were made to justify the 1985 cuts in supervision on technical grounds, rather than admitting them to be entirely a matter of financial exigency, the tutors rose to defend what they perceived as the core identity of MG's work. Finally the AGM endorsed a resolution presented by the Wakefield Marriage Guidance Council calling for a wide-ranging review of the organisation by an outside agency to be undertaken by the middle of 1986 and to cover strategic, structural and practical issues. One representative, himself a management consultant, cautioned the organisation about the choice of a consultant and recommended that it opt for a participative rather than a directive approach to the business of the review. After calling for bids, the executive committee later decided to appoint Coopers and Lybrand to carry out the task. While their methods might be described as consultative, they were not participative and they resulted in major changes in personnel and in the ethos of the organisation. For in the face of continuing financial stringency the therapeutic culture of MG bowed before an increasingly powerful managerial structure by which regional officers finally achieved primacy over tutor consultants and 'technical' staff felt themselves to be squeezed out of processes of central decision-making.

THE PROBLEM OF ACHIEVING CHANGE IN MG

The suddenness of the change in 1985 came as a surprise to a majority of workers within MG and particularly to the staff of NMGC and the chief officer, who was forced onto the defensive at the 1985 AGM and who felt sorely rebuffed by the resolutions that were passed.

In all likelihood the events of 1985, which simultaneously defeated a proposal for change in terms of supervision and called for a major overhaul of the organisation, had more than one origin. The financial crisis was the catalyst and the officers recommended cuts without thinking through the effect they might have on the large group of tutors, who gained their credibility from the elaboration of MG's therapeutic culture and perceived themselves as its most active defenders. This group, whose power had increased substantially during the 1970s, had yet to have its 1974 pay agreement honoured. In addition, members of the executive, who brought the proposals for cuts to the 1985 AGM following the recommendations of Rugby staff, were sufficiently perturbed by the reception they received to give their firm backing to a call for an external review. It was undoubtedly significant that in 1985 the chairman of the executive was one of the regional officers who had called on the executive to review its position in 1975; she had resigned in 1978 because of the lack of support she felt that she had received from the chief officer. Above all, behind the suddenness of change in 1985 lay the problem of why there had been so little success in effecting fundamental change during the previous fifteen years. In retrospect, the history of MG appeared to be littered with reports that were never implemented, of which, in 1985, the tutor pay review of 1974 was only the most obvious.

MG appeared busy, expanding and therefore successful, but this masked a sense of drift in regard to the way in which problems were addressed. Many of the issues identified in the early 1970s, especially by the Gowler and Spoors Reports of 1973, were restated during the early 1980s. In particular, the standards of many local councils remained poor, largely because the NMGC allowed small and weak councils to gain constituent status. Problems regarding counsellor retention and the hours of work of counsellors were never tackled. The document on implementing the new training merely noted that it was not possible to make legally binding contracts with volunteers, but said nothing about the possibility of contracts for paid counsellors. Many of MG's problems with taking steps to secure the professional workforce it desired as an organisation delivering a professional service revolved around the perceived antagonism between voluntary and professional, in the sense of unpaid versus paid, and the belief that in order to remain a voluntary organisation MG had to retain a voluntary workforce. Many counsellors were committed to the idea of 'volunteers' working alongside 'professionals' as part and parcel of a peculiarly English way of doing things. This carried an implicit rejection of the North American model of the non-profit organisation, which relied on salaried workers while remaining in the voluntary sector. Nor did MG effectively confront the issue of whether it was meeting client needs. The identification of the primary task of the agency as 'marital counselling' did not go far enough towards resolving the issue of whether MG should offer a variety of forms of marriage counselling in a number of different settings (e.g. long-term or short-term, and crisis counselling, in drop-in centres or health centres as well as in councils' own premises), let alone whether local councils should diversify in terms of the groups to whom they offered counselling (e.g. to families, the divorced, the unemployed). Nor, at another level again, was the continuing demand on resources, exerted by those committed to education, resolved. According to Handy's (1981) analysis of effectiveness in voluntary organisations these were second level problems – the hard issues that lay behind first level presenting problems, such as leadership style or resources. In 1985 it was first level problems that provoked a demand for change, but there was no guarantee that the deeper issues would also be addressed.

The reasons for MG's failure to take action to remedy its fundamental problems are many and relate to the quality of the leadership offered by its paid and unpaid officers; the extent to which the organisational structure impeded reform efforts; and the extent to which the culture of the organisation militated against effective management and resulted in MG becoming inward looking to the point of being relatively unresponsive to external changes in marital behaviour, theories of marriage and the family, and government policy. It may be argued that this is to posit a one-way relationship between MG and its external environment and to place too much responsibility on the organisation for guiding change, when the absence of money in particular was crucial in determining its development. But the deeper second level issues were ones that MG itself had to come to terms with and it seems reasonable to seek the reasons for its failure to address them, even when they were identified by internal *ad hoc* working parties and individuals within the organisation. One of the most conspicuous aspects of MG's failure to undertake fundamental reforms or to come to an agreement as to future directions was the fact that such issues were avoided rather than an attempt made at solutions that failed.

The leadership style of both the paid and unpaid officers of the NMGC was on the whole *laissez faire*. Tyndall was concerned above all to establish a place for marriage counselling and MG as a voluntary organisation in the context of an expanding statutory social work sector. The model he seems to have implicitly relied upon was the one most common to the British voluntary sector, which viewed the service offered as supplementary to the welfare state (Kramer 1981). Nowhere was marital counselling offered on a systematic basis by the statutory social work services and from the beginning it had been considered by Parliament to be too intimate a service to be delivered by the state. While MG was jealous of its status outside the state, the chief officer was anxious to secure government recognition for marriage counselling and thus in turn to make a case for increased government funding. The major role he played in setting up the Home Office working party on the marital agencies during the late 1970s should be located in this context and grew out of a concern as to the professional quality of MG's service *vis-à-vis* the work of the newly established local authority social service departments. Tyndall's emphasis on marital counselling as the primary task of the organisation was designed to sharpen its focus and to encourage greater professionalism in the activity it was acknowledged to know best. Innovation thus tended to be limited to further elaboration of supervisory and training structures and techniques. The needs of the organisation were perceived in terms of sharpening and refining rather than radically altering. MG was a firmly established voluntary organisation and, to use Gerard's (1983) classification, was more concerned with order than with change, and with supplementing the work of statutory services.

Within MG, Tyndall tended to give his fellow paid officers at national and regional level and local councils a free hand. The Wheeler working party on staff structure endorsed his style of management, but like any management style it suited some and needed modification to be helpful to others. This was particularly the case in respect of the regional officers, who were often isolated and hard pressed to exert authority over autonomous local councils. Having appointed staff to do a task the amount of direction and/or support forthcoming from the chief officer was often minimal, and if the task was poorly done, as was certainly the case in regard to some of the work by paid staff at Rugby, action was rarely taken. When Tyndall arrived as chief officer in 1968, the report he wrote on the structure of the organisation at the behest of the executive favoured a strong headquarters and much more direction from the chief officer than had been the case under the 'triumvirate' that had followed Brayshaw. Tyndall came in every bit as much a 'strong man' as his successor in 1986, David French. But in the end the management of MG was characterised more by *laissez faire* and drift than by strong central control. Many respondents used the analogy of 'a family' to describe the way in which MG worked as an organisation during the

1970s. Nicholas Tyndall and Joan Sullivan, the head of counselling, were seen as father and mother and each part of the 'technical' workforce related to its own 'mother figure': counsellors to tutors, tutors to tutor consultants, and tutor consultants to the head of counselling. The whole organisation operated as a rather closely knit system. Anyone entering it had to learn the rules by osmosis: very little was written down; local councils had their own ways of working, often relying heavily on the personality of the secretary and the chairman; and very little direction could be imposed on either local councils, voluntary counsellors or self-employed tutors. Above all the 'family' of MG was held together by a commitment to its therapeutic culture, which is what enabled its workers to continue to speak of it throughout the 1970s as a movement.

In many respects the organisation was over-reliant on the chief officer for leadership. The executive of the 1970s did not exhibit the kind of leadership it did in the 1960s under Paul Cadbury. Indeed it was heavily dependent on the chief officer for advice and did not provide the strategic thinking MG really needed. Executive members acknowledged the complex structure of advisory boards and *ad hoc* working parties to have been confusing. Only the chief officer knew precisely who was looking at which issue when. Eighteen of the executive's 30 members were regional representatives who only sometimes succeeded in thinking nationally. Influential people whom leading officers felt should be on the executive either gained membership through their position as chairs of advisory boards or were coopted year after year. Under two successive chairmen, revisions to the constitution were discussed with the chief officer, but somehow were never accomplished. Similarly, the executive never insisted on the implementation of the recommendations of the various *ad hoc* working parties, and never challenged the increasing number of often weak councils seeking constitutional status during the decade. In the recollection of one member: 'it had a curious habit of stifling people with reform ideas'.

As the Gowler Report of the early 1970s clearly indicated, the crucial linkages between the fundamental problems facing MG as an agency wishing to deliver a service were best revealed at the local level. The issues revolved around what was being delivered to whom and at what cost. But it was very difficult for anyone at the national level to tackle problems from the bottom up. In a sense, the NMGC concentrated on developing those parts of the work over which it did have direct control: the training of counsellors and the development of supervisory structures. Beyond these, it was forced to acknowledge its lack of authority to compel local councils to act, whether in the matter of introducing paid counsellor schemes or amalgamating with another centre to form a more cost effective unit. The only really widespread channel of communication to the local level the NMGC possessed in the 1970s was the tutors, and they were an increasingly disaffected workforce. Rather than taking a strong directive stand, the chief officer and the head of counselling were more often than not forced into a power-broking role, seeking to balance tutors, tutor consultants, regional officers and local councils. Local councils had considerable power to affect crucial decisions at the annual general meeting. Representatives, who might be chairmen, managers or counsellors, were rarely well-informed and were often swayed by the mood of the occasion rather than by strategic considerations. This was probably a key factor in the support given in 1985 to the motion calling for an external review.

MG's main strength and its main weakness lay in its work culture. This was what held such a structurally diffuse and ill-managed – some would say under-managed – organisation together. Virtually all members of MG shared a belief in and an understanding of counselling. The vast majority of its paid staff, including the chief officer, were trained counsellors. Many might have been wary of the power of 'Rugby magic', but they understood it and the organisation was proud of the cohesive technical workforce that it had built up. Workers came up through the ranks to occupy the position of tutor, tutor consultant and often regional officer, and were thus fully imbued with MG's way of doing things and with a commitment to the organisation as well as to the task. Increasingly, MG counsellors were accepted into other agencies. At the same time, this powerful therapeutic culture was inhibiting. The few technical staff members who happened to come in from outside with alternative views as to which therapeutic interventions might be used soon lost their reforming zeal in a manner not dissimilar from new executive committee members, or quickly left the organisation. At worst, the culture became the kind of self-serving vehicle for the counselling workforce described in such scathing detail by O'Connor in 1980. Equally serious was the charge that the method of non-directive counselling penetrated the whole fabric of MG's structure and organisation. In the crisis of 1985 especially there was a tendency to attribute the drift in the organisation to the self-indulgence and dominance of the technical workforce without any thorough attempt either to analyse the precise nature of MG's problems or to acknowledge the structural impediments to solving them. Given the strength of MG's therapeutic culture and its intrinsic connection with the agency's task, it would have been wrong either to ignore or to downplay it. During the 1970s, commentators on local government and health service reorganisation wrote at length on the folly of trying to impose rational structures without due account being taken of work cultures and of the need to secure the commitment of the workforce to the changes (Dearlove 1979; Haynes 1980; Brown 1979). More recently, management literature relating to private industry has also begun to stress that 'effective organisations talk more of culture than structure and strategy' (Peters and Waterman 1982: 7). To blame 'non-directiveness' and implicitly the power of the technical workforce was too simple and too dangerous a diagnosis and one that was to have unfortunate repercussions in the 1980s.

However, there was no doubt but that the culture of MG was inward looking during the 1970s. Lacking confidence in its public stand for marriage and the family, particularly in face of changing public attitudes and behaviour in respect of premarital and extramarital sex, MG had taken refuge in the private work of marital counselling and made it its primary task. Within the non-directive counselling room any outcome was possible. In continuing to uphold and elaborate the method that it had made its mission – non-directive counselling – MG was unable to offer a flexible response to changing client needs. In particular it offered a very confused response to the dramatic increase in the divorce rate and the idea of conciliation. Nor, despite the Rugby research seminars held during the years following the publication of *Marriage Matters*, did it take on board much of the new research on marriage, especially by feminists, which meant in turn that counsellors were ill-prepared to recognise either the different meanings marriage might hold for husband and wife, or the importance of understanding other aspects of the social context of the client, for example the 'help seeking career', the effect of unemployment or of friendship and kin networks (Brannen and Collard 1982; Timms and Blampied 1985). Nor did the agency exhibit any great awareness of the significance of changes in government policy towards voluntary organisations. It was slow to comprehend the strength of the ideological underpinnings of the real cut in the government grant from 1979 onwards, and the implications for MG's financial structure.

The reasons for MG's drift in respect of the fundamental issues that needed to be addressed were therefore complicated: the result of the failure 'to grasp the nettle' of change was that change was effected by crisis rather than by management. O'Connor had perceived a feeling of 'crisis' in the organisation during the course of his research on training. He noted that tutors lived with the permanent crisis of underfunding and 'making do' and had to be ready to respond most to 'crisis calls' from counsellors. He asked whether the prevalent air of crisis in the organisation was not actually about maintaining the status quo rather than about growth.[72] His comments were perceptive: while MG was expanding it was doing so within its existing organisational framework. The failure to address fundamental issues inevitably meant that those issues became more serious, and this in large measure accounts for the explosive crisis of 1985. It was clear from the early 1970s that MG could not continue to expand without giving more thought to the retention and output of counsellors and to changing client needs. But change as a result of crisis is never comfortable and so it proved in the aftermath of 1985.

NOTES

Unless otherwise stated, all materials held in the Relate – NMG Archives.

1 *Newsletter* no. 36, June 1969, p. 5.
2 Nicholas Tyndall, 'The Structure and Staffing of the NMGC. Final Report to the Executive of the NMGC', July 1968.
3 Notes of a discussion on the Seebohm Report, 6/1/69.
4 Nicholas Tyndall, 'Marriage counselling services in the future'. Address to CMAC Annual Conference 1971.
5 Chief officer's column, *Newsletter* no. 37, July 1969, p. 1.
6 *Newsletter*, No. 43, May 1970, p. 7. In support of his views Tyndall cited the findings of the 'Change of Name Committee' which reported that 'It would seem that counsellors are looking, not so much for a new name as for a new task specification.'
7 Report to the Executive Committee from the Sub-Committee on Education for Marriage (The Collier Report) 1973.
8 Gratton Endicott, letter, *Newsletter* no. 35, May 1969, pp. 4–5.
9 Report on the Working Party on the Organisation of Marriage Guidance at the Local Level, 'The Spoors Committee' to the Executive of the NMGC 1973; Dan Gowler and Karen Legge, Final Report on the Organisation of Local Marriage Guidance Councils, March 1973.
10 Peter O'Connor, 'The NMGC. A Review of Training' 1980.
11 Chief officer's column, *Newsletter* no. 53, Jan. 1972, p1.
12 Chief officer's column, *Newsletter* no. 58, Nov. 1972, p. 3.
13 Gowler and Legge, Final Report.
14 *Ibid.*, p. 2.
15 *Ibid.*
16 *Ibid.*, p. 114 App. V.
17 *Ibid.*, Interim Report App. I, p. 52.
18 Report of the Spoors Committee, p. 5.

19 Gowler and Legge, Final Report, pp. 64–85, App. II.
20 Report on a Visit to Leicester and Salop MGCs, 1976.
21 NMGC Executive Mins, 18/7/73.
22 Liz Bostock, Report, *Newsletter* no. 61, May 1973.
23 'Visit of the Maces', Report, *Newsletter* no. 58, Nov. 1972. See also Mace (1972) and P. T. Brown, Report to the counselling advisory board of the NMGC of the Research Work of the Marital Dysfunction Project, Oct. 1973 – Aug. 1976, 31/8/76.
24 David Barkla, 'Group and Education Work in MG: present position', July 1977.
25 NMGC Executive Minutes, 24/9/77.
26 Nicholas Tyndall, 'Towards a Definition of Groupwork in MG'. Memo on Group Work for the Executive Committee, 1977.
27 Report of the Working Party on the Tutor System to the NMGC Executive 1974.
28 Tutor Jobs Specification, February 1975, p. 4.
29 NMGC Executive Mins, 17/5/72.
30 Nicholas Tyndall evidence, Notes of a Meeting of the Wheeler Working Party, 28/11/75.
31 Report of the Working Party on Staff Structure to the NMGC Executive 1978, p. 2.
32 Nicholas Tyndall evidence, Notes of a Meeting of the Working Party on Staff Structure, 18/4/77.
33 *Ibid.*, 20/5/77 and 29/6/77.
34 Dan Gowler and Karen Legge evidence, Notes of a Meeting of the Working Party on Staff Structure, 19/7/77.
35 Dan Gowler and Karen Legge, Some Notes on Regional organisation with especial reference to the roles of RO and TC, nd, circa 1978.
36 O'Connor, 'Review of Training', p. 2.
37 *Ibid.*, p. 4.
38 *Ibid.*, pp. 8, 10, 39.
39 An Initial Response by the Tutor Consultants to Peter O'Connor's Review of Training, Dec. 1980; Peter O'Connor's Review of Training: An interim comment from ANMGCT, 7/3/81.
40 O'Connor, 'Review of Training', p. 26.
41 *Ibid.*, p. 44.
42 NMGC Executive Mins, 20/9/75 and 18/9/76.
43 This view was confirmed by many of our tutor respondents. The importance of not doing crisis intervention work, but rather more 'professional' in-depth counselling was also an assumption informing O'Connor's 'Review of Training'. There are also occasional casual confirmations to be found in the literature, e.g. the statement of Barbara Newton, a Basingstoke counsellor (see below p. 154).
44 Hooper cited Murch's evidence from two surveys of families involved in divorce proceedings during 1973 and 1974. This research was published in 1980.
45 Nicholas Tyndall to Richard Fox, 22/8/79.
46 P. Mears, 'Conference 1972', *Newsletter* no. 58, November 1972, p. 6.
47 See, in particular, Bernard (1973).
48 Chief officer's column, *Newsletter* no. 58, Nov.1972, p. 1.

49 NMGC Executive Mins 22/10/83.
50 Chief officer's column, *Newsletter* no. 46, Nov. 1970, p. 1.
51 Griew (1972) presented a powerful case for distinguishing conciliation from reconciliation.
52 Chief officer's column, *Newsletter* no. 59, Jan 1973, p. 2.
53 M. O'Leary (Director, CMAC), D. Woodhouse (Chairman of the Executive, IMS), and N. Tyndall to Sir Arthur Pearson (Perm. Under Sec., HO), 2/7/73.
54 Woodhouse to Tyndall, 5/2/73.
55 NMGC, IMS, CMAC Progress Report on Marriage Matters, November 1981.
56 Report of the Working Party on CMAC/NMGC Relations, Aug. 1986.
57 The Proceedings of two of these meetings were published: see the special issue of the *International Journal of Sociology and Social Policy* 2, no. 3 (1982) and of the *International Journal of Social Economics* 12, no. 2 (1985).
58 'Professionalism in MG' 1981.
59 'Professional Standards in Local MG Management', A Consultative Document 1982.
60 'Report and Recommendations to the Executive of the NMGC by the Education Projects Officer', May 1979; and 'A Follow Up Paper', Oct. 1979.
61 'Report of the Education Review Group', May 1980.
62 'EPO's Report to the NMGC Executive', Sept. 1981.
63 'An Education Strategy for MG. Recommendations to the NMGC Executive', April 1983.
64 'Report of the Education Officer to the NMGC Executive', July 1986.
65 Bernard Davies, 'MG Training in Context. A Speculative Essay' 1982.
66 'Review of Training for Marital Counselling', June 1983.
67 'The New Training', 1983, p. 5.
68 David Barkla, Note on Finances, 12/9/85.
69 Sir Philip Allen to Cadbury, 6/1/67.
70 NMGC Executive Mins, 10/7/85.
71 NMGC Minutes of the AGM, 1985.
72 O'Connor, 'Review of Training', p. 32.

5 From marriage guidance to Relate

After the call for an external review of marriage guidance, a group of honorary officers met to consider the options. They asked four bodies, felt to be representative of particular types of consultants, to submit bids: Coopers and Lybrand Associates for large commercial firms offering management consultant services; the Grubb Institute for institutions specialising in the study of organisations; Local Authority Management Services representing management consultancy services offered by local government institutions; and the Department of Management Studies at Sheffield City Polytechnic for departments of academic institutions specialising in management studies. The total costs quoted ranged from £10,000 to £60,000. The group decided to appoint Coopers and Lybrand, who quoted a fee of £40,000, representing a 25 per cent discount on their normal scale of fees, which it was agreed would be funded 50 per cent by a £12 levy on active counsellors and 50 per cent by the National Marriage Guidance Council (partial funding was obtained from the Charities Aid Foundation and by a private donation).[1] Coopers and Lybrand reported in August 1986 and their recommendations set in train a prolonged period of structural change that was by no means complete at the conclusion of the research for this study in the autumn of 1989.

The decision to achieve change by radical means was not entirely new in marriage guidance's history. The departure of each chief officer (Mace excepted) had been marked by conflict: in the case of Brayshaw, the dispute had remained internal, but Sanctuary's departure had been heralded by a report commissioned from a partial outsider, Nicholas Tyndall. However, since 1970, MG had experienced some fifteen years of commissioning reports from internal working parties, occasionally with assistance from outsiders (for example from Gowler and Legge of the Manchester Business School), all of whose findings had been for the most part ignored. Both the appointment of a large firm like Coopers and the decision to implement its report thus marked a significant departure. Furthermore, the frank use of a large management consultancy company as a means of achieving change was increasingly a feature of the management of voluntary organisations in the 1980s. The CMAC had called in Coopers and Lybrand as early as 1975 to advise on its management structure, the Family Service Units did the same in 1987 and the Family Planning Association followed in 1988. This trend towards using such companies was also a feature of developments in the public sector during the last decade, but the advantages and disadvantages of applying techniques developed for use in the private sector to both the public and voluntary sectors has received surprisingly little attention.[2] In the case of marriage guidance, there is a sense in which the NMGC wanted to secure a demonstrably professional assessment of its position which it could use to good effect in its negotiations with the Home Office. In the 1980s management consultancy companies have been widely believed to provide this. Certainly MG opted fully to accept the findings of Coopers and Lybrand and to do its best to implement them, although other organisations have been more circumspect in the reception they accorded their respective reports, accepting only some of the recommendations.

Coopers and Lybrand was asked to undertake 'a wide ranging review' and to pay special attention to six major areas: the objectives of NMGC and how they were being achieved at all levels of the organisation; the structure of the organisation; its staffing; finance; organisation, in terms of decision-making, planning and consultation and communication procedures; and its context, including its underlying philosophy and culture, its clientele, possible changes in its nature – from a 'marriage movement to a service agency' – and the definition of its mission.[3] The Coopers Report focused particularly on the changes needed in staffing and structure, confining its comments regarding the essence of the organisation – its philosophy and mission – to the recommendation that MG raise its profile. In response to the latter, MG hired the services of an advertising company, Dorlands, which provided it with a 'relaunch' early in 1988 and a new name – Relate. To implement the changes suggested by Coopers (together with the costs of the report itself) involved an organisation already in deficit in a further financial gamble. Towards the end of 1987, in face of a deepening financial crisis and with no immediate promise of help from the Home Office, Relate, as it officially became on 14 February (St Valentine's Day) 1988, embarked on a further and more radical restructuring of its finances, which was in turn tied to reform of the constituent standards of membership for local marriage guidance councils, now called local Relate centres. The outcomes of the Coopers Report thus proved considerably more far-reaching than had been predicted and involved the organisation, a considerable proportion of whose paid management staff were newly hired in 1987, in charting a complex new strategy.

The changes were radical and painful. In particular the therapeutic culture, which was so highly developed during the 1970s, was ruptured and in the longstanding conflict between 'technical' and 'administrative' staff, the former perceived themselves to have 'lost the war', to use the words of one. The widespread feeling was that technical wisdom was subordinated to administrative (renamed management) expertise and that solutions to the organisation's problems were money-led rather than technically-led. A number of issues remain on the agenda. Both the Gowler Report of 1973 and the O'Connor Report of 1980 demonstrated the importance of examining the linkage between the issues of the organisation's objectives, structure, finance and organisation and their relationship to the kind of service that was delivered by whom to whom. However, in the strategies developed by the organisation during 1987/8, issues concerning the nature of the service and more specifically the needs of clients and ways of securing a greater output from counsellors were addressed but indirectly, through the acceptance of new constituent standards for local Relate centres and through a new financial structure, which was designed to increase the proportion of monies coming from the local centres. In large part, this strategy was dictated by MG's federal structure; counsellors work for local centres and not the NMGC, which has never been able to tell local centres how to run their affairs. But the changes in the relationship between the national and local bodies, in terms of both finance and standards of work (which will not be fully accomplished until the end of 1993) are highly complex and raise in an acute form many issues for Relate as a voluntary organisation: the extent to which the nature of the changes is fully understood at all levels of the organisation and the degree to which there is room for participation as well as consultation; whether the organisation can continue to sustain a volunteer workforce or whether, in pursuit of the North American non-profit model, it will move towards paid technical as well as managerial staff; and whether, in steadily decreasing its reliance on state funding in accordance with government policy, and in increasing its reliance on client contributions, its services will remain accessible to a cross-section of the population. Finally, and most fundamental of all, there remains the issue of Relate's mission. The previous chapters have argued that this has been in doubt since the 1960s. While the policy documents of 1989 have addressed the matter directly, this chapter suggests that it is still not entirely clear whether Relate is about marriage, couples or families, or counselling. Certainly, the immediate post-Coopers and Lybrand changes seem to have served to increase rather than to clear the confusion.

THE COOPERS AND LYBRAND REPORT: MANAGEMENT CONSULTANTS MEET 'RUGBY MAGIC'

The atmosphere in which the management consultants began their work was far from harmonious. The chief officer was unhappy that the AGM had insisted on an external review and warned in the *Newsletter* that the organisation had already gambled on an increased Home Office grant and gone into debt as a consequence; the review would cost yet more money (Tyndall 1985). In the spring of 1986 he chose to reply to Robert Chester's influential article, 'Shaping the Future: From Marriage Movement to Service Agency', published in the autumn of 1985. In his 'Open Letter' he questioned the need for further paid 'professionalisation', stressing the recognition that *Marriage Matters* had given MG and the extent to which future developments would be determined by 'external forces', principally by MG's government paymasters. His only reference to the Coopers review was made when he wrote of the way in which the organisation's decision-making process tended 'to reflect more the community and voluntary ethos of marriage guidance councils than the professional aspirations of the counselling workforce', which he felt explained the resolution put at the AGM to review the structure of the NMGC (Tyndall 1986:24). Tyndall thus made clear his commitment to volunteerism and his view that the Coopers review had come about as a result primarily of tutor intransigence. His attitude towards it was correspondingly cool.

The business of the Coopers review occupied the first eight months of 1986, during which time paid staff felt anxiety about the effect of any restructuring on their jobs. Some who either resigned after the Report was circulated, or reapplied for their revamped jobs, claimed – albeit with the benefit of hindsight – to have 'seen the writing on the wall'. The position of the national staff at Rugby was particularly difficult given the tensions surrounding the chief officer's position and the fact that many MG workers blamed national staff for allowing a situation to develop which required external review. The palpably tense atmosphere that prevailed among paid staff during the review period may have proved an additional factor in pushing Coopers towards making radical recommendations for changes in MG's management structure.

The Coopers Report invited MG to seize the challenge of radical change and become authoritative, innovative, and dynamic, with a higher public profile, expanded services and the capacity to attract and retain good staff. Critically, MG had to operate as 'a unified organisation' in order to achieve all this, with all the elements in the organisation accepting the national body's need to intervene in order to raise standards and expand the scale and scope of MG's services.[4] To this end, the new 'director' of the NMGC should act as a leader of the whole organisation, not just of the Rugby staff, and call on the support of both a national management team and a more responsive representation/democratic control structure.[5] The emphasis placed by the report on restructuring the national management organisation was therefore underpinned by a belief in the need for the new structure actively to shape the organisation as a whole.

The report noted the division between the technical and management strands of the organisation at both the national and regional levels and further noted that the links between the counsellors, tutors, tutor consultants and head of counselling provided 'the only coherent "backbone" to MG as a whole'.[6] In contrast, the support structure on the management side was found to be poor and, furthermore, Coopers reported that 'our interviews indicated that the tutor organisation is also widely perceived as operating too independently of the rest of MG'.[7] The report recommended appointing a director with a larger brief to develop MG at all levels; a regional manager for each region responsible to the director for the preparation of a regional plan; and, at Rugby, three assistant directors responsible for the development of services, public relations and fundraising, and finance and administration. Together, these would provide a direct line of communication to the local centres and a management 'backbone' comparable to that enjoyed by the technical staff. It was stressed that all these appointments should be opened to external as well as internal candidates.

The role of the new regional managers was of particular strategic significance in providing the crucial link between local centres and the national organisation that was necessary if the 'interventionist' policy advocated by the report was to be pursued. Coopers noted that MG had only rarely sought to enforce standards for counselling, management and administration in local centres. Reiterating that the future successful development of MG depended on acceptance of the idea that the national body should be expected to intervene in the affairs of local centres, the report stressed the need for regional managers to work with local centres to raise standards in accordance with the priorities to be set out in the regional development plans.[8] The purpose of national intervention was to enable local centres to merge or federate (in the manner of the Spoors Report). In 1985/6, forty councils reported having fewer than six counsellors. In its turn, the NMGC was urged to create a national development fund with which to offer discretionary help to local centres planning to launch new initiatives. The Report acknowledged that 'it has often been argued that under the present constitution of NMGC, the autonomy of local MGCs has precluded positive intervention by the national organisation to raise standards and promote the development of MG services at the local level'. It went on to reject this view: 'We do not support this view because, regardless of the precise constitutional position, an interventionist policy can be made to work if there is the *will* to do so and a commitment – at both local and national levels – to the objective of expanding MG's capacity to provide high quality services' (our ital.).[9] Nevertheless, within MG's constitution, it was not possible for the consultants to give the new regional managers any new powers to help them carry out their crucial development role *vis-à-vis* the local councils.

The report addressed three further areas of concern: first, the need to strengthen the representation/democratic control structure, second, to improve service delivery and support and, third, the need to secure funding. Under the first, in an effort to confine the executive to policy direction rather than day-to day administration, the report recommended that the membership of the executive be reduced from 26 to no more than 15, and in particular that the number of regional representatives be reduced from 3 to 1, and that the chairs of advisory boards no longer automatically be given seats on the executive. However, these measures proposed to reduce democratic representation from the regions at a time of radical change and to abolish the method by which many interested outsiders had found a place on the executive. Arguably, the problems of the executive in setting policy arose as much from its lengthy agendas and from its heavy reliance on the chief officer for information as from its size. The difficulties experienced at the 1985 AGM also led the consultants to propose changes in the workings of the council: first, to have the elected chairman of the executive act as chairman of the council (one of the very few recommendations not adopted because of the danger of further identifying proceedings at the AGM with the hand of the executive, and, second, to award local councils a number of votes according to their size. In the light of the pivotal role to be played by regional managers, the report stressed the need for two or three regional consultative conference meetings a year and for a review of communication mechanisms more generally within the organisation.

In regard to services, the report was rather more vague. It identified as major concerns the tendency for counsellors to be middle class and white; the degree of uniformity in residential and in-service training required by the NMGC; the high cost of training relative to counsellor output and length of service; and the problems of motivating and retaining counsellors and of evaluating the effectiveness of the counselling performed. The report then acknowledged that 'it became increasingly clear that many of these issues were inter-related and that it would be necessary to consider both the technical and management implications of possible changes'.[10] A separate working group of two consultants and nine MG people was therefore established to consider 'The Training and Counselling Conundrum'. Given the findings of previous working parties, a successful resolution of this 'conundrum' was crucial to any interventionist strategy that MG might develop. However, the working group produced a rather lacklustre document, which reviewed the need for better selection procedures to reduce counsellor wastage; more flexible basic and in-service training, using external trainers and shared tutorials where appropriate, with some proportion of basic training delivered in the regions; reception interviews; and increased client contributions.[11] Nowhere was the nature of the inter-linkages, which Gowler and Legge had seen clearly in the early 1970s because of their 'bottom-up' approach, spelled out.

MG as an organisation desperately needed some indication as to the way in which to tackle the training and counselling conundrum. In many respects the last and shortest section of the report's chapter on services, entitled 'Evaluation', provided the best chance of doing this. MG needed to know more about client needs. Only then could issues regarding the nature of training and the kind of flexibility required be addressed. Nor could the problems of tutor deployment be treated entirely separately from those of counsellor work output and retention. The therapeutic culture of MG was, as the report began by observing, but then ignored, its 'backbone'. Moves towards further 'professionalisation' of counselling, by introducing national contracts, salaried work and a scheme of accreditation for counsellors, and salaried, fixed-term posts for tutors with recruitment from outside the organisation, threatened to change the whole structure of MG's therapeutic culture without necessarily ensuring that client need would be met or the costs of training reduced. Elsewhere the report stated its commitment to 'a mixed economy' which included volunteers and paid staff,[12] but nowhere raised the issue of whether paid staff should pay for their training. Any interventionist policy needed a clear idea as to the kind of service it was trying to promote at the local level, otherwise standards of efficiency would inevitably be developed in relation to existing models of services and ways of working. The failure adequately to unravel the issues at the heart of the 'training and counselling conundrum', which were linked directly to the wider issue of MG's objectives and mission, was in and of itself an invitation to fragmentation, rather than to the unification urged in the report. Counselling, counsellors and their structure of support were treated in the report as a problem of management rather than part and parcel of the core problem of values that had to be translated into goals.

Finally, the report tackled the question of finance. It recognised the need of the organisation to increase its level of funding and suggested that it do this by expanding the scale and range of its services and by mounting campaigns to raise its profile,[13] thus yet again begging the question as to what exactly MG as an organisation was about. As the response of one member of the Rugby staff pointed out, the report

> includes no analysis of the forces at work within MG or in its immediate environment. Some of the rhetoric of the report suggests that there is no real problem about deciding what MG should or could do. This is very far from the case. Many of the present difficulties of MG arise because there are differences of value and interest between various categories of people in and around MG – counsellors, tutors, a chairman, treasurers and so on . . . what consensus now exists about MG's 'distinctive position' is far too narrowly based to sustain a high profile.[14]

Interestingly, a very similar criticism was raised in response to the Coopers Report on the CMAC in 1976; the consultants were accused in the CMAC *Bulletin* of 'a certain amount of woolly thinking about the fundamental principles' informing the basis of the Council's work (Nugent 1978).

By raising its profile, the consultants predicted that MG would be able to achieve a 50 per cent increase in funds within 3–4 years from client contributions, local authorities and fundraising campaigns. The report suggested that in the interim it should be possible to seek one-off funding from the Home Office to tide the organisation over.[15] As with counsellors and counselling, the goal was essentially a simple one of achieving real growth; little attention was paid to the problems posed by the organisation's financial structure. The report pointed out that just under 50 per cent of NMGC's expenditure was incurred on activities in direct support of local councils, including national selection and training, in-service training and support, marital sexual therapy and education. A further 16 per cent went on the six regional offices, whose primary task was to provide support to local councils. Local councils supplied the NMGC with only 8 per cent of its income through their constituent membership and training fees.[16] The report assumed that once a substantial increase in MG's income had been achieved, then the national body would be able to introduce more discretion into its funding of local councils based on the priorities established in the regional plans, and the contributions of local councils could also be differentiated according to size, income and whether the council was contemplating a major new initiative. The report supplied no guidance in the event either that Home Office support was denied during the crucial period of transition or that increased funds were slow to be realised.

The consultants suggested a tight timetable for implementing their recommendations, beginning with the report going for consideration to regional consultation conferences the following month (September 1986) and then for approval to the AGM in October. They also recommended that their assistance be retained in appointing and briefing the new management staff of director, assistant directors and regional managers. In the meantime, they advised that MG should begin a vigorous campaign to persuade the Home Office and private donors to supply interim funding and should set up task forces to take forward the report's recommendations on service delivery and support.

In one of the many immediate responses to the consultants' work, Chester cautioned that the report did not necessarily provide a blueprint for structural and functional changes and that there might be alternative ways of doing things.[17] He also warned that acceptance of it would necessarily involve a commitment to change, not only on the part of the national staff at Rugby, but also by local councils, who would need to 'sacrifice in some measure' their autonomy. Others also took issue with particular recommendations, for example the lack of any precise reference to the fate of education in the report,[18] but Chester's comments provided the best marker as to the most significant assumption underlying the report. While his analysis of the shift from 'movement to agency' had already proved influential within the organisation, there is little evidence that his comments on the Coopers Report received widespread circulation. This was important because the report, while relatively short at 34 pages, was densely written such that it was possible to miss the full import of its assumptions regarding the desirability of a more unified and integrated organisation. David Barkla, the national development officer, also pondered the limits of an 'interventionist strategy', reminding his readers that the Coopers review had been called for largely because of 'NMGC's power to affect the operation of local MGCs in apparently arbitrary and damaging ways' [by reducing support for counsellors in the form of tutorials and case discussion groups].[19]

Notwithstanding these well-considered doubts, the recommendations of the report were accepted with very little change. The tensions within the organisation that had formed the backdrop to the review itself undoubtedly played a major part in securing the kind of wholesale acceptance that was not granted by the CMAC, the FPA or the FSU. Just before the presentation of the report, the chief officer was asked by the executive to give six months' notice.[20] Details of his farewell speech at the same AGM that accepted the Coopers Report were remembered *verbatim* by many respondents, particularly his reference to having previously been in the same hall in order to give blood – voluntarily. He referred to the previous year as 'a baffling time . . . in which key concepts to MG, such as processes of separation and attachment and of transition had somehow appeared forgotten'.[21] Certainly, the tendency within MG's therapeutic community to make analogies between the workings of the organisation and the work of counselling had cut little ice with a firm which was more likely to accept the view that the work culture of the organisation militated against effective management. But Coopers and Lybrand had presented a full and coherent report and there was 'nothing else' on the table. The AGM thus accepted the report and the organisation entered a difficult period of 'interregnum' until the new director, David French, arrived in February 1987. In November of 1986, a steering group followed Coopers and Lybrand's suggestion and set up four task forces, with the intention of tackling each of the major sections of the report – the development of an interventionist policy, representation and control structure, service delivery and funding – rather than focusing primarily on service delivery and support as

Coopers had advocated.[22] In December of 1986, MG heard that the Home Office had refused its request for a one-off grant to implement the Coopers Report. While there could be no turning back, the whole exercise of restructuring was thus made considerably more risky.

MANAGEMENT FIRST

While the Coopers Report was divided into chapters of roughly equal length, each dealing with a particular issue, the need to restructure national management was placed first and was obviously viewed by the consultants as the key underpinning for the development of an interventionist policy, improving service delivery and raising funds. From the first, MG showed itself willing to implement the recommendations regarding the hiring of a new director, three assistant directors and six regional managers. Indeed, many respondents, including a substantial number of those paid staff remaining in post, regarded the Coopers and Lybrand exercise primarily as an elaborate means of justifying the executive's desire to replace the chief officer. While such an agenda may well have played some part in the decision to commission a review by Coopers, as an explanation it ignores both the long term difficulties MG had experienced in achieving managed change and the immediate source of the call for the review, which came from a local council at the AGM. Nevertheless, MG as an organisation and its executive in particular were as prone to expecting deliverance at the hands of a new set of managers as were Coopers and Lybrand, and during 1987 considerable amounts of time and money were devoted to putting the management structure in place.

The Coopers management structure was very simple:

Director

Field Work	National Office
Regional Managers	Asst. Dir. Finance and Admin., Asst. Dir. PR and Fundraising, Asst. Dir. Services

In the view of the chairman of Manchester MGC, it was much *too* simple and ignored a 'multiplicity of invisible dotted lines'.[23] This view finds considerable support from the management organisation literature. For example, Rowbottom and Billis (1987: 7 and 12) have suggested that the true variety of relationship types within all kinds of organisations is much more complicated than 'functional' or 'line and staff' organisation charts would suggest and that often at least two lines of authority need to be identified. In the case of MG, Coopers' structure was notable first for the way in which it omitted the tutor consultant at the regional level and second for the way in which the counselling officer, education officer and MST officer acquired a staff rather than a management function and became accountable to the assistant director of services. The 'technical' line of authority, which by the late 1970s and early 1980s had terminated in the powerful figure of Joan Sullivan, had no place in the new management structure.

Two new assistant directors were hired in September 1987, Richard Redmond as director of services and Ric Holland as appeals director; the former administrative officer Bryan Owen remained in post as the new director of administration and finance. The two new appointees both left the organisation within eighteen months, largely because their ideas failed, and were generally described by respondents to have been unsuccessful appointments. This was particularly difficult in view of their lack of understanding of the organisation's therapeutic culture at a time when technical staff were already feeling threatened by the form of the new management structure. Holland rapidly changed his title to that of 'marketing director' and pushed hard for a diversification of MG's services – particularly into work with children – which could not readily be sustained by the training and expertise available within the organisation. Redmond's lack of appreciation of MG's therapeutic culture was more immediately and more directly felt. The interpolation of an assistant director of services presented special problems. The role of the assistant director was described in terms of policy development, but he had no direct control over the regional managers on the one side and was distanced from the sources of expertise in the form of the three officers in charge of counselling, education and MST on the other. Most of the tutors and tutor consultants were not eager to welcome an outsider to the post. But even those who were prepared 'to wait and see' were rapidly disillusioned by Redmond's failure, first to appreciate the particular strengths of MG's training with its mixture of residential and non-residential components and of practice and supervision, and second to sustain the therapeutic culture. The structure by which the head of counselling had 'nurtured' the tutor consultants, who had in turn made the needs of tutors their first priority while tutors attended to those of counsellors, was rudely shattered. The tutor consultants were made formally accountable to the new regional managers and thus had much less direct contact with Moira Fryer, who took over from Joan Sullivan as counselling officer in 1984, than they had hitherto enjoyed.[24] Finding the tutor consultants to be without effective power the tutors increasingly approached the Rugby staff directly, using their staff association.

The tutor consultant group was perhaps the most sorely affected by the management changes. Considering the prestige and authority they had achieved during the 1970s and early 1980s, their role attracted very little attention in the Coopers and Lybrand Report. They were mentioned but once as part of the in-service training and tutor support given to local councils and with input to the development of the regional plan.[25] Given the longstanding issue of boundaries between the tutor consultants and the regional officers, the tutor consultants were bound to experience the new structure as a demotion. One described how in 1986 she took responsibility for drawing up her region's budget, only to pass the job over to the regional manager the following year. Two tutor consultants described feeling 'muzzled' by the new arrangement. Their complaints about the lack of a technical forum anywhere in the upper reaches of the new management structure resulted in the establishment of a senior technical group, but the director of services did not encourage discussion outside this group. As a result, the tutor consultants began to experience acute tension arising from their position as national employees on the one hand, and from their traditional allegiance to the self-employed tutors on the other. The position was complicated considerably by the fact that the regional officer posts were made redundant. Their incumbents had therefore to compete for the new job of regional manager. Only two of the original six were reappointed as regional managers. One new regional manager had previously been the tutor consultant in her region, but on the whole the new regional managers were rather younger and possessed somewhat fewer formal qualifications than did some of the tutor consultants. In many instances the boundaries between tutor consultant and regional manager remained unclear and the tutor consultants objected to their exclusion from the management structure and from the national management team, to which all the regional managers were appointed.

The tutors, who were perceived to have formed a block to oppose the cuts in tutorial and case discussion group support proposed in 1985, continued to feel threatened under the new arrangements. In accordance with the suggestions in the Coopers Report, the new director of services pursued ideas about regionalising training and recruiting tutors from outside MG. Outsiders recruited onto the training team during 1988 were not always specialists in marital work. In one tutor's estimation the new management team 'think we're an anachronism rather than the backbone'. A member of the national staff concurred: 'Coopers were right, the supervisors are the backbone, but they put a new backbone in and didn't make the links'. While the tutors saw themselves as the flagbearers, protecting national standards of practice, they found themselves with no formal means of influencing national management strategies other than participating in regional consultation days. Furthermore they were pinpointed as the single most costly item in NMGC's budget, while their own pay claim remained unmet.

In the absence of clear communication about the rapid changes in the management structure, and even more perhaps as a result of their sense of being beleaguered, fears and rumours spread quickly through the tutor body. For example, regional managers were said to be taking over consulting rooms for administrative purposes and new assistant directors to have negotiated high salaries and good perks. In March 1988 the chair of the supervisors and trainers association of Relate (STAR, formerly the Tutors Association) wrote to both the chairman of the executive and the director to impress on them the need for 'clear feedback' and the feeling of STAR members that:

> the strategy adopted is resulting in almost all the organisation's limited financial resources being devoted to the establishment of a strongly hierarchical line management structure in Rugby and the Regions, to PR, marketing and fundraising, and to highly speculative long-term planning ventures.

Furthermore, the lack of openness had created considerable anxieties on the part of the tutor body who believed that the amount spent by the new management team was too great and who felt that their own contribution was undervalued.[26]

The new management culture also affected the tutors at the local level. One group of tutors described the manager of a local council as having traditionally been 'a good soul' behind a desk. But over a period of some ten years most 'good souls' had been transformed into first receptionists, then secretaries, then organising secretaries, coordinators, and finally 'managers' with a status, in the perception of some tutors, equivalent to their own. Partly in response to this, the tutors developed a new 'realism' of their own, becoming increasingly prepared to operate their own 'mixed economy' and engaging in more and more private practice (a tutor working full time for Relate could hope to earn only £10,200 a year in 1989).[27] Large numbers of tutors, including those working on the training team, left MG from the summer of 1987 and there was considerable anxiety during 1988 that basic training courses might have to be cancelled.

MG's therapeutic culture has already been described as both its weakness and its strength (see above p. 176). There were longstanding problems associated with the development of 'Rugby magic' and with the imbalance between the power and authority achieved by the technical as opposed to the administrative structures within MG. But to alienate what the Coopers and Lybrand Report had acknowledged to be the organisation's 'backbone' in the shape of its technical staff was to imperil the future success of the reorganisation. As many studies of organisational change have shown, it is crucial to retain the commitment of participants to the changes (see especially Haynes 1980: 113).

MG'S MISSION AND MG'S PROFILE

As if to confirm the fears of the technical workforce, the task force on service delivery, identified by the Coopers and Lybrand Report as having the most important work to do, proved the least successful.[28] The group got no further than reiterating some of the ideas in the Coopers Report with the addition of a few examples. Thus, for example, it advocated extending the range of services provided by MG to telephone counselling, workplace counselling and drop-in centres.[29] But it did not attempt to begin the work of unravelling the more fundamental issues to do with the nature of training, and counsellor retention, output and support. Significantly, the group felt it necessary to spend some considerable time deriving a 'statement of common purpose'. This much needed mission statement reflected the ambivalence and uncertainty felt by the organisation and contrasted greatly with the clear and confident statements of MG in its early years (see Appendix 2). Beginning by reiterating MG's primary commitment to 'helping couples and individuals in the context of their marriages', the rest of the statement then struggled to be more inclusive both of 'other adult relationships which are comparable with marriage' and of other family members especially children. The focus of MG – whether marriage, families or counselling – was by no means clearly established although, in the formal list of services it gave, the statement returned more firmly to an emphasis on counselling and education for marital problems (including divorce). Perhaps, like the East Region in its report to the task force's steering committee, the group wished to avoid the vexed question of 'are we into marriage or counselling?'.[30]

The Coopers and Lybrand Report had spoken forcibly of the need to extend the range and coverage of MG's services, but had left unspecified the nature of the services to be provided. In a lengthy review of the report in the light of the work done by the task forces, David French returned to the issue of what MG should be doing: 'In addition, I believe the task group should be prepared to address the fact that we remain predominantly a single-service agency in which new initiatives are comparatively rare and do not readily flourish'.[31] The Coopers Report had held out the vision of growth – in funding and in services – but the issue as to *how* to extend MG's work was not rigorously addressed either by the report or in the work that followed it. As a regional officer and a tutor consultant commented immediately the report was issued, one of the major issues was how far MG should aim to become a more generalist agency. In common with most of the technical workforce, they strongly defended the image of an MG counsellor as a specialist (Applegarth and Hunt 1986).

However, as the Coopers Report recommendations were picked up by the incoming managers, they were read as advocating substantial 'diversification'. Thus Richard Redmond (1987) wrote of the importance of establishing 'family counselling centres' as the way forward for the organisation and Ric Holland, the marketing director, highlighted the importance of providing services for children, for example in cases of divorce.[32] Such an approach infuriated tutors and tutor consultants, who did not believe that the training MG provided equipped counsellors to undertake this sort of work and who felt that MG was in danger of becoming all things to all people – 'a sort of marital CAB' – and, in the process, doing none of them well. Had the extension of services been approached in terms of increasing specialisation on the basis of MG's established strengths, stressing, for example, outreach programmes, short-term work, work with different kinds of couples, then, its technical staff believed, it would have gained in credibility. As it was, this crucial issue remained unresolved and during 1987 became submerged in the excitement of the 'relaunch'.

The Coopers Report had mentioned in passing that a new or modified name for MG, to reflect more closely 'its current profile' would have 'greater public appeal' and would enhance its fundraising capacity.[33] In July 1987, the advertising agency, Dorlands, was appointed by MG to give it a 'new corporate profile'. In his review of the situation in March 1987, David French wrote: 'I believe we cannot over-estimate the importance of getting our profile right . . .

that we replace the somewhat negative image with an altogether more positive and professional one'.[34]

Dorlands prepared a video presentation to explain their work for the organisation. In this they described themselves as a 'communications agency' and their task in respect of their clients – whether Heinz, the Halifax Building Society or MG – as assessing in commercial terms 'where MG is and where MG needs to be' and recommending ways of bridging the gap. Dorlands reported that the public perception of the organisation was that it was established, reliable and affordable, but that its cause was not one that attracted public sympathy. It also tended to be regarded as somewhat staid and 'preachy'. It was, in short, viewed as a low status, undeserving charity. It therefore needed to raise its profile and present itself to possible donors as a 'modern self-help charity'. Dorlands suggested that the gap between the current perceptions of MG and what it needed to become was such as to justify a 'relaunch', the main feature of which would be a change of name. As the agency explained, the *act* of changing the name of the organisation was in and of itself important because it forced a reassessment of the organisation and provided MG with an opportunity to talk about itself and to re-pitch its approach to sponsors. Dorland's proposals were approved by the executive and ecstatically received by the delegates to the 1987 annual general meeting, who at the end of Dorland's presentation were invited to find the organisation's new name fastened to the bottom of their chairs.

Thus on 14 February 1988 MG took the new name 'Relate', which, Dorlands argued, is what 'you teach the consumer to do'. The name change also provided for a measure of continuity, in that each local council could retain its name as a subtitle, thus Rugby Marriage Guidance Council became Relate: Rugby Marriage Guidance, while the national body became Relate: National Marriage Guidance. While there were inevitably objections to the change, the new name was on the whole well-received by the local centres; after all MG had agonised many times in its history over the word 'marriage' and even more especially 'guidance'. Considerable publicity attended the change in name and Relate has largely succeeded in keeping a much higher public profile since, aided substantially by Princess Diana becoming its patron in 1989. But as the chairman of Manchester MGC wrote some twelve months before the change of name was decided upon, the problem with the determination to raise MG's profile was that it assumed unity as to the organisation's purpose and glossed over issues on which the organisation remained unclear.[35]

The more fundamental issue of which consumers the organisation was teaching to 'relate' and by what means had not been addressed. Nor had the problem of the place of education within MG been resolved and, in those areas attempting to mount an education programme, the parallel (and expensive) system of education workers, organisers and supervisors limped on. In the surge of energy that followed the relaunch, many local Relate centres picked up the idea of diversifying their services, some promising family therapy, and others crisis counselling. The promotional video for Relate, shown at the 1988 AGM, promised to deliver an extremely wide variety of services to individuals, couples and families; to the unemployed and to ethnic minority groups; and in a wide variety of settings: the workplace, drop-in centres and by telephone as well as in more traditional office premises. While examples of these services could be found within its existing Relate network, many centres experienced difficulty in introducing new schemes. In one example offered by a respondent, a counsellor engaged in reception interviewing found herself one morning with a free slot because of a broken appointment. This was filled by a client demanding instant help because he had heard that this particular centre was offering a drop-in service. The client was abusive and the counsellor shaken. The incident forced the centre to reassess the extent to which it was prepared even for changes in the way it delivered marital counselling. In the case of the largest local centre, London, the reaction to the relaunch was very different. London remained indifferent to the change of name and confident as to its purpose. Its director, Renate Olins, insisted that 'the reason . . . London is successful is that we know what we're doing . . . we exist to provide a married or couples counselling service, which is a specialist service'.[36] London had also chosen not to be involved in NMGC's education programme, preferring to run its own group counselling department and training groups for professionals, such as health visitors, who wish to know more about counselling. In addition, by 1990 plans were under way for a London-based training programme for counsellors.

Irrespective of the merits or demerits of the course that London has chosen to pursue, it is clear that a firm definition of and faith in its 'product' seems to have served it well. The recent literature on management in the private sector has stressed the importance of 'product champions' (Peters and Waterman 1982), but in the absence of a clear sense of direction in terms of service development, it becomes increasingly difficult to sustain the level of conviction necessary to maintain a high profile. As Handy (1981: 7) pointed out in his discussion of the second level problems encountered by voluntary organisations, 'values are part of the essence of voluntary organisations': 'why values' demand to know the purpose of an activity and its worth, providing the organisation with its mission, and 'how values' determine the way in which the work is done. During a period of considerable pressure to achieve rapid change, survival is likely to become more important than reflection on purpose and goals, and operational goals are likely to supplant purposive ones (Harris 1989; Powell 1987). In the Coopers Report and in the work done by Dorlands, the main impetus to raising MG's profile was the need to attract more funds and this quite legitimate sense of urgency about the organisation's survival was not accompanied by any thoroughgoing discussion of its purpose. It is notable that in the case of the FPA, clarification of the organisation's mission was made one of the priorities for the Coopers review, although in the event the organisation decided to reject Coopers' recommendations in this crucial area.

Relate's confusion about its mission became yet more tricky to manage as the 'politics of the family' acquired new significance during the 1980s. In the first place, the family has achieved much greater prominence, together with the voluntary sector and the private market, in the government's approach to social policy formation since 1979 (Wicks 1983). However, the prescriptions as to family relationships and responsibilities have been by no means uniform. While Ferdinand Mount (1983), sometime family policy adviser to the Thatcher government, has adopted a libertarian position, viewing the increase in divorce, for example, as reflecting higher expectations of marriage and as a matter of free choice rather than a cause for concern, government policies, especially regarding the care of the elderly and children, have stressed the importance of the responsibilities family members bear one for the other, which in turn rest on the assumption of the two parent family form (Lewis 1986b, Lewis and Meredith 1988). In terms of the mainstream of government policymaking, the assumption regarding Relate's activities probably remains similar to that of government during the late 1940s and 1950s: that the organisation helps to mend marriages. On the other hand the desirability of any intervention into the private world of the family by social workers in particular has increasingly been called into question. Thus, while from early 1983 leaks as to the discussions of the government's Family Policy Group made it clear that more importance was being attached to the family both as a provider of welfare and as a solution to social problems, individuals and organisations, including those, like Relate, whose aim it was to encourage greater self-sufficiency, were discouraged from making any claims on state funds.

In these circumstances, when the family is uncharacteristically high on the political agenda and also a delicate political issue, it may be additionally tempting to refrain from strong mission statements. On the other hand, having spent part of the 1960s and much of the 1970s substituting counselling for the promotion of marriage as the main purpose of MG in a society which no longer appeared particularly committed to marriage, there has also been a temptation (expressed by a number of national staff) to swing back to a firmly pro-marriage position. But as has been well documented (Burgoyne and Clark 1984; Eversley and Bonnerjea 1982; Finch 1989) and as counsellors know from their practice, notwithstanding government's desire to bolster 'traditional' family values and form, the social reality comprises a high divorce rate and increasing rates of second and third marriages. Furthermore, Relate has to address the actual needs of clients. While the most recent (1989) strategic plan for Relate emphasised the importance of marriage counselling as the core task, the desirability of this was questioned by STAR, who would prefer to see the use of the phrase 'couples in trouble'.[37] Relate's ideas, purpose and mission were as vulnerable to political as to financial pressures in the 1980s. This is inevitable, but it proved difficult to acknowledge and discuss the conflicting pressures.

A STRATEGY FOR SURVIVAL

The commitment to implementing the recommendations of the Coopers Report involved MG/Relate in adopting a further high-risk financial strategy when the financial position of the organisation was already shaky. Prior to its 1985 AGM, the organisation had gambled on receiving a vast increase in its Home Office grant and spent accordingly. In addition, it was agreed at the AGM to pay the tutors an extra 10 per cent and to commission a review from Coopers and Lybrand. At an extraordinary general meeting in March 1986, the executive presented council with ten different options for increasing the training contributions payable by local centres and counsellors. The executive favoured an option which kept the increase relatively low but which also restricted to 200 the intake of new counsellors for training. The council opted for somewhat higher charges and an intake of 300 counsellors, reflecting the fact that MG continued to lose as many counsellors as it trained. The increased charges imposed on local councils were justified in terms of the 43 per cent increase in income they had enjoyed since 1981, in contrast with the 9 per cent real cut in the value of the Home Office grant received by the national body (*Newsletter* No. 93, Jan. 1986, pp. 2–3).

At the end of 1986, the Home Office refused a one-off grant to implement the Coopers Report and stated its hope that local centres would soon become self-sufficient such that the organisation would be able to meet the 'full costs of its training and other services'.[38] This smacked of MG's own early hopes in the late 1940s, but in practice, and particularly during the late 1960s and 1970s, MG had come to expect regular upratings in its government grant as befitted a voluntary organisation delivering a supplementary service outside the welfare state. However, the Home Office had never given MG any firm idea as to either the size or nature of service it was prepared to support. In the post-war decades, voluntary organisations which served as the primary providers of services enjoyed substantial leverage in their relationship with state funders (Kramer 1981), especially when, like MG, their goals were widely supported. But since 1979 the government's role shifted dramatically from that of provider to that of change agent, for by withholding funds it has forced a fundamental reassessment of the funding patterns of voluntary organisations which in turn forced the pace of change.

MG was thus bound to implement the changes in its management structure without assistance from central government. In the view of one respondent, the organisation thus became increasingly involved in 'selling the family silver'. Very little detail as to costings was provided by the Coopers Report, but the total costs of the management restructuring were estimated at within 2 per cent (£10,000) of its payroll.[39] One of the recurrent criticisms of the Report by the paid staff of Relate was the extent to which this figure proved to be an underestimate. The new management staff of director, three assistant directors and six regional managers was hired at substantially increased salaries and, confirming the worst suspicions of the tutors, the directorate was provided with 'company cars'. In their defence, the Coopers and Lybrand consultants said that they had recommended some reductions in the staffing budget, but that these recommendations had not been followed. In the event, the NMGC decided not to ask the local councils for further monies to cover the cost of the management reorganisation, fearing widespread objection.[40] Rather, the costs would be met by the national body, which in turn pinned its hopes on the fundraising capacity of its new marketing director. The latter promised MG that he could raise half a million pounds in the first year (between March 1987 and March 1988). However, only £100,000 was raised in the first twelve months. During the period 1988/9 £240,000 was raised at a cost (mainly in salaries for the fundraising team) of £174,000. While many businesses would regard a new venture that more than recovered its costs in the first year as better than satisfactory, half a million pounds had been written into MG's budget. It was therefore inevitable that the next round of rethinking within Relate would be money-led.

During 1988, Relate began to tie the major elements of what the Coopers Report had dubbed 'an interventionist strategy' to a new financial plan, the development of which had very little to do with the Report's recommendations. The task force on developing an interventionist policy, to ensure that national staff in the regions worked with local centres to plan and to set priorities, had stressed the need for local councils to reach new constituent standards of membership in terms of their capacity to improve the standards of their premises; to offer an interview within two weeks of initial contact; employ a minimum number of counsellors; perform a minimum number of units of work (roughly equivalent to hours of work with counselling hours counting as one full hour); and to employ a full-time manager and appointments secretary.[41] During 1988, these standards for constituent membership of Relate were further elaborated and at the 1988 AGM the vote was overwhelmingly in favour of requiring local centres to produce plans as to how these were to be achieved by the end of 1990 – in many cases centres would be forced to federate or amalgamate – with December 1993 being set as a deadline for their implementation. The efficiency of local centres was intimately linked to the new funding strategy, which proposed to shift the burden of funding from the national body to the local centres. The motion on the new funding strategy attracted considerable opposition but was passed when put to the vote.

The rationale for the new financial structure was provided by the Coopers Report, but the strategy itself was very much the work of Relate NMG. The Coopers Report had pointed out that just under 50 per cent of NMGC's expenditure went directly to support local centres with a further 16 per cent to regional offices, whereas the constituent fees paid by local council comprised only 8 per cent of the national body's budget. Given also the 9 per cent decline in the real value of the Home Office grant since 1981, the 36 per cent rise in the number of cases dealt with and the 43 per cent increase in the income of local councils over the same period (mainly as a result of increased client contributions), the national body felt ready to insist on financial restructuring. It set out first and foremost to show that volunteers did not in fact come 'free'. The cost of training and supervising a counsellor over two years was computed early in 1988 to be £3,800, which was met by the national body and thus comprised a hidden subsidy to the work of the local councils. The director of administration and finance calculated that, in 1986/7, 29 per cent of the costs of the work delivered by the local councils was covered by local authority grants, 0.7 per cent by local fundraising, 28 per cent by client contributions and 35 per cent by national subsidy.[42] National Relate therefore proposed to continue to pay for the costs of selection, basic residential training and regional training days, but to pass the costs of supervision to the local centres over a four-year period.[43] It was envisaged that such a strategy would have a number of additionally desirable spin-off effects. Local centres would be forced to become more efficient and to raise more income; one way of doing this, it was pointed out, was by securing more work from counsellors. By making centres responsible for a large proportion of training costs, they would also be forced to confront the fact that a counsellor working three hours a week cost as much to train as one working 20 hours. Similarly, it would be in the interests of local centres to develop a career structure for counsellors, with the aim of retaining a greater proportion of their workforce. For its part, the national body proposed to increase the number of training places for counsellors to 400, thereby assuring a real growth in the workforce and providing the basis for expanding Relate's services. In addition, any centre able to pay the full cost of training a counsellor over two years would be able to buy additional places at full cost. Thus, together, the financial strategy, the first stage of which was also accepted at the 1988 AGM, and the new constituent standards made a bid to put Relate's finances on a secure footing and also to break the 'sausage machine' aspect of the organisation, whereby it continued to train and lose counsellors in equal numbers.

The dual strategy, designed to be implemented during the early 1990s, nevertheless faces some substantial problems. In regard to the achievement of the new constituent standards, some 158 local centres were asked to undergo swift and radical transformation. Many of the smaller centres must either amalgamate, federate, associate or collaborate to achieve the new standards; the variety of terms used reflects the uncertainty about the degree of restructuring that may be required. Some centres have already merged. Paradoxically, for an organisation seeking to increase the numbers of paid counsellors, this has resulted in a need for an increased number of voluntary workers in the form of 'chaperones' to work alongside the outposted counsellors. But some centres, for instance in Cumberland, face real geographical problems in attempting to amalgamate, while others might find themselves next door to a strong centre with no need or inclination to merge. In addition, agreement must be reached between local (honorary) chairmen and (paid) managers as to who will take charge of any new unit. Given local loyalties, local pride and, among chairmen, the strength of motivation prompting voluntary work in the first place, this is far from easy to achieve. In one region, the regional manager suggested that two centres amalgamate and that one of the chairmen take on a development job in the new unit. The regional manager met with a blank refusal and, because of the autonomy enjoyed by local centres, this centre has not amalgamated and may or may not meet the constituent standards demanded by the end of 1993.

The regional manager was envisaged by the Coopers Report as being the key to implementing an interventionist strategy, but the Report stressed the extent to which his or her ability to do so rested on the local centre's willingness to cooperate. Most regional managers referred to the tension they experienced as a result of being expected to act as the agents of the national body on the one hand, and to support the local centres on the other. They described their work with local centres in terms of 'facilitating', 'persuading' and 'consulting', and expressed varying degrees of frustration at their lack of power to direct. One commented ruefully that he could exercise authority only in respect of his secretary; most local centres merely used him as a shoulder to cry on. On the other hand, he felt very uncomfortable about earning five times as much as most local managers and about presuming to direct local affairs when, in his view, both the finances and management of the national body left much to be desired. While, according to the management chart drawn up by Coopers and Lybrand, regional managers were shown as 'managing' the local centres, in practice it is not even clear whether they have any powers of supervision over the local manager, who is the employee of the local centre's executive and therefore under the direction of the local chairman. From the local centre's point of view, the regional manager is perceived as often divided in his support, between both the national body and the local centre, and locally between the chairman and the manager. Many local managers complained that their regional manager was hopelessly tied up in national meetings and was not available for consultation, indicating further that little had changed in practice from the days of the regional officer.

The position of the local managers themselves is far from secure. Many still work part-time, something the new constituent standards seek to correct. Fifty per cent earn between £1,500 and £10,000 a year and there are still some working only for an honorarium, in much the same way as the local receptionist or secretary would have worked for a local council during the 1950s. No two local centres operate in the same way. Traditionally the organisation of most local centres has depended heavily on the commitment of the chairman and secretary who, in the manner of most volunteers, harboured no ambitions as to cost effectiveness and efficiency and who, unlike many counsellors, have not envisioned themselves as 'professionals'. Furthermore, the low volume of work done by small local councils was easily handled by minimal managerial capacity. The demand for a more 'professional' operation and a 'manager' capable of negotiating higher grants from the local authority, of fundraising and working with an executive (who might be either ill-informed or possibly recalcitrant) in order to secure more work from counsellors has placed considerable pressure on this group of workers. In addition, the position of many local centres may be more fragile than appears at first sight. Managers with some twelve counsellors to call on may find that the bulk of the work is in fact being done by three or four, with the result that if one or two of those are temporarily or permanently lost, the viability of the centre is threatened. Unlike counsellors, managers have only recently begun to receive training and their calibre varies considerably. Many complain that counsellors continue to treat them more as 'person Fridays' than managers, while their relationship to the chairmen of their executives remains ill-defined. The manager is usually the person to 'talent spot' a member of the executive for the position of chairman but, once appointed, the chairman is formally the manager's employer and if he chooses to ignore some or all of the directives from the national body there is little the manager can do about it. The fact that managers are usually female and chairmen male means that the relationship tends to slip into that of boss and secretary, especially from the chairman's perspective. The managers may remind chairmen that, after 1993, if constituent standards have not been met, national support for training and supervision will be withdrawn, but some chairmen, albeit a minority, were reported either to be 'putting their heads in the sand' over the issue, or asserting their rights 'to do what I want'.

From the manager's point of view, and ideally in Coopers and Lybrand's view as well, a 'modern self help charity' would run better as a genuinely unitary body. However, not only is 'management' as understood by the private sector impossible in Relate, but the organisation has lacked any set of unified and written procedures to deal with, for example, the induction of new staff hired from outside, any redundancies that might result from amalgamation, or the formulation of contracts for paid counsellors. As a 'family organisation' MG had developed an oral culture, and senior staff, whether tutor, tutor consultant or regional officer, had come up 'through the ranks'. In the absence of written guidelines, the new staff, including management staff, often found themselves initially dependent on those they were meant to supervise; in the case of new tutor consultants recruited from outside the organisation since 1986, this played a part in the rupture of the traditional relationships with the tutor body. The loose federation that suited the marriage guidance movement in its early days does not serve a professional service agency well. But, at the local level, many of those committed to voluntary work with Relate continue to be inspired by values that are closer to those that influenced workers during the 1950s (albeit that their commitment may be more to helping couples in trouble than to marriage mending), than to the professional and managerial concerns that inspired the changes begun by the Coopers Report.

Just as many local centres will experience difficulty in achieving the growth necessary to meet the new constituent standards, so many will also find difficulty in raising sufficient funds to pay the new fees. Neither national staff nor managers are convinced that all local executives understand exactly what they are being expected to pay for. Some may hope that if they manage to raise a little additional money they might carry on as before. The dual strategy of new constituent standards and a new funding structure is complicated and, while a great number of memoranda have been sent to local chairmen from the Rugby staff, the pace of change has been rapid and the full implications of the strategy may not yet be clear. Local centres, and in particular local managers, must be prepared to develop their own strategic plans. For example, well-off centres who are in a position to buy in more training places on top of their allocation must calculate whether this is a wise investment. Increasingly, centres are realising that they will need some compensation for counsellors who move and join another Relate centre at no extra training cost to that centre.

The prospect centres have of raising additional funds varies. In respect of local authorities, the national body has argued that it will be easier to prepare grant applications with realistic costings. But local authorities might not be so happy if they understood how much money was being paid to the national body for training rather than being spent in the local community. The public expenditure cuts of the 1980s have affected local authorities as much as voluntary organisations and have reduced the level of funding to some local centres. Birmingham City Council demanded a more specific commitment from Relate that it would tackle the kinds of need specified by the authority. Other local centres are also in the process of negotiating sometimes lucrative counselling contracts with local authorities, whereby counsellors promise to be on call to provide assistance to local authority employees for work-related problems, but this again raises the issue of identity: what kind of counselling does Relate intend to provide and why?

Client contributions have provided local centres with the bulk of the increase in their revenues during the past decade. In most places these are still rising, but in some parts of the north are nevertheless not meeting the targets set. But while the average contributions per interview may vary, especially between north and south, training costs will be the same for all centres. Most counsellors have overcome their lingering doubts about the ethics of soliciting contributions from clients, but many continue to express fears as to whether Relate will increasingly serve those who can afford to pay. In this regard, it becomes more than ever crucial to receive funding from local authorities to cover those who cannot pay. Finally, local centres have been encouraged to engage actively in their own fundraising efforts. This responsibility tends to fall on the managers' shoulders; very few counsellors want to have anything to do with fundraising. The team of regional fundraisers appointed by the ill-fated director of marketing proved to be a short-lived phenomenon, but some evidence of their work in the form of charity shops (for which managers must find volunteer staff) remains. The national body did draw up guidelines on fundraising in order to avoid overlap in approaches to donors between the national and local bodies, but boundaries remain fuzzy and local expertise in fundraising poorly developed.

It is difficult to predict the outcome of the dual constituent standards and financial strategy. In the course of formulating the 1989 strategic plan, the director outlined his vision of the organisation in the future, which included some '120 centres'.[44] There are now 158, so there must be the anticipation that some of the weaker and poorer ones will not survive into the 1990s and the organisation will emerge 'leaner and fitter'. Given that the tutor body has warned that the financial calculations may be an underestimate in the light of their demands for a pay increase, still greater contributions may be demanded from local centres and more may fail. Opinions as to the justice of the strategy vary considerably. Some, including some of the managers of large centres, feel that it is inevitable that small centres should disappear and refer back to the 1973 Spoors Report, which had recommended amalgamation, but which was never implemented. But the question remains in the minds of many as to whether too much is being expected of local centres too fast.

When the NMGC was founded in 1946, it was fully intended that local councils should be both independent and self-supporting. The Home Office grant was provided to cover the costs of training and national administration. But the rapid expansion of the work of the organisation from the mid 1970s quickly outstripped the value of the grant. Thus, in the 1980s, for a local centre to be 'self-supporting' meant something very different and necessarily involved the centre in bearing a portion of the training costs for its counsellors. Nor in an agency delivering a professional service may local centres be permitted to go their own way. During the 1970s, the NMGC exercised an ever tighter grip on technical standards through the elaboration of the tutor system. The late 1980s have seen a similar tightening in the exercise of managerial control. But the constitution of Relate remains that of 1946, which makes direct intervention in local affairs by the national body an impossibility. Relate National Marriage Guidance possesses sanctions in respect of standards of practice. Thus, if a centre defaults, the national office can withdraw the services of its staff and forbid the use of the name 'Relate', but there is nothing to prevent the centre using another name (possibly 'Marriage Guidance') and employing tutors for its counsellors on a freelance basis. As both the Coopers Report stated and some of the commentators on it warned, the new policies require local cooperation, yet there is little evidence that local centres are prepared fundamentally to compromise their autonomy. Indeed, crucially, it was resentment about the NMGC's attempt to cut its training support that prompted the call for a wide-ranging review in the first place. As in many voluntary organisations loyalties are primarily to the local community rather than to a regional manager or a national management team. Thus, in significant ways the behaviour, if not the beliefs, of those involved with Relate at the grass roots resembles that of the early marriage guidance movement more strongly than 'a modern self help charity'. It was survival that demanded acceptance of the new financial strategy at the 1988 AGM, leaving many local centres feeling resentment that there appeared to be no other options. Given the wide variation in the standard of managerial efficiency between centres, enormous responsibility for the future survival of the organisation is being devolved upon them;

small wonder that one paid officer referred to a 'planned entry into a period of turbulence'.

FROM 'FAMILY BUSINESS' TO 'FRANCHISE ORGANISATION'?

Given the difficulty of grafting the apparatus of a professional service agency onto an organisation with a constitution designed for a different purpose, it is not surprising that a number of new trends have emerged, some of which appear paradoxical. Most striking is the way in which the encouragement given in the Coopers Report towards a unitary structure and as much line management as the organisation would tolerate is threatened three years later by increased decentralisation and fragmentation. The effect of developing the dual constituent standards and financial strategy has been effectively to set managerial and financial targets for the local centres, but to leave them free to decide how, or indeed whether, to meet them. The setting of uniform standards to be met by each local centre and charges that reflect the real cost of training needs must result in considerable changes in the way in which local centres relate to each other and to the national body, and the way in which nationally employed managers relate to technical staff.

Local centres will be asked to buy from the national body whatever they can afford by way of basic training (over and above their allocations) and supervision. Some local centres, particularly London, are already buying in extra supervision and planning to train their own counsellors. Others believe, in all probability wrongly, that it might be cheaper to provide their own training. Still others may find themselves cut off from the national body because they fail to meet the constituent standards, and be forced to look elsewhere for trainers and supervisors. As a self-employed body already engaged in a substantial amount of private practice, there is nothing to prevent Relate tutors supplying this need if the local centre is able and prepared to pay them. Similarly, there is no means of dictating to local centres what kind of service to supply. Until the mid 1980s the core service of marital counselling was sustained by a shared belief in its worth and by a cohesive technical structure geared to its supply. With the encouragement given to centres to diversify, increased recruitment of technical staff from outside the organisation, and continuing lack of clarity as to what Relate's purpose and mission should be, centres may well choose to go very different routes in terms of the types of marital counselling they offer (long-term or short-term, by telephone, on a drop-in basis or by appointment) and of whether they offer more by way of other kinds of personal and family counselling. But this in turn only serves to weaken the image of the 'trademark' – Relate – that they are buying. The new constituent standards did not lay down specific guidelines as to the nature of the service local centres were to provide, which makes sense in terms of maximising the possibility of a flexible response to local need but, in the context of a managerially rather than a technically dominated organisational culture, may result in increased fragmentation. Once begun, fragmentation may prove hard to halt.

Marriage guidance began as a profoundly decentralised organisation. The elaboration of its closed and cohesive technical structure increased the control the national office was able to exercise over the practice of counselling within the organisation. But that control remained of an essentially familial type. It was not for nothing that Joan Sullivan and Nicholas Tyndall were often referred to as 'mother and father'. The tendency for technical staff to use marital and familial analogies when discussing the problems facing the organisation remains. While the marriage guidance movement had already become an agency offering a professional service by the 1970s, it had not acquired the managerial trappings of professionalism. Rather, it continued to operate without formal procedures according to the tenets of an essentially oral and therapeutic culture. The Coopers Report sought to introduce a greater measure of managerial centralisation but, given the lack of power of the new regional managers over local centres and the 'unmanageable force' (in terms of organisation charts) of the tutor workforce, this hope was doomed to disappointment. The unintended outcome has been a restructuring which owes but little to the original Coopers Report and which, while it accepts the federal nature of the organisation, seeks to devolve considerable financial and managerial responsibility to the local centres, thereby profoundly changing the organisation's culture. Marriage guidance always had constituent standards for membership, but in the past these were not very stringent and were rarely enforced. Under the current arrangements, the standards have been raised and will be enforced. In return for their increased fees, local centres will be looking for greater value for money from the national body. In short, as one respondent observed, the ethos of the franchise organisation bids fair to prevail over that of a therapeutic culture, albeit the power of the purse will probably rest firmly with the local centres, and the power of the national body to enforce standards of practice may be compromised.

The logic of the new strategy has been boldly and tightly argued, but its foundations may not be solid. Uniform constituent standards must presume the delivery of a particular set of services, but the purpose of Relate in this regard is far from clear. Furthermore, uniform standards and fees may serve the organisation *qua* organisation well, but may not provide adequate flexibility for the delivery of the very different kind of service needed by Cumbria on the one hand and London on the other. The Coopers Report envisaged a situation in which the organisation moved away from the principle of fixed charges payable by all local centres to differential charges for training, and the replacement of the constituent fee and possibly part of the training charges by a levy based on the total cash income of a centre or, at least, its income from client contributions and other private (other than public sector) sources.[45] Some flexibility in such a diverse organisation would seem to be essential if the tension between local autonomy and national control is to be contained. The logic of the current strategy requires an eventual shift towards a unitary organisation but, by the time the council is ready to accede to such a policy, a high degree of fragmentation might already have taken place.

The new management structure was intended to resolve long-standing disputes such as that between tutor consultants and regional managers and to put an end to a situation in which it was perceived that the therapeutic culture had essentially thwarted effective management. The new managers tended to regard the technical workforce, and in particular the tutor group, as 'unmanageable' and obstructionist, for example in the matter of acceding to different types of training. The tutors saw themselves as the standard bearers and the keepers of technical expertise, their loyalties being in the end to the work itself rather than to the organisation. They refused to contemplate that one kind of counselling might be preferable to another (for example, short-term rather than long-term) and resisted the implicit assumption behind the new director for services' support for diversification: that the training MG provided equipped counsellors to counsel most people and most problems. With the rupturing of MG's therapeutic culture, their position became more beleaguered, but no less powerful. After all, the withdrawal of their services represents the national body's only sanction against recalcitrant local centres and their self-employed status means that suitable incentives must be offered to secure their cooperation. But the strong feeling on the part of the tutors and tutor consultants that technical matters have become second order considerations within the organisation has only served to deepen the tension between the technical and managerial branches of the organisation, which in turn militates against Relate operating as a unified organisation.

A large part of the difficulty in developing both a viable management structure for Relate and a workable financial strategy, whether for a unitary or a franchise organisation, is the lack of a clear sense of what it wishes to deliver. The dual constituent standards and funding strategy was prompted by the organisation's financial crisis, but in 1989 the drafting of a Strategic Plan promised to address directly the nature of Relate's services. The Plan put forward firm proposals regarding the accreditation of counsellors and measures to provide a quick and effective response to clients. It emphasised that the core of Relate's work is marital counselling, and gave less encouragement than previously to widespread diversification. But it is also stressed that conciliation work and family counselling should be considered and that services should be delivered through a variety of means including telephone and short-term counselling.[46] However, there was no attempt to formulate a firm mission statement and the emphasis in the documents from which the Strategic Plan was prepared was on the level of client contributions achieved by Relate for marital counselling compared to that achieved by other organisations in the field. This suggests that the thinking has again been derived more from financial considerations than from a rigorous interrogation of values and purpose. By the end of our study period the Strategic Plan, which had been widely debated before and during the 1989 Annual conference, was being passed to the Executive Committee for further consideration and elaboration. While the Plan goes some way towards listing the variety of services in which Relate is and might be involved, and was portrayed by management as providing a clear sense of direction, beyond a commitment to the 'primary task' of a 'service of marital counselling to individuals and couples in need', significantly it contains no clear statement about the *goals* of such intervention.

NOTES*

1 'External Review. Report of the group set up by the National Executive to explore the options for the commissioning of a review of NMGC', 8/1/86.
2 In the case of the voluntary sector Billis and Harris's (1984, 1986) ongoing research programme is designed to address this issue. See also the recent contributions from Handy (1988) and Poulton (1988).
3 'Consultancy Brief for a Review of NMGC', 8/1/86.
4 Coopers and Lybrand, 'Seizing the Challenge of Change. Strengthening MG's Capacity to meet Society's Needs. A Report to the NMGC', August 1986, paras 1.13–14.
5 *Ibid.*, para. 1.15.
6 *Ibid.*, para. 2.3(b).
7 *Ibid.*
8 *Ibid.*, paras 3.1, 3.18.
9 *Ibid.*, para. 3.18.
10 *Ibid.*, para. 5.3.
11 'The Training and Counselling Conundrum. Summary of Recommendations', nd. circa 1986.
12 Coopers and Lybrand, 'Seizing the Challenge', para. 1.18.
13 *Ibid.*, paras 6.6–7.
14 David Barkla, 'Note on Coopers and Lybrand Report to MG', July 1986, p. 2.
15 Coopers and Lybrand, 'Seizing the Challenge', paras 6.8, 6.16.
16 *Ibid.*, para. 6.2.
17 Note by Robert Chester on Coopers and Lybrand, Sept. 1986.
18 Sarah Gammage, 'Seizing the Challenge for Change: some implications for education', Sept. 1986.
19 Barkla, 'Note on Coopers and Lybrand', p. 5.
20 NMGC Executive Mins, 11/6/86.
21 NMGC Executive Mins of Oct. 1986 AGM.
22 Coopers and Lybrand, 'Seizing the Challenge', para. 7.10.
23 Chairman of Manchester MGC to David Barkla, 30/1/87, Papers of Task Force 4 on PR and Funding.
24 The title 'head of counselling' was changed to 'counselling officer' when Moira Fryer succeeded Joan Sullivan in 1984.
25 Coopers and Lybrand, 'Seizing the Challenge', para. 2.9.
26 Enclosure in David French to Divisional Directors and Regional Managers, 'Development Activity within Relate', 16/3/88.
27 'Review of the Tutor Role. Report presented to the Executive', Jan. 1989.
28 Coopers and Lybrand, 'Seizing the Challenge', para. 7.10.
29 'Final Report of the Service Delivery Task Force', 1987.
30 'Report to the Task Forces Steering Committee by the East Region', 4/4/87.
31 David French, 'Seizing the Challenge of Change: Implementation', 3/3/87.
32 NMGC Executive Mins, 20/1/88.
33 Coopers and Lybrand, 'Seizing the Challenge', para. 6.11.

34 French, 'Seizing the Challenge'.
35 Chairman to Barkla, 30/1/87.
36 Interview 15/2/89.
37 STAR response to 'Relate 2000 Strategic Review. A Consultative Document,' April 1989.
38 Paul Osmond to Chairmen of local MGCs, Dec. 1986.
39 Coopers and Lybrand, 'Seizing the Challenge', para. 2.22.
40 Raymond Frostick (Chair EC) to all Chairmen of local MGCs, 20/2/87.
41 'Membership of National Relate. Rights and Obligations', 21/9/88.
42 Bryan Owen to National Management Team, 'Costs of National Relate', 8/4/88.
43 'Funding Relate: A Discussion paper', 12/8/88.
44 David French, 'A Personal Vision', In 'Relate 2000 Strategic Review', cover.
45 Coopers and Lybrand, 'Seizing the Challenge', para. 6.24.
46 'Relate 2000. Meeting Client Needs. A Strategic Plan'. Draft For Consultation. Pts 1–3, October, 1989.

Conclusion

Issues in the life history of a voluntary organisation

Older theories of the life histories of voluntary organisations stressed the idea of cycles of growth, whereby organisations start out as movements and move through a process of formalisation to death or become subsumed within statutory services. Kramer's (1981) extensive comparative study of voluntary organisations identified four common weaknesses: institutionalisation, referring to the process by which the organisation becomes more bureaucratised and professionalised, thus losing flexibility and responsiveness (albeit too little institutionalisation would result in inefficiency); goal deflection, by which means become ends; minority rule by a self-elected and self-perpetuating group; and ineffectuality, including inefficiency and insularity, poor accountability and a 'muddling through' philosophy. It is possible for any or all of these to triumph over the competencies Kramer identified: specialisation, advocacy, consumerism and service provision. Recent work has questioned the existence of an evolutionary model and has pointed rather to the manner in which voluntary organisations actively seek new survival strategies, a process that requires both a reinterpretation of goals so that means do not become ends, and administrative acumen (Sherrington 1985). In all likelihood, few voluntary organisations, which after all tend to attract a committed workforce, are prepared to be passive participants in a cycle of growth and decay. However, it may be difficult for the members of a voluntary agency successfully to identify weaknesses and to achieve change.

Marriage guidance certainly exhibited many of the common weaknesses of voluntary organisations at different points in its history. It could be argued that, during the late 1960s, the power of the small hand-picked group around John Wallis grew to the point where Wallis was determined that only like-minds should have administrative power within the organisation. During the 1970s, the elaboration of the organisation's technical structure represented a species of professionalisation and was also responsible for the increasing insularity of MG. Nor did these issues pass unnoticed but, as an organisation, MG proved incapable of addressing them without external intervention and a certain amount of blood-letting. Thus, after writing his report in 1969, Nick Tyndall was brought in as a strong man at the head of a hierarchically organised structure, only to be replaced in a not dissimilar fashion in the course of the Coopers and Lybrand review fifteen years later. In each instance, however, the diagnosis of the problems was only partial. It was not until 1985 that Robert Chester identified the shift from 'movement' to 'agency', which in technical, if not in managerial, terms had been evident from the late 1960s. Most importantly, there was a lack of rigorous discussion about the goals of the organisation. After 1969, MG increasingly managed to submerge uncertainties about its public voice and its commitment to promoting marriage beneath the work of professionalising training and the supervision of counselling, hitherto the 'means' rather than the 'end'. Little evaluation of the service was undertaken and little assessment was made of client needs. This strategy was premised on substantial government support. The chief officer clearly saw MG providing a complementary social service, to which there was no access within the welfare state, and for which increasing amounts of government money might therefore be expected. With the setting up of the government sponsored review of the marital agencies (which resulted in the publication of *Marriage Matters*), it seemed that this anticipation was about to become a reality. To this extent, the dramatic change in government attitude towards public expenditure after 1979 was the key factor in prompting MG to seek a new survival strategy. But this would be to ignore the difficulties the organisation had experienced throughout the 1970s in dealing with problems that emerged as a result of grafting the mechanisms necessary to deliver a professional service onto the organisational structure developed to facilitate the growth of a 'marriage movement'.

It was this sense of drift, together with deepening financial crisis, that explains the determination on the part of the organisation as well as the consultants they hired to promote 'radical change'. In their study of 31 voluntary organisations, Butler and Wilson (1989) found that change strategies were usually developed in response to crisis. The focus of the 1986 Report was not so dissimilar from that of Tyndall in 1969, concentrating on a fairly mechanistic review of the organisation's management structure. However, the setting up of a clearly visible line of management accountability from the regional manager to the assistant directors and director was insufficient to create a unified organisation; MG remained a loose federation of autonomous centres. Nor was sufficient attention paid to the strengths as opposed to the weaknesses of MG's therapeutic culture, which had succeeded in holding the organisation together. The ethos of MG's technical work was the ethos of the organisation and could not lightly be displaced. The rhetoric of the post-1986 strategy therefore rang somewhat hollow. In particular the urge to raise the organisation's 'profile' lacked concrete foundation in a consensus as to what Relate's purpose was. The technical staff saw the various suggestions for service development as being driven not by technical expertise, but rather by what would prove most marketable. Neither the technical nor managerial branches gave the assessment of client need or the evaluation of the service much higher priority than it had been given in the 1970s. Relate's current strategy is the boldest of all and will inevitably put considerable pressure on poorly developed local centres.

The apparent incapacity of the organisation to achieve change other than by dramatic means and the social costs of such change raise important questions about the kind of management models suitable for voluntary organisations, especially at a time when the rate of change is accelerating. Billis's (1984) research has suggested that the models developed for use in either the statutory or for-profit sectors will not necessarily be suitable for use by voluntary organisations. It is difficult to devise rules for organisations in which the lines between the bureaucratic and the informal and between employer and employee may be blurred. Relate manifests both these difficulties. For example, it still lacks clear written guidelines for even straightforward procedures, reflecting the days when senior paid staff started at the bottom of the organisation as counsellors and absorbed its ways of working, values and the cohesive properties of the therapeutic culture by osmosis. The relationship between local managers and local chairmen is a good example of the blurred lines between employer and employee: the manager usually becomes the paid employee of a volunteer executive member she has 'schooled' for the office of chairman, the situation being additionally complicated by the customary gendered division of labour between the two, something that extends to the organisation as a whole. Of the original management team of a director, three assistant directors and six regional managers hired in 1987, only two regional managers were women, while the technical workforce was overwhelmingly female. Many respondents viewed the new management structure not only as destructive of the organisation's therapeutic culture, but also as quintessentially 'masculine' and inappropriate to the 'feminine', nurturing qualities of the organisation. The management structure devised by Coopers and Lybrand looked simple and straightforward, but was roundly condemned by all those respondents who had weathered the period of change, although it should be acknowledged that the interviews took place at what may well prove to be the bleakest time for the organisation in terms of its financial prospects (late 1988 and early 1989). The consultants were referred to as 'asset strippers', as having done nothing but 'moved the furniture around', and as having encumbered the organisation with a management structure 'suitable for a legion', although in fact only one other national charity of a comparable size has a smaller headquarters' staff. Furthermore, at a time when the pace of change was extremely fast, MG found itself with only two people with considerable experience of the organisation on its national management team.

The Coopers and Lybrand management model made no concessions to the blurred relationships that tend to characterise all voluntary organisations or to the special tensions between the technical and administrative workforces within MG. The latter remain problematic. The technical workforce has only one representative on the national management team in the form of the female assistant director in charge of services appointed in 1989, and there remains the tension in the regions between tutor consultants and regional managers. Replacing the unsatisfactory parallel structure of the 1970s with one in which the regional managers were given clear authority has not proved a solution. Within a service agency, technical expertise will always provide legitimacy (as it does in the case of the second person appointed to the post of assistant director for services), and it is likely that two similarly qualified regional staff, with both technical and management expertise, working as a chief officer and a deputy would do best. Problems arising from any perceived insensitivity on the part of management staff are always more acute when the agency is involved in counselling.

The new management structure was also encouraged by the Coopers Report to lead the organisation as a whole. It has done so boldly in respect of the current constituent standards and financial strategies. But this dual strategy is complex and the consultation process regarding it was very tightly scheduled to meet the deadline of the October AGM. In addition, consultation has tended to be from the top down, which poses problems for a voluntary organisation in which the members may perceive that they have the right to make decisions about the organisation's future, whether as a result of their commitment to the organisation, or of the organisation's loose, federal structure that encouraged a *laissez-faire* leadership style in the past. The AGM as the final decision-making body remains whimsical in the way it operates, first because the status of the representatives attending on behalf of centres is often very different. If a (paid) manager attends on behalf of a centre, she may well feel unable to vote against the wishes of her (volunteer) employer (the chairman) no matter what the course of debate. In the second place, proceedings of Council may be increasingly subject to control by a more sophisticated management, which consults and lobbies in advance. There is also the danger that with a new and active director, the executive will again take a back seat rather than take full responsibility for policy direction as happened after the appointment of Tyndall in 1969. At the 1989 AGM, the chairman of the executive expressed pleasure in the fact that with an active national management team the executive had been able to play more of a mediating role between the national body and local centres. But this is not necessarily to fulfil the vital work of policy direction which, in common with other voluntary organisations, seems increasingly to rest with paid officers who in turn seek external help from consultants. The management of a voluntary organisation must take account of the democratic and participatory structures of the agency, although in MG the parlous financial state of the organisation and the importance attached to firm central direction by the Coopers Report have encouraged a style of management familiar to the private sector. But the degree to which the national body can actively manage an organisation in which the local centres enjoy complete autonomy is severely restricted.

The life history of MG/Relate reveals the way in which the development of the organisation has been characterised by a series of dysfunctions which began to emerge as soon as MG's faith in its mission to promote marriage faltered. Above all, the development during the late 1960s and 1970s of a sophisticated technical structure for the delivery of a counselling service raised the related issue of what to do about MG's educational role, the vehicles best suited for delivering a counselling service, and the problem of counsellors' work output and retention. These were not resolved. The current financial strategy may well force a change in the pattern of recruitment and work of counsellors. Indeed, the 1989 Strategic Plan made substantial recommendations on the improvement of career structures for counsellors, including accreditation, contract counselling and more highly developed paid counselling schemes. But the larger issue remains of what the essential qualities of Relate's work are and should be. Until the nature of the 'product' is clear it is difficult to be sure that management and funding structures are appropriate.

In the future, Relate faces considerable competition. Work for the 1989 Strategic Plan estimated that its share of marital counselling work fell 10 per cent between 1979 and 1989 and could fall another 10 per cent between 1989 and 1992. The largest growth in counselling has been in the private sector, where the client pays £20–25 an hour, as opposed to the average client contribution of £6 collected by Relate.[1] But other charitable counselling organisations have also experienced considerable growth. For example, the Westminster Pastoral Foundation (WPF), founded in 1969, employed 137 staff in 1988, all of whom were paid and 12 of whom were full-time and salaried. It saw 650 clients per week for counselling. In comparison, Relate's 1,890 active counsellors gave some 265,000 interviews a year. Thirty five per cent of the WPF's clients were unemployed, but its average client contributions per session was £9.50. Over 70 per cent of its income was derived from counselling contributions and training fees, 15 per cent from central and local government and 14 per cent from donations. Relate still relies on government grants for 40 per cent of its income, on client contributions for 42 per cent and on fundraising for 10 per cent. In 1988, the WPF recorded a surplus of £62,912 (Westminster Pastoral Foundation 1988). The WPF is also clear about its role as a service agency aiming to provide high quality counselling and psychotherapy for a wide range of personal and family problems.

If Relate is to continue the process of becoming a fully professional service agency, then it must face the crucial issue of further refining its purpose, together with the counsellor and client issues that flow from it. At present, while Relate's share of the marital counselling market is diminishing, it still trains the bulk of marital counsellors. Many of its own counsellors and tutors are engaged in private work, and technical staff report that increasing numbers of counsellors are giving the minimum required voluntary service to Relate in order to gain the certificate of recognition (three hours a week for forty weeks for three years) and then leaving to do private work. This must raise the issue of Relate's position as a training organisation and the desirability of moving towards contracts for counsellors and fees for training.

Increased reliance on client contributions raises the issue of whom Relate intends to serve. During the 1970s, MG's research officer stressed that the organisation saw a cross-section of clients roughly equivalent to the population at large, but recent data show that higher socio-economic groups are over-represented among Relate's clients, while lower socio-economic groups – those most likely to divorce – are under-represented.[2] The type of counselling Relate offers is intimately linked to the kind of clients it is likely to attract. Better-off clients are likely to want appointments for a number of sessions. Poorer clients are more likely to use drop-in centres or telephone counselling and may desire a more task-centred approach. Relate has been inclined to offer a service more geared to social classes one and two, although for these the long waiting lists must act as a deterrent, especially in an expanding market. There may well be a tension between Relate's desire as a charitable organisation to serve the population as a whole and its increased reliance on client contributions as its main source of funding. The desire to elicit payment from clients may also require additional skills on the part of counsellors. The husband prepared to pay £50 a session (a not unknown sum in some southern regions) for counselling for himself and his wife may also expect the counsellor to change his wife's behaviour. But, basically, Relate has a fund of goodwill to draw on in terms of public opinion, which might, as Dorlands found, perceive it as somewhat staid but also reliable, and in terms of its workforce. Inevitably, both paid workers and volunteers have their own reasons for getting involved with Relate; personal satisfaction as much or more than altruism has always been the main motivating force. Nor is this necessarily incompatible with the delivery of a professional service, but more research and evaluation of client needs and of the precise ways in which Relate feels able to meet them is crucial.

NOTES

1 'Relate 2000 Strategic Review. A Consultative Document', April 1989.

2 *Ibid.*, p. 7.

Part III
David Clark

Introduction

In this third and final part of the book we return to that area of work which, over time, came to be seen as the primary task of the NMGC: marital counselling. In Part II we explored how counselling approaches developed in the context of specific organisational changes, and in particular a growing uncertainty about the extent to which marriage guidance could continue to speak with a public voice on issues concerning marriage and family life. Here, our emphasis will be more upon the debates which affected the growth of counselling as a specialised, technical activity within marriage guidance. We shall see that counselling did not develop in a linear, uninterrupted manner, but has been subject to conflicting tendencies, oscillating between change and stability. In making sense of this, some of the concepts introduced in Part I are of value; there are issues here concerning the role of key individuals, both as initiators of particular developments and as 'theorists' about these; there is also the question of 'medicalisation', which asserts and reasserts itself at various points.

The following chapter therefore takes as its main theme the relationships between 'guidance', 'counselling' and 'therapy' in the work of the NMGC from the early 1950s onwards. Out of these inter-relationships we are able to construct a marriage guidance 'model' of intervention in marriage. This 'model' came to comprise an admixture of approaches deriving from a number of different sources: non-directive counselling (albeit with occasional elements of 'guidance' still retained), psychodynamic theory and practice, behaviourism, and counselling 'skills' approaches. The adoption of this eclectic approach was partly incremental, for example during the 1970s, when links with the Institute of Marital Studies brought in a heavier emphasis on psychodynamic theory and when the experiments with marital sex therapy (MST) introduced counsellors to behaviourist ways of working. Then, following the major review of training which took place in the early 1980s, a new legitimacy was given to this mixing of influences, and a further dimension added in the emphasis on counselling skills. By the end of our study period it appeared that this eclectic formula had achieved a broad official sanction within Relate.

As we shall see, however, these increasingly sophisticated debates about theories and methods of intervention were obfuscated in three ways. First, they allowed the focus to move away at times from the couple and their marriage, to the individual needs of the client and the client's inner worlds. This was a particular danger of non-directive approaches, practised in the main with lone clients, rather than couples. Second, these debates often took place in the absence of any parallel discussion about the goals of intervention. What was the aim of counselling: reconciliation, conciliation, divorce counselling? As the 'public' doubts surrounding these questions became such an important feature of marriage guidance, so the tendency to avoid them by attention to 'technical' questions appeared to grow. Third, the lack of clear agreement about goals prevented the development of a sound strategy for research and evaluation. Non-directive styles of counselling, based on humanistic principles, were clearly ill-suited to 'positivistic' research concerned with effectiveness and for many years little research was attempted. When research did take a more important place on the organisation's agenda it was often poorly resourced and tended to focus on practical questions of service development. Where work was conducted on questions of counselling process and outcome, the results were only partially reassuring, showing the service to be limited in scope and effectiveness.

In the chapter which follows, these issues are traced mainly through their representations within the marriage guidance literature, drawing particularly on the in-house bulletin (later journal), *Marriage Guidance*, as well as a variety of other publications produced by the organisation. We also make reference to literatures developed elsewhere, particularly at the Tavistock, which made a major contribution to the development of ideas about intervention in marriage. In taking this material as a basis for analysis, it has to be recognised that the sources used may not always be typical of more rank and file thinking within marriage guidance or of overall standards of service delivery. It is likely that the ideas expressed in the journal may be to some degree in 'advance' of those more widely disseminated through the organisation. Accordingly, a reading of this material tends to have the effect of 'bringing forward' the chronology of changes described in earlier chapters, such that, for example, non-directive counselling or therapeutic approaches appear rather 'earlier' than they may have done on the ground.

Another characteristic of this material is the extent to which it emphasises the thinking and reflection about marital work which has gone on in marriage guidance over several decades. The house journal has undoubtedly played a major role in this, providing an outlet not only for the organisation's own thinkers and writers, but also for others outside who, through its pages, have been able to contribute further ideas for development. The demise of the journal in the mid 1980s may well be symptomatic of the diminished place for such reflection within the organisational culture; and, certainly, for as long as the journal remains absent it creates a significant *lacuna* in our understanding of the organisation's thinking on technical matters. At the same time, it is a striking feature of most of the literature explored in this chapter that it is more concerned with advancing *theoretical* understandings about marital problems and marital work, than with the evaluation of service outcomes. This observation is a general one, by no means limited to the marriage guidance material; but while the journal has fallen into abeyance, and in the absence of other outlets, it does raise the question of which groups and organisations are currently pursuing such questions within the spectrum of marital work in Britain.

It is the aim of this chapter to show how a variety of influences (didactic, non-directive, medico-therapeutic, 'skills'-based) have been brought to bear within marriage guidance over four decades. We shall see how these have vied for attention, displaced or unbalanced one another and come to co-exist in a fragile, eclectic combination. Some may see echoes here of a post-modern formulation, which is lacking in core values, de-centred and sceptical of any one prevalent rationality. Such an analysis may prove helpful in understanding future changes within Relate. It also suggests a bridge to one area of enquiry which we have not been able to develop here. This study has not, within its terms of reference, given detailed attention to the client perspective, and has relied on the research efforts of others for insights into this. Within the 'cat's cradle' of linkages between organisational, marital and societal changes, referred to in Part I, a crucial question for further development would be the extent to which the present combination of models is able to 'fit' with the changing experiences and constructions of marriage in a society characterised by 'post-modernism' (Featherstone 1988).

6 Counselling, therapy, efficacy

Within the space of a decade a small number of individuals working within marriage guidance were responsible for the introduction, acceptance and eventual wide dissemination of a radically new approach to the issue of helping those experiencing problems in marriage. The adoption of *counselling* as the main mode of intervention in marriage was a remarkable achievement, though one which, as we have seen, brought several complications in its wake. David Mace had been an early convert to the counselling approaches being developed by Carl Rogers and his colleagues in the United States. These placed a major emphasis on counselling as a process, rather than a set of diagnostic and treatment techniques, through which clients were enabled to reach some measure of self-understanding. The role of the counsellor in this process would be one of giving unconditional positive regard to the client, in such a way that unwelcome behaviour and bad feelings could be explored openly. But in the early 1950s, marriage guidance was still not ready for such an approach. The movement remained heavily dominated by doctors, lawyers and ministers of religion and a philosophy that complex problems in a marriage could only be dealt with adequately by professionals. Volunteer counsellors were therefore largely restricted to the role of initial interviews with clients, followed by referral to a specialist consultant, and this division of labour was one of the characteristic features of 'guidance'.

Mace's departure to pursue his interests more vigorously in the United States and the appointment of officers eager to develop the work further, particularly John Wallis, contributed to a climate in which counselling ideas and practice could become more central to the movement's activities. Wallis was iconoclastic and inspirational; counsellors trained under new techniques which emphasised the importance of thoughts and feelings in relationships and they became increasingly eager to work with clients themselves, utilising a new-found confidence in the value of counselling. But the nature of this activity often remained unclear. The movement repeatedly asked itself what *is* counselling? And there were doubts and disagreements about the extent to which it could be described, learned and taught.

Despite these, marriage guidance became increasingly recognised for its rigorous approach to the selection and training of volunteer counsellors. Methods of training and tutorial supervision, developed in-house, became more refined. With the appointment of Nicholas Tyndall as chief officer in 1968 the organisation looked for a source of intellectual and theoretical validation for its work. It found this in a new rapprochement with the Institute of Marital Studies (formerly the Family Discussion Bureau), which provided a highly developed framework for understanding the psychodynamic aspects of the marriage relationship. These ideas joined Rogerian principles at the centre of the marriage guidance approach to counselling, drawing it in some instances in a more overtly therapeutic direction. In parallel to this, the organisation explored the possibilities for a specialist service offered by counsellors with a further training in working with sexual problems. Following initial pilot experiments, a marital sex therapy service was developed during the 1970s which made use of a radically different set of theoretical and practice principles, drawn from behaviourism.

It would be a mistake however to suggest a clear linear progression, wherein the work inexorably moved from 'guidance' to 'counselling' to 'therapy'. Although 'guidance', with its overtones of advice-giving, became less favoured, some elements of it lingered on, for example in the application of a medical model to marital problems, which were seen in the early days as having an organic quality, amenable to 'treatment'. While this approach had become less favoured by the 1960s, it did reassert itself in the 1970s, when some counsellors became absorbed in the theories of marital and sexual therapy; even so there remained some resistance to the medical model, and there was little attempt to develop clinical principles of research and theory building within the organisation. Likewise, non-directiveness, while it usurped 'guidance', did not entirely pave the way for 'therapy'; John Wallis in particular was concerned about such a transition and seems to have exercised a moderating role, which allowed the organisation to hold on to its 'lay' traditions. In this way 'guidance', 'counselling' and 'therapy' seem to have existed in overlapping, oscillating relationship: an in-house fusion which came to characterise the marriage guidance approach. Indeed, during the 1980s, *eclecticism* became an explicit hallmark of the marriage guidance style, selectively drawing on elements from a variety of models: non-directive, skills-based, psychodynamic, medicotherapeutic, behavioural. This more pragmatic approach seemed to find particular favour in the cost-effective atmosphere of those years, steadily shaping the organisation's view of marital work following the Relate relaunch of 1988.

Eclecticism may, however, have been a response to deeper contradictions. Despite all the attention given to the selection and training of counsellors and to the development of local marriage guidance councils, little effort was made to address questions about the efficacy of the service. Research in the organisation has never held a high priority and has been dogged by a number of constraints: confidentiality, methodological difficulties, and lack of resources. However, the available evidence does cast doubt on the extent to which marriage guidance has provided a comprehensive service to the population of those experiencing marital difficulties. It also shows that only about one half of clients appear to be satisfied with the service they receive. More fundamentally, there remained the problem of evaluating the success of the service in terms of the organisation's own goals. In so far as the goals of intervention remained unclear, there were limits to how far evaluation could be developed.

FROM GUIDANCE TO COUNSELLING

When marriage guidance first began there were limited expectations as to what could be achieved by volunteers working face-to-face with clients in difficulty. Writing in 1966 from the United States, David Mace, one of the founders of the movement, looked back on the original work.

> Our first concept of a British marriage counsellor was that of a 'first aid' worker, who did what he could to help, but in the knowledge that he had behind him a team of specialized consultants whom he was expected to bring in when he got out of his depth.
>
> (Mace 1966: 7)

In his book *Marriage Counselling*, Mace (1948b) had seen two particular tasks for the counsellor working with couples in need of help. Counsellors must know enough to be able to 'diagnose' the cause of clients' troubles with reasonable accuracy and they should also be qualified to give simple treatment in uncomplicated and non-technical situations (Mace 1948b: 7). However, it was deemed preferable for husbands and wives to be seen separately, rather than together (Mace 1948b: 45) and Mace's approach to the interview in those days was in marked contrast to the later orthodoxies of the non-directive school: counsellors were encouraged to sit behind a small writing desk, and in the early stages of the first interview would note down a range of 'essential details' about the case, including the history and nature of the presenting problem (1948b: 45,46).

At this time there were clear limits to the expertise which counsellors had at their disposal and marriage guidance remained primarily a referral service. Following the counsellor's initial 'diagnosis', the usual practice was to refer the client to one of a range of consultants. Depending on the nature of the 'problem', these included psychiatrists, psychologists, general practitioners, solicitors, social workers and ministers of religion. Providing 'guidance' on marital problems in the 1950s was therefore actively multi-disciplinary and brought the lay counsellor, the doctor, priest and lawyer into collaboration. This combination of legal, spiritual and medical influences was the key framework for the work of marriage guidance at this time and was reflected in the training programme for counsellors, which contained numerous lectures on these subjects. It is interesting to note the range of intellectual influences to which trainee counsellors were exposed, however, and the extent to which the organisation constructed marriage and its problems as both a private relationship and a public phenomenon, interlocking with wider elements of the social structure. This emphasis upon the institutional aspects of marriage and the role of a multi-disciplinary service was considerably eroded by the mid 1960s, and in the intervening years elements of the 'guidance' model, such as the role of religious and medical ideas, struggled to remain influential.

The rise of counselling

Throughout the 1950s there was a growing debate about the nature of counselling in marriage guidance. As it developed, volunteers became less willing to refer cases to specialised consultants and increasingly eager to work with clients themselves. In so doing they were able to generate a self-image as caring, skilled 'professionals', albeit while working as volunteers. They were helped in this by the writings of NMGC's own paid staff, such as John Wallis (Wallis 1955, 1960), who was appointed counselling officer in 1955 and who, as we have seen, was to have a major role in promoting counselling approaches both within and beyond the organisation. But the growth of counselling was not only about organisational imperatives; counselling was supported by, and itself helped to generate, a belief that in the increasing affluence of the post-war success story, problems rooted in economic disadvantage had been largely supplanted by those which lay in the realm of interpersonal relationships. These problems were not easily labelled as spiritual, medical or psychological, though practitioners of each of these disciplines continued to speculate on their cause and cure, and to bring an influence to bear within marriage guidance. As features of a new post-war era, these personal and emotional problems, as they related to marriage, were thought amenable to innovative approaches, which the emergent ideologies and practices of counselling seemed suitably poised to develop.

When David Mace, writing in *Marriage Guidance* in 1951, asked 'What *is* counselling?' (see above p. 103) he suggested that the question could only be answered by reference to the considerable American literature on the subject, and in particular the debate on the merits of 'directive' and 'non-directive' approaches. Mace clearly identified himself as a follower of the teachings of Carl Rogers on client-centred, non-directive counselling and sought to put to one side the historic notion of counsel as advice or recommendation, such as that practised by priests, doctors, lawyers. Instead, counselling should be understood as a 'relationship' which '. . . should aim at a situation in which the counsellor does no more than provide a sounding board to enable the enquirer to think out and feel out the solution to his problem, relying almost entirely upon his own innate resources' (Mace 1951: 2). For Mace, this was the model of counselling towards which the movement should progress, recognising always that 'both directive and non-directive methods, mingled in proper proportion according to the nature of the situation with which the counsellor has to deal, will have their part to play in the total therapeutic task' (Mace 1951: 3). It was precisely this question of the 'proper proportion' which would become the issue of contention.

Two years later, in the September 1953 issue of the journal, J. B. Alfred, a counsellor, bemoaned the new extremes of non-directive theories which proscribed any advice or information being given, in favour of allowing the 'client' to talk endlessly and un-prompted (Alfred 1953: 5). The article produced a correspondence which continued until February of the following year. Two psychiatrists wrote pointing out the importance of unconscious motives in determining both the client's utterances and the responses of the counsellor, emphasising that non-directive counselling should be seen as an *active* rather than a *passive* process. More characteristically, a counsellor from Uxbridge pleaded that 'true counselling' should take the 'middle way', being 'both directive and non-directive and, paradoxically, neither'.[1,2]

Border skirmishes between the advocates of person-centred approaches to counselling and the holders of reductionist and medical based viewpoints, as well as more 'directively' inclined counsellors, continued for several years. For example, some doctors involved in the movement made counter-suggestions which tended to point up the contrasts between the non-directive approach and a style of intervention based more rigidly on a medical model. Alfred Torrie, a general practitioner, though much impressed by the value of counselling, saw marriage breakdown as a 'social disease' requiring treatment by a psychiatrist only when 'everything else has failed' (Torrie 1958: 380). But David MacLay, a psychiatrist, suggested a 'positive approach', prompted by his idea for a more specialised service dealing with sexual problems (MacLay 1955: 4). Likewise, another psychiatrist could be quite categorical on the requirements for effective marriage counsellors, who should be able to distinguish between manic, depressive, neurotic and psychopathic states (de Rudolf 1955).

Nevertheless, during the 1950s these medical influences, which had an important early role in the 'guidance' model, were gradually being filtered out of the organisation's official thinking about intervention in marriage, particularly on the part of its paid officers. Following the appointment of Wallis, counsel would increasingly be replaced by counselling, an approach which placed considerable emphasis on the practitioner's self-awareness. The influence of North American, person-centred theories now came fully to the fore.

Non-directiveness in the ascendant

When NMGC's education secretary, Alan Ingleby, returned from a study visit to the USA in 1956, he had two important experiences to report. Firstly, he had met Carl Rogers and participated in one of his counselling workshops, run on 'client-centred' principles. The language of Ingleby's description clearly prefigures some of the elements which were later to congeal into what became known as 'Rugby magic'.

> . . . the workshop became a living experience of what is meant by the 'client-centred' approach and from start to finish the group

was thrown on its own resources . . . In the first few days, we
felt all the frustrations of people accustomed to some form of
organisation and direction in their lives, and in consequence the
staff had to put up with a good deal of hostility . . . until gradually
we began to realise that the answers lay in ourselves. That there
were no ready-made solutions. That here was a climate in which
we could experience that individuals have within themselves the
seeds of their own fulfilment. That an atmosphere of complete
unconditional acceptance of people as they really are, 'warts and
all', can demolish defences and release a latent capacity for growth.

(Ingleby 1957: 58)

Secondly, in participating as a staff member in a workshop run
by family life educator, Nelson Foote, Ingleby was exposed to
the notion that family stability is a product of the interconnected
personal *competencies* of family members; and moreover that these
competencies can be learned and improved on. Crucially, Ingleby
learned how this notion could be explored through the use of *role-play*,
which later became an important tool within the training of volunteer
marriage guidance counsellors.

At a more fundamental level, however, Ingleby in this article had
articulated a significant shift in the organisation's thinking. Here at
last was some form of theoretical underpinning to the growing practice
of non-directive counselling. Most important of all, it represented an
appeal to a theory which was explicitly counterposed to deterministic
Freudian ideas of the personality:

While having direct links with Freud, Rogerian 'client-centred'
theory is as different from Freudian psycho-analytic concepts as
chalk is from cheese; the positive view that it is of the very nature
of man to move forward towards maturity contrasts sharply with
the idea that the individual is constantly frustrated by the conflict
between his instinctive needs and the environment in which he
lives his social life.

(Ingleby 1957: 59)

Nonetheless, such a position also carried an inherent weakness,
apparently unrecognised by those who were attracted to it. Person-
centredness was a practice based on *individual* theories of psychological development, and not on issues relating to the marriage
relationship or marital interaction. Accordingly, as these Rogerian
ideas became more established within the organisation they tended
to redirect the focus of practice away from marriage and towards

individual counselling. The point was further reinforced later the same year when the *Marriage Guidance* journal published an address given by Rogers in which he explored the role of psychotherapy in easing problems of communication, thus giving further encouragement to those within the movement who wished to take their practice to 'deeper' levels (Rogers 1957).

Though its most important champion within marriage guidance, Wallis nevertheless seems to have been concerned about non-directive counselling slipping imperceptibly into psychotherapy. His enthusiasm for new approaches had its limits. Wallis wished to see counselling established as 'an entity in its own right and not . . . "the poor relation of psychotherapy" ' (1959: 29). But his justification for this was always paradoxical: counsellors *could* work with issues of unconscious motivation and not 'run away with self-protective cold feet, muttering that it is all too dangerous and difficult'. But at the same time they should not expect to learn about such issues through academic study, since 'much reading of text-books can hinder rather than help' (1959: 29). For Wallis there was no substitute for the experiential learning of training and of practice.

By the late 1950s marriage guidance was poised to become synonymous with non-directive counselling. When Margaret Torrie wrote an article in the journal describing the emergence of the Cruse organisation for widows, she was able to point out that '. . . counselling was not enough. The Cruse Club had to go beyond the scope of marriage guidance . . .' (Torrie 1959: 213–14). Non-directive theories appeared to find especially fertile ground in the expanding number of case discussion groups which became available to counsellors under Wallis's encouragement. One counsellor, writing in 1962, recalled her first experience of such a group:

> It soon became apparent that counselling by proxy or theoretical solution was not in demand. What then was supposed to be happening? I was mystified, I was restless, I wanted to *know*. Going straight for the ball, I finally asked 'What do other group members think the purpose of this is?' It is significant that I remember nothing of their replies, or even if there were any. I only remember the ball being returned to me – 'Well, what do you think it is?' and my reply 'Self discovery'. This is in fact a partially correct answer but was given without comprehension.
>
> (Stafford 1962: 201)

This account also showed how case discussion might be used to deal with 'blocks' which resulted when a particular case found echoes in a counsellor's own earlier experience and she needed as a result to be 'helped through it' in order to return to being 'client-centred'. *Group* dynamics were used to illustrate the dynamics of the counsellor-client relationship and the role of the group leader in case discussion consequently assumed greater importance. As one informant remarked, it was also a feature of this period that the early case discussion leaders, mainly psychiatrists and psychiatric social workers, were gradually replaced by tutors from within the movement.[3] While this was seen as a sign of growing confidence within marriage guidance and must undoubtedly have produced greater consistency of style within the groups, it also promoted insularity and sealed off at least one door through which the organisation might be exposed to new ideas from the 'external' world.

A further feature of the non-directive counselling approach was the increasing tendency to ignore or devalue the importance of wider structural factors in the creation of marital problems. Addressing an international marriage guidance conference in June 1963, Wallis identified three dimensions of counselling: 'impersonal', 'personal' and 'relationship' aspects. While it was important to 'take into account' the first of these in counselling, it could often be seen that some clients were themselves the cause of their apparently 'external' problems (Wallis 1964: 67–9). This tendency was discussed at a more general level by Halmos (1965) in his *Faith of the Counsellors*, where he explored 'the discrediting of political solutions' within contemporary society. The NMGC in these years certainly showed little interest in the political aspects of marriage, preferring as Halmos put it in a 1966 *Marriage Guidance* article 'to correct the complainer and not the cause of the complaint' (Halmos 1966: 117).

Nevertheless, there was evidence of an increasing demand for the services provided by Wallis's new-style counsellors and the number of cases seen for 'remedial' counselling more than doubled in the period 1955–65, to 16,000 (NMGC 1954–5, 1964–5). Related to this there was a growing disinclination for counsellors to refer their clients to expert consultants. Indeed, as Wallis pointed out in a 1966 article, some of these professionals were now inclined to refer their own patients and clients *to* marriage guidance, and to look to the organisation for training in marriage counselling (Wallis 1966). The era of 'guidance' was largely over and indeed the term itself had become something of an embarrassment. In the succeeding years it was dropped from the organisation's vernacular, giving way as we have seen to the widely used term, 'MG'. By the 1970s there was little enthusiasm for the kind of 'guidance' favoured in the early 1950s, which had served to project the organisation as one composed of 'experts' on marriage.

The ascendancy of counselling did not lead automatically to more *therapeutic* pretensions however. Although in the years after Wallis there would be a growing interest in the use of more overtly therapeutic approaches, these were less to his own taste:

> Counselling is not a science or a technique, since the counsellor is personally involved in the process. He is not an aloof practitioner or technician, an unmoved mover, like the First Cause. He gives of himself, he shares with and receives from the people who come for his help . . .
>
> (Wallis 1968: x)

There seems to be a rejection here of counselling being aggrandised into some more inclusive, all-seeing, clinical gaze (Foucault 1973) in favour of retaining a more liberal, egalitarian approach to counsellor-client relations. Indeed, in another piece, published in 1968, Wallis asked the question 'Is the therapist a real person?' and felt able to reply in the negative, arguing that in psychoanalytically based interventions the 'emphasis tends to be put on interpretation rather than involvement as the true essence of casework, leaving the urgent, practical, everyday problems as little more than symptoms or unwelcome intrusions from outer reality into the therapeutic task' (Wallis 1968b: 167–8).

But Wallis may have by this stage led his audience too far to draw them back from the brink of therapeutic aspirations. Although some of the 'first aid' counsellors still remained in the movement, the gold standard in counselling work was soon to become that which was constructed on the foundations of psychoanalytic theory and in which the methods and techniques of the therapist would hold greater cachet than those of the counsellor. Certainly the pages of the *Marriage Guidance* journal during the 1970s, following Wallis's departure, carried a far greater proportion of material than before on issues of a psychotherapeutic nature (e.g. Skynner 1975, 1976; Thornborough 1975; Williams 1975; Ness 1976; Gray 1976). All these would serve in general to encourage the psychotherapeutic aspirations of many counsellors and to stimulate movements towards a model of practice within marriage guidance which, while holding on to Rogerian self-centredness, fused this with approaches involving the overt use of psychodynamic theories and techniques of intervention.

Therapeutic drift

The early 1970s saw a number of longstanding practitioners within marriage guidance writing at length on the theory and practice of their work (Guiver 1973; Holt 1971; Mann 1974). Although these publications appear in the Tyndall years, they are better seen as an important legacy of Wallis's contribution, with its ambivalent stance on counselling versus therapy. While they were not yet typical of mainstream practice within the organisation (their ideas were probably in advance of most counsellors and tutors of the time), we see in these writers something of the drift towards therapy which Wallis, despite his apparent intentions, had engendered. For example, Nancy Holt, who had trained as a counsellor in the late 1940s and who subsequently took a variety of roles within marriage guidance, felt able in her book *Counselling in Marriage Problems* to describe the nature of 'marital *therapy* as practised by many NMGC counsellors' (1971: xi, our emphasis). Drawing on the influences of psychodynamic theory, she could also describe the approach as one in which 'sympathy and science meet and mingle' (1971: 1). This picture is reinforced by Pamela Guiver, in a book interestingly sub-titled *Counselling in Personal Relationships*:

> Counsellors are trained in psychoanalytical theories to provide a firm basis for their work, but the art of counselling relies on the skill with which the counsellor exercises her own intuitive and perceptive faculties.

> (Guiver 1973: 15)

The uneasy relationship between theory and intuition is at the heart of much of this writing. Anthony Mann, a counsellor and later regional officer within MG, in a work with both Jungian and existentialist overtones, could offer an elaborate account of the paradoxes of human relationships but seemed unable to advance beyond a position in which the counsellor's 'own person is the main tool in the counselling process' (Mann:1974b: 136). In this way the model of practice within MG in the 1970s came to represent an in-house blend of Rogerian-inspired non-directiveness with psychodynamic insights. A further addition to this would be the behavioural principles which were developed in the marital sexual dysfunction project; we shall discuss these in the next section.

It is perhaps characteristic of these rather inward-looking years that it took the observations of some relative outsiders to draw attention to the mounting contradictions which lay within the MG approach to marriage counselling. Douglas Hooper, a university academic and chairman of the NMGC Counselling Advisory Board, questioned whether an organisation developed to respond to marital problems within post-war British society was well equipped to deal with the social trends of the late 1970s. In particular he emphasised that the mode of practice within counselling ought 'probably [to] swing now to *active*, *accessible* and *positive* counselling in which the problems which are produced by the clients are delineated sharply and attempts made to help the couple solve them' (Hooper 1976: 151, original emphasis). He went on to suggest that GPs and lawyers, as practitioners greatly concerned with couples in difficulty at various stages of the life-course, could make suitable partners for the development of counselling services in shared premises, which should be explored through carefully designed and evaluated experimental projects (1976: 152). There were warnings here about a drift into therapeutic approaches which might not fit either the needs of clients or the organisation's structure for service provision.

Hooper's article was said to have caused some controversy within the organisation and when he followed it up in 1977 with a speech at the NMGC's conference at Swanwick, he claimed there had been public criticism and private praise for its content. In the Swanwick speech he anticipated, in a way which others had not done (not least the authors of *Marriage Matters*, which was to appear two years later), how MG's service should be seen within the context of a 'market-place of inter-personal help' (1978: 5). In a direct attack on the growing therapeutic aspirations within MG he went on:

> The image of the market is a very different one from that of the clinic which perhaps we have had with us for too long. The notion of 'withdrawn sanctity', if I may phrase it thus, does not for me square with counselling in 1977.
>
> (Hooper 1978: 6)

Hooper's voice was joined by another outsider and fellow member of the Counselling Advisory Board, William Parry-Jones, a psychiatrist who was also a consultant to Oxford MGC. Parry-Jones, writing in 1978, took the view that MG had reached a 'critical time' and identified three key background themes: the rising incidence of divorce, economic restrictions on service development, and a growing concern about the professionalism of counselling within society in general. While recognising the need for innovation, he nevertheless expressed reservations about the possible proliferation of 'sexual dysfunction clinics under the auspices of the MGC' and saw this as 'flirting with a therapeutic approach which conflicts so clearly with orthodox counselling approaches and, in fact, is a non-counselling method' (Parry-Jones 1978: 77). He did not defend the counselling *status quo* however and went on to criticise

> the time-honoured marriage counselling techniques that are derived from psycho-analytic methodology [which] can be seen, at their worst, to be devices for evading responsibility and doing nothing more than playing the part of the good listener, who facilitates the ventilation of feelings and promotes insight.
>
> (Parry-Jones 1978: 77)

For Parry-Jones the issue centred on the extent to which counsellors were able to accept their own authority in relation to their clients and on occasions to use more directive methods. For this to take place, however, the training of counsellors would have to be revised, and even then there remained the problem of 'part-time semi-professionals' (1978: 81) being able to accept the additional responsibilities of a more directive approach to changing the lives of clients. As one influenced by behavioural principles, Parry-Jones argued that counsellors in future should feel as comfortable with this framework and its associated techniques as with those deriving from non-directive teaching. They should feel able to reach some *diagnosis* of their clients' problems and make a clear offer of help. His recommendations added fuel to a debate which would explode with the publication two years later of the O'Connor report on the training of MG counsellors.

We have already described in detail the findings of the O'Connor report (see above pp. 149–51), which did so much to expose the theoretical limitations and absence of skills training within the NMGC's programme. The report highlighted the consequences of an uncritical blending of non-directiveness with psychodynamic interpretations: counsellors were shown to have few diagnostic skills at their disposal, in a context where their own need for 'personal growth' through training appeared to take precedence over their ability to serve the needs of clients. Following a review of training in 1983[4] there would be a far more considered approach to the relationship between person-centredness, psychodynamics and counselling skills within the MG house-style. Henceforth the influence of Rogers would diminish; this would be accompanied by a growing acceptance of therapeutic approaches, as found especially in the work of the Institute of Marital Studies; and these would be joined in turn by a new emphasis on the development of counselling 'skills'. Counsellors would be taught more systematically to assess the presenting problems of their clients and to adopt a structured approach to intervention. But the psychodynamic theoretical underpinning to this work would be further highlighted, rather than eroded. Henceforth the psychodynamic perspective, clearly labelled as such, would be the central theoretical model within MG's teaching and practice and although experimentation with behavioural models would occur in the marital sex therapy programme, these would not have a wide-ranging influence upon counselling practice.

THERAPEUTIC APPROACHES

While during the 1970s there was a growing interest in broadly *therapeutic* approaches to working with 'marital problems', this was not an inevitable process and there had been various examples of earlier resistance to moves which might seem to make the counselling work too technical and less personal. For example, as early as 1961, when the influence of John Wallis was becoming more and more visible, one writer in *Marriage Guidance* could make a case for the 'ordinary counsellor' and pleaded:

> Let us not try to transform these excellent people into pseudo-psycho-therapists, insecure in their new knowledge, their confidence in their own wisdom disturbed. Let them continue to be what they are (and what they are is more important than what they do) and they will, within these limits of courtesy, discretion, patience and confidentiality, do a power of good and a minimum of harm to the clients they seek to serve.
>
> (Jackson 1961: 58)

It is unlikely that this represented an isolated, revisionist position. Indeed, the doubts accompanying the shift towards a Rogerian model, which we explored in the last section, reveal major concerns about departing from an empirical and commonsense approach to problem-solving in marriage guidance. Wallis himself would probably have found little to disagree with in such a view, given his own concerns about the transition from counselling to therapy. Jackson's anxiety however was in response to processes which were already under way within the organisation by the early 1960s and which would continue to gain momentum. Later, two important therapeutic influences would find their way into marriage guidance, one of these deriving from the psychodynamic approaches being developed at the Tavistock and the other stemming from ideas based on behavioural theory, which found a ready application in working with sexual difficulties in marriage. Each of these would have an influence on the training programme for counsellors in the organisation and would lead to the adoption of an increasingly eclectic model of intervention.

The influence of the FDB/IMS

The word 'psychodynamic' had already begun to appear in the *Marriage Guidance* bulletin by the mid 1950s. Articles at this time, however, such as those by Winnifred Doherty, a doctor, reflected little of the sophistication with which the concept was being used within the Family Discussion Bureau. They may though have been closer to what the journal's readers wanted to hear at that time, as they tentatively enquired into what could be learned from the theoretical realms of psychology and psychoanalysis. Doherty was unequivocally prescriptive about marriage:

> For its normal functioning marriage should include the comfort and companionship each can have in the other, but it is conditioned very profoundly indeed by the full blossoming and fruition of normal sexuality between the partners.
>
> (Doherty 1956: 13)

And when she came to the unconscious motivations which may draw spouses into marriage, her principal objective seemed to be the reinforcement of traditional gender stereotypes (a theme which we have also explored in Wallis's writings):

> If a woman enters marriage with a marked 'masculine protest' she will become a competitor with her husband. Should a husband have not emerged from the adolescent homosexual stage he may despise his wife for her true femininity, because he is afraid of it, and only accept her as a mother figure.
>
> (Doherty 1956: 15)

So much of the thinking and development about psychodynamic approaches to marital work took place at the Family Discussion Bureau (FDB). It is therefore interesting to note how little Douglas Woodhouse (1990), in a chapter devoted to the history of the FDB/ Institute of Marital Studies (IMS), has to say about connections with marriage guidance, which are mentioned only in passing and in the context of a wide range of similar training consultancy collaborations with other agencies. Seen from the other side, the relationship between marriage guidance and the FDB appears far more significant, if not unproblematic. In 1955 the bulletin carried on facing pages an article summarising a talk at the AGM by John Wallis on the perennial 'What is counselling?' and another reporting Kathleen Bannister's address on 'A professional casework approach to marriage counselling.' Wallis opened by asserting that 'we deal with people and not with "cases"' and emphasising the importance of meaning rather than facts (Wallis 1955: 6). Bannister described the task of the FDB as being that of evolving new methods of working and training for social workers grappling with the emotional difficulties of their clients, especially their marital problems. Within a psychoanalytic framework of understanding the marriage, she felt that they had evolved a 'teachable technique' of interviewing (Bannister 1955: 7). This seemed a far cry from Wallis's view on the opposite page, to which we have already referred, that 'Counselling . . . is not just a matter of technique or psychology; it rests on a sensitive and intelligent understanding of the terms on which we all live, learnt mainly from the counsellor's own experience' (Wallis 1955: 6). Bannister's conviction that work of the kind conducted at the FDB 'could not possibly be undertaken by counsellors working in isolation' also seemed to point up the differences with marriage guidance, where at that time counsellors were in general left unsupported after initial training (Bannister 1955: 7).

The first full description of the FDB approach appears in a work by Bannister *et al.* (1955) and is followed by that of Lily Pincus (1960). Henry Dicks (1967), although working mainly in the Tavistock rather than the FDB, developed this further in a work which set out in detail the application of Freudian and object relations theories to the treatment of marital disturbance in a National Health Service setting.

Dicks makes some interesting observations about the work of Mace, which appear to characterise the view of marriage guidance as seen from the Tavistock. Mace, 'the Marriage Guidance Council's theoretician' is praised for his mistrust of psychiatrists and for being in advance of medical attitudes in his thinking about marital problems (Dicks points out how these were often seen in the post-war period as amenable to ECT and other aggressive therapies). But at the same time Mace was inclined to rely on clichés in his exposition and in particular 'shared the prevalent dread of the joint interview' (Dicks 1967: 2). Dicks's lukewarm enthusiasm for marriage guidance is further revealed, as we noted on p. 110, in his history of the Tavistock, where he felt it necessary to refer to marriage guidance counsellors in inverted commas, implying some ambiguity in his view of them (Dicks 1970). Nevertheless, Dicks's key work on

Marital Tensions appeared on the reading list for trainee counsellors soon after its publication and was to have a major influence on thinking and practice within MG throughout the 1970s and into the 1980s. In 1968 the FDB, reflecting a growing concentration on research and intervention in marriage, changed its name to the Institute of Marital Studies (IMS) and then became the Tavistock Institute of Marital Studies (TIMS) in 1988.

Looking back on the early development of the bureaux, Woodhouse, a former chair of the IMS staff executive, explains that initially the FDBx had three tasks:

1 'Consumer research' in two areas of London to assess the needs and relevant approaches for working with marital and family problems. This took the form of group discussions, which gave rise to the name: ' "Family discussion" was neutral, applicable alike to preventive and therapeutic work, and suggested the joint client/worker nature of the task' (Woodhouse 1990: 77).
2 The application of psychoanalytic theory to casework with marital problems.
3 The investigation of patterns of living in ordinary urban families, which led to Elizabeth Bott's (1957) work on family and social network.

This account makes it clear that 'The marital relationship was conceived in systemic terms from the start as was the family of which this relationship is the nucleus' (Woodhouse 1990: 78). Woodhouse also emphasises that 'The concept of the practice, training and research "mix" as a total function was implicit in the pilot experiment' (1990: 82), though practice was always given prominence. He recognises however that FDB staff were not the first to apply psychodynamic theories to marital problems: 'It was the function of the working group and the four-person therapeutic relationship . . . that could claim to be unique' (1990: 84). The use of the 'therapeutic pair' with the client couples developed out of the pilot experiment and was to become a hallmark of the work at the Family Discussion Bureau/Institute of Marital Studies, albeit one which marriage guidance, with its more limited resources and far wider service provision, could never emulate. In particular, this approach placed a growing emphasis on the way in which the relationship between the therapists could reflect problems within the couple relationship, highlighting the importance of case conferences for these elements to be explored by the whole group, and not just the therapist pair. This, as we have seen, was to become a feature of working in marriage guidance, where the case discussion group could provide an opportunity for the exploration of feelings as well as facts relating to the counselling process.

The psychodynamic approach of the Institute of Marital Studies (IMS) has been described in a number of publications, including the chapter by Diana Daniell (1985), which distinguishes three key concepts within the IMS understanding of marital interaction.

1 Many problems of adulthood and of marital relationships stem from each partner's infantile and childhood experiences.
2 Motivations which underlie the choice of a partner sustain the relationship and give it a particular quality, which is related to unconscious as well as conscious factors.
3 There is a system of shared fantasies and shared defences which operates in a marriage, an unconscious 'contract' incorporating what each spouse expects of the other (Daniell 1985: 171).

Accordingly 'marriage has to be viewed as a psychic entity in itself – a system greater than the sum of the personalities of the two partners' (1985: 171–2). This approach represents a modification of classic Freudian psychoanalytic theory through the application of the ideas of the object relations theorists, principally Melanie Klein (1932), but also W. R. D. Fairbairn (1952) and D. W. Winnicott (1958); for some it also relies on Bowlby's theories of attachment and loss, which themselves represent further modification of the work of the object relations theorists. As Daniell explains:

> Bowlby has reformulated what, in traditional theory, is termed a 'good object' as an attachment figure who is conceived as accessible, trustworthy and ready to help when called upon; similarly, what, in traditional theory, is termed a 'bad object' he reformulates as an attachment figure who is conceived as often impossible, unhelpful and at times even hostile.
>
> (Daniell 1985: 173)

This application of object relations theory allows marriage to be understood as a 'transference relationship' in which 'the partners become a fundamental part of each other's environment; each is both subject and object and each is the object of the other's attachment' (Woodhouse 1990: 84). As John Sutherland, an early collaborator at the Tavistock, put it: 'A critical advance in marital work was to see that what the partners complained of in each other was an unwanted part of themselves' (Sutherland 1962: 9). A further important element of the IMS approach is the notion of the *reflection process*, in which the conflicts exhibited by client couples may manifest themselves not only in the relationships between their therapists, but also in the wider context of the organisation in which they work. This principle was demonstrated to good effect by Mattinson and Sinclair (1979) in their study of marital therapy in a local authority social services department.

The criteria for seeing partners conjointly or separately were debated at length in the IMS, where increasingly the tendency has been for couples to be seen by *two* therapists, both in 'doubles' and 'foursomes', according to the nature of the presenting problem and the stage in the therapeutic process. As Skynner has pointed out, the preferred mode may also relate to the perceived psychological nature of the marital problem, so that, for example, conjoint therapy is of particular use to those who utilise 'paranoid schizoid' processes, with the extensive use of denial or splitting, whereby parts of the self are projected into the other, and so are not 'true' individuals with separate identities and boundaries (quoted in Daniell 1985: 178–9). Nevertheless, IMS work also emphasises that therapy 'is based on an attempt to understand a process of interaction, rather than applying a set of techniques' (Daniell 1985: 182). Daniell also quotes Dick's description of the process of treatment as being like a symphony in which 'the chief themes are stated early; the rest of the movement is occupied with their development and working out, ending with a restatement' (1985: 183).

Several difficulties are apparent when exploring the conceptual influences of IMS work upon thinking and practice within MG. By the mid 1980s still only 36 per cent of interviews were with couples seen together (Tyndall 1985c: 108). This must surely have inhibited the development of counsellors' understanding of some of the psychodynamic elements within the marriage relationship and its application in the counselling process. Also non-directive counselling approaches tended to be seen as more appropriate for working with individual clients and it should be clear from earlier sections that most of the theoretical debates going on within the movement in the 1950s and 1960s were about counselling in general, rather than *marital* counselling. There was also the issue of how far the work in MG should be influenced by a medical model of aetiology and intervention. Although Woodhouse (1990) describes the work of the IMS as 'non-medical therapy', this is drawn into question by our discussion in Chapter 3 and, as he acknowledges: 'Once within the Tavistock, the FDB was located on the boundary between the medical and social spheres of operation and was confronted with tensions inherent in that position' (1990: 79–80). Certainly, FDB/IMS writings frequently drew on medical models of 'illness' and 'treatment' in marriage, something which may have been reinforced rather than diminished by the decision in the mid 1980s to adopt the term 'marital therapist' rather than 'caseworker' to describe those employed in the IMS (Woodhouse 1990: 80). Woodhouse also points out that, following the move to the Tavistock in the early 1950s, medical referrals, mainly from general practitioners, progressively replaced those from Citizens Advice Bureaux. In a reference to David Morgan's (1985) work he goes on:

> Thus, operational connectedness shifted towards the medical network and, while the unit's experience has been that the distinction between the 'social' and the 'medical' in this field is unhelpful, some sociologists and social theorists remain critical of what has been called the 'medicalisation of marriage'.
>
> (Woodhouse 1990: 81)

These influences, insofar as they impinged upon MG, would certainly have run contrary to some of the assumptions underpinning non-directive counselling. But a further factor might explain why medico-therapeutic models could never predominate within MG. This is the absence of a theoretical and research based approach to the work. Whereas the FDB/IMS was able to pursue a strategy which gave considerable, if not equal, prominence to the activities of research and theoretical formulation, this could never be possible within MG, with its increasing orientation to service delivery. It would be uncharitable to suggest that in this respect the IMS came to be the 'brains' of MG (and as we shall see there were significant influences from other sources), but it does appear from the evidence presented below that MG was able to draw judiciously upon the technical and theoretical advances taking place in the IMS in the 1970s and 1980s.

The training work of the FDB/IMS developed in and with the more general group relations conferences at the Tavistock, which were attended by a number of key NMGC officers in the years following Tyndall's appointment as chief officer. Extramural courses also attracted MG personnel and probation workers, some of whom undertook marital therapy at the Tavistock unit. Later NMGC tutors took one-year registrarships at the IMS. One respondent we interviewed, who occupied a senior tutorial position in NMGC in the late 1960s, recalled being discouraged by Wallis from going to the FDB for further training, whereas Tyndall 'came along and backed it straight away'[5] This was symbolic of the new rapprochement between the two organisations. By sending the most experienced counsellors from MG to the IMS, something seems to have been done to deflate the notion that MG's standards of work were seriously below those of the Tavistock. As the same respondent put it, the two organisations 'related better and better', laying the foundations for a range of collaborative activity over the next two decades.[6]

In 1972 a joint NMGC/IMS Workshop on marital work was begun at Rugby. Described as a 'staff development programme' for experienced MG counsellors, the core activity of the workshops was the discussion of members' own current cases. Case discussion and study groups were co-led by one staff member from each organisation and the course consisted of three one-week residential units (increased to four in 1977), held over a three-month period. From 1974, members of the Probation and After Care Service also participated. Between 1972 and 1985 over 150 MG counsellors and tutors attended the workshops, which must have played a significant part in disseminating psychodynamic approaches to marital work throughout the organisation.[7] IMS and NMGC staff also collaborated on the *Marriage Matters* working party from the mid 1970s and Janet Mattinson, Woodhouse's successor, was a member of the group set up in 1981 to review the NMGC counsellor training programme in the aftermath of the O'Connor Report.[8] There was regular IMS representation at the Rugby research seminars held in the first half of the 1980s and Christopher Clulow, who went on to succeed Mattinson as the chair of the IMS staff executive, spoke at NMGC annual conferences, including the key meeting held in Manchester in 1989, which debated the ramifications of Relate's strategic plan.

Such activities reflect the wide-ranging influence of IMS thinking and practice upon the work of MG; it is likely that they had the effect of pushing the aspirations of some counsellors and tutors in a more overtly *therapeutic* direction. Indeed by 1985, in an enthusiastic review of Clulow's *Marital Therapy*, the NMGC counselling officer revealed her wholehearted admiration for the IMS approach, referring to a 'treasure trove of a book' the experience of reading which was 'like listening to a favourite Bach fugue' (Fryer 1985: 13). But as Woodhouse himself later reflected, the development of marital therapy and the mutual collaboration of the two organisations was increasingly beleaguered in the changed political climate of the 1980s when the 'external boundaries of groups and organizations tended to become less permeable as preoccupation with survival and stress among practitioners increased' (1990: 94).

Marital sex therapy

Certainly, as we have already noted, the 1980s did produce a new emphasis on a skills-based approach to the work of marriage counselling. But in another area of MG's work a more task-focused and skills orientation had already been explored and adopted. This line of development, in the introduction of a programme of marital sexual therapy (MST), although based on the contrasting theoretical formulation of behaviourism, can be seen running in parallel to the growing links with the IMS in the 1970s. Because of this, therapeutic models of working should not be seen as wholly dependent upon psychodynamic, Tavistock-inspired approaches for their development within MG.

The adoption of behavioural approaches to marital sex therapy also provides a further example of how the medical model has retained a place within the organisation's thinking and practice.

As early as 1955, David MacLay, a psychiatrist writing in *Marriage Guidance* and working as a 'tutor' leading case discussions, had raised the issue of dealing with psychosexual difficulties and proposed that a number of counsellors should be chosen 'to improve their skill by extra study and by supervised work in this direction' (MacLay 1955: 4). It was not for another fifteen years that this proposal was taken up and, significantly, the important decision to launch an experiment in the field of sexual therapy saw the NMGC paid staff in reactive rather than proactive mode, with the initial inspiration coming from elsewhere. But NMGC was nevertheless in the forefront of the development of sex therapy services in Britain and, paradoxically, also with the evaluation of models of training and intervention, something which it has significantly failed to address in relation to marital work more generally.

It was in 1970 that Masters and Johnson's widely influential work on *Human Sexual Inadequacy* was first published. The authors made three critical observations:

1 Since sex tends to happen between two people, it is preferable for both to be seen together in therapy.
2 Since a male therapist is unlikely to appreciate fully the sexual experience of a woman, and vice versa, it is advisable to have a male and female therapist present with the couple.
3 Since sexual arousal and response is a physiologically normal function, problems in sexual relationships (dysfunctions) might be approached through the processes of education rather than psychopathology (Masters and Johnson 1970).

Building on these insights, the authors went on to propose a fourteen-day rapid treatment programme for couples, working with co-therapists. In late 1971 David Mace, on a visit to NMGC headquarters, showed a range of sexually explicit film material which was being developed in the USA for educational and research purposes (Brown 1979: 11). In the following year Mace published a short book with NMGC in which he outlined his ideas on sexual problems in marriage, but was forced to acknowledge the limited availability of skilled help for couples experiencing difficulties (Mace 1972). The same year two MG counsellors described their own self-tutored attempts at offering a sexual therapy service in their local setting (Harris and Usborne 1972). This particular initiative had provoked concern at Rugby and the head of counselling had visited the counsellors to learn more, even though by that stage the tutors had tried to 'stamp on it'.[9] But interest was growing, and another local marriage guidance council invited Paul Brown, a clinical psychologist, to conduct a series of training sessions on the work of Masters and Johnson. Soon afterwards, the head of counselling worked as a co-therapist with Brown, on an experimental basis,[10] and following this experience Rugby senior staff recommended that the implications of this style of work for MG should be investigated. In an atmosphere of considerable anxiety and caution, the Department of Health and Social Security was approached to support an experimental programme of training and intervention, which would be directed and evaluated by Brown. Since the department was concerned that only married couples should be seen, the initiative, which did receive support, was named the Marital Sexual Dysfunction Project[11] (Heisler 1983).

The project addressed five key questions:

1 How readily and effectively do marriage guidance counsellors assimilate a body of knowledge about sexual dysfunction grounded in the work of Masters and Johnson?
2 How successfully is this knowledge applied in treatment?
3 Can co-therapy treatment procedures be carried out satisfactorily by a single therapist?
4 Does a training in essentially behavioural and directive treatment techniques influence counselling skills? And if it does, how?
5 What evidence can be established about the incidence of sexual dysfunction in the general population as a basis for establishing resources to meet the need perceived?[12]

Six women counsellors took part in the project in the first year, when they were trained by Brown: the following year they too took on trainees. This apprenticeship model was unprecedented in MG and represented a radical departure from the received wisdom of the Wallis years which argued that trainee counsellors could not observe the work of their more experienced colleagues, principally for reasons of confidentiality. The study concluded that counsellors could develop the relevant knowledge and apply it with increasing accuracy to diagnosis; there were no significant differences between single and co-therapy procedures; but also little evidence that training in this particular work improved counselling skills more generally. The report estimated an annual incidence of cases of sexual dysfunction at around 50,000, of which some 14 per cent were referred.[13]

Brown presented his final report in 1976. It was enthusiastically received and the organisation went on to secure further DHSS funding for a project which would extend the MST training and service provision to all areas, under the direction of a Rugby-based officer who was one of the original trainees. From the beginning of the 1980s, MST activities were funded from within NMGC's mainstream budget. By 1985, 130 counsellors were doing this specialist work in 68 MST 'clinics' (Tyndall 1985c: 103). Tyndall distinguished several features which differentiated those taken into the sex therapy programme from other MG clients. Couples had to be willing to attend together and were seen as 'very much their own therapists', being set 'homework' tasks. There was an extensive diagnostic stage to sex therapy, with comprehensive questions and answers and forms to be completed; the nature of the helping relationship was described as that of 'educator giving instruction'. Departing from the Masters and Johnson model, couples were seen weekly, often by therapists working alone (Tyndall 1985c: 103–4).

Training

The development of a more overtly theoretical and therapeutic orientation to the work of counselling couples, whether inspired by psychodynamic or behavioural perspectives, placed increasing strain on the programme of training for counsellors. We have seen that MG training was the subject of a thoroughgoing critique in the O'Connor Report of 1980. Three years later a review of training for marital counselling was produced, the implementation of which coincided with the major crisis which beset the organisation in the mid 1980s. NMGC training had remained unchanged since 1975, when a two-year course was designed around six residential two-day events, held at Rugby. The members of the working party which produced the 1983 report set their recommendations in the context of a broad appreciation of the changing social and economic context to which clients belonged, of the demand for the service, and of developments in professional thinking. While they recognised that there had been a great expansion in the knowledge base surrounding counselling, they also noted that the introduction of such material had been 'piecemeal and unsystematic'.[14] The working party made a total of forty-one recommendations, the most significant of which for the purposes of this chapter were to do with the content of basic training. It recommended that a more theoretical orientation should be introduced, with the main focus on psychological and social perspectives and counselling practice. Trainees should be introduced to an understanding of the interactive processes between couples. There should be 'systematic attention to the teaching of counselling skills of attention-giving, observing and listening'. In particular, trainee counsellors would be given more help in 'assessing and understanding clients' problems and making a selective response to them'.[15] A key agent in this, as explained in the *Counsellor Basic Training Prospectus* (NMGC 1987), would be the adoption of a three-stage model of *exploration, understanding* and *action* in the counselling process, as adapted from the North American work of R. R. Carkhuff (1969) and Gerald Egan (1975).

Commenting on the merits of the NMGC programme in a chapter on issues in the training of marital therapists, Windy Dryden and Paul Brown argued that the 'new' training was far superior to the 'old' in its ability to deal adequately with the theoretical, practical and personal aspects of preparing to undertake marital work and suggested that counsellors on the 'new' programme were likely to receive more in the way of skills training. However, they reserved judgement on the extent to which the mixture of traditional MG person-centred approaches, along with psychodynamic and skills elements, was likely to bear fruit:

> Time will tell whether the 'marriage' between the person-centred view of the person, the psychodynamic perspective on marital interaction and Carkhuff's three-stage model of counsellor intervention will be a happy one.
>
> (Dryden and Brown 1985: 314–15)

They noted also that, as elsewhere, little had been achieved in the formal evaluation of training programmes. Perhaps the most serious area of criticism, however, was that relating to the assessment of trainees' work with clients:

Although skill acquisition is emphasized on the NMGC training course, the most appropriate supervision methods to aid the learning process of trainees in this respect (ie those that allow supervisors to directly monitor trainees' actual work with clients) are *not* routinely used by NMGC supervisors. It is still possible for MG trainees to complete their training programme without their actual counselling work being *directly* supervised.

(Dryden and Brown 1985: 307, original emphasis)

They went on:

Despite the lack of research on the outcome of training in marital therapy in Britain, the NMGC claims in its *Basic Counsellor Training Prospectus* (1984) that the service provided by NMGC counsellors is 'highly professional and *comparable in standard* with that offered by formally qualified counsellors in other fields' (p2). Such a statement is not warranted . . .

(Dryden and Brown 1985: 311, their emphasis)

These are important criticisms and it appeared that, by the late 1980s, such observations had not gone unnoticed by Irene Short, the newly appointed director of services at Relate, who launched a major policy initiative on the accreditation of counsellors. This would seek to develop counselling qualifications at both certificate and diploma level, awarded by Relate's own proposed Institute for Marital Counselling, but accredited by an external organisation. There were also suggestions that the changes which had taken place in the basic training in the mid 1980s had been 'too cosmetic' and had provided no mechanism for the integration of theory and practice; further developments in the training programme were also being considered.[16] By early 1990 Relate seemed poised, not to push its aspirations further into the medicalised arena of marital therapy, but rather to see itself as the premier provider of training in marriage *counselling*, using a model which would make electicism its key strength.

With the possible exception of the mid 1950s to mid 1960s, the organisation has generally eschewed a doctrinaire approach to marital work, and the pages of its house journal bear testimony to the wide-ranging influences which it has been prepared to tolerate. 'Guidance', 'counselling' and 'therapy' have co-existed in complex and shifting relationship and each has posed its own problems for the organisation. Person-centred approaches never quite usurped some aspects of guidance, but the Rogerian approach had its own limitations and crucially lacked a model of marital interaction, so vital to an organisation claiming to specialise in the marriage relationship. This was provided through the influence of the FDB/IMS and took an essentially psychodynamic form, with more overtly therapeutic overtones. Client-centred counselling could also be seen as vague, woolly and lacking in clear objectives. This criticism would be answered through the introduction of a skills-based, contractual approach, influenced in part by the behavioural methods used in MST. Against this background of conceptual development, the technical aspects of work in the organisation also struggled with a number of other tensions, which we shall turn to in the final section, when considering the nature of the service which marriage guidance has offered to its clients.

EFFICACY

There has never been within marriage guidance a well-defined tradition of research aimed at establishing the efficacy of the counselling service, though undoubtedly the tutorial system has provided a mechanism for the critical scrutiny of practice. On the whole, client-centred approaches were not seen to lend themselves to or to invite evaluative research. Indeed it was not until the 1970s that research issues were given much consideration. Some of the work which resulted sought to focus on questions of client satisfaction; but in general the findings raised as many problems as they clarified. Of course, there is a range of methodological difficulties attaching to this kind of research, which will cast doubt on the validity of findings. Nevertheless serious concerns were exposed: only about half the clients appeared to be satisfied with the service they received; clients were not representative of the population as a whole, and of the divorcing population in particular; and a high proportion were still seen without their spouse. More fundamentally, however, the best of this research work raised questions about the goals of intervention and the broader aims of providing a service in marriage counselling. Given the intractability of such issues, it is perhaps not surprising that a good deal of the research effort focused on more specific organisational issues and problems: reasons for resignation among counsellors, reception interviews, counselling in GP surgeries, and so on. Following the Relate relaunch, research activity became further restricted, though plans were made for new developments which would form part of a wider strategy aimed to give the organisation a more public voice in issues of social policy relating to family life.

Empathy versus efficacy?

A crucial feature of the non-directive approach to counselling that developed in marriage guidance under John Wallis was that it had little or no place for a research-based strategy on questions of effectiveness. In collaboration with a university academic, Wallis had conducted a research study in the early 1950s which asked counsellors to record their perception of the outcome of cases (Wallis and Booker 1958), but in general Wallis remained opposed to the notion of evaluation. He began one of his later books by explaining that:

> . . . . by its very nature Marriage Guidance has to deal with imponderables. There is no yard-stick of success or failure, no valid frame of reference for an accurate assessment (or even definition) of its effectiveness.
>
> (Wallis 1968: ix)

This disarming observation was further elaborated in subsequent passages where Wallis went on to describe counselling as a 'craft' rather than a science and to state that the 'awkward question of success' should be turned back on the questioner, who should be asked 'to explain what he means by success and then try and answer accordingly' (Wallis 1968: 5, 6). This 'reflecting back', which had become such a common element within the empathic practice of non-directive counselling, was clearly of less utility in dealing with questions of efficacy. Yet Wallis had to admit the importance of the issue, 'since the training and administration are subsidised by government and local authority grants and by donations, covenants and subscriptions from individuals and groups, all of whom have the right to know their money is being usefully spent' (Wallis 1968: 5–6).

This lack of a research base was probably not unusual in counselling organisations in the 1950s and 1960s. Moreover, as Douglas Hooper points out, British writing on marital work has in general been more preoccupied with issues of theory development than with questions of empirical evaluation (Hooper 1985: 290). A major difficulty which inhibited the growth of research thinking within marriage guidance for many years was the fear that research could lead to breaches in confidentiality (Tyndall 1985c: 110). Client confidentiality was paramount in an organisation dealing with aspects of intimate life and this may in part explain the fact that there were more than twenty years between the Wallis and Booker research, conducted in 1952–53, and the next survey, of NMGC clients, in 1975. There also seems to have been some resistance to the *idea* of research, as something inadmissible within the humanistic counselling philosophy; for example, one writer asserted in *Marriage Guidance* that counsellors only do the work 'because they believe in it' and because they 'have values about their work which are outside scientific assessment' (Baker 1978: 91). To this might be added the notion that volunteer counsellors should not be subject in their practice to levels of scrutiny which might be more appropriate to the evaluation of the services provided by paid professionals.

During Nicholas Tyndall's years as chief officer, however, there was a growing recognition of the importance of research and evaluation as a significant activity within all organisations concerned with aspects of social welfare. Again, some of the stimulus for this came from outside, with academics and practitioners from other organisations (some themselves engaged in the newly developing field of social work research) contributing articles to the *Marriage Guidance* journal, and participating in conferences and working groups. NMGC established a Research Advisory Board in 1969 and appointed a research officer in 1972 (see p. 151), though it was not until 1983 that the promotion of research became one of the organisation's stated objectives. During the intervening years a number of projects were undertaken, some of them focusing on surveys of MG clients and counsellors. At times this work could again exhibit an in-built resistance to the notion of evaluation. Thus even the research officer could suggest that most requests from counsellors for evaluation of their work are born out of the need for 'personal reinforcement', rather than any wider goal of improving service provision (Heisler 1977b: 234). In a revealing passage Heisler continued:

> Obviously it is pleasant to be told that what we are doing is good and useful, and the reverse applies equally. In an area as nebulous as human relations it is difficult to have measures.

> (1977b: 234)

In the light of such remarks it is perhaps not surprising that research work within the organisation was slow to develop. By the late 1970s *Marriage Matters* could still speak of the need to 'foster a research minded attitude' in the marital agencies (Home Office and DHSS 1979: 91). This was partly addressed by the Rugby research seminars, held between 1979 and 1985, which brought together a number of MG personnel interested in research with academics and social researchers from outside. But as some research projects got under way, it also became clear that their findings highlighted fundamental and longstanding problems in the provision and quality of the service offered by the organisation.

Problems and contradictions exposed by research findings

In April 1975 and October 1982 detailed surveys of the total monthly intake of clients were carried out (Heisler and Whitehouse 1975; Heisler 1984). Tyndall (1985c) summarised the findings of this work. The majority of clients were in the 20–40 age range, with nine years of marriage as the median. The proportion of clients in first marriages fell from just under 80 per cent in 1975 to around 70 per cent in 1982. The surveys were also said to reveal a 'striking correlation between the social class of MG clients and of the general population' (Tyndall 1985c: 108). Tyndall made it clear that women were more likely to use the service than men: '53 per cent of first interviews are conducted with women, which shows little change from 56 per cent in 1975 and 58 per cent in 1953' (1985c: 109). The proportion of men having a first interview alone however dropped from 37 per cent in 1953, to 25 per cent in 1975, to 19 per cent in 1982, while first interviews with both spouses seen together increased from a mere 5 per cent in 1953, to 19 per cent in 1975 and 27 per cent in 1982. This bias towards sessions with individual clients is further emphasised when looking at the total number of interviews given in one year. In 1983–84 from some 215,000 interviews 44 per cent were with women, 20 per cent with men and 36 per cent with couples (Tyndall 1985c: 109). On the question of clients' presenting problems, although there were difficulties for counsellors in giving an unequivocal categorisation of these, 'personal traits' and 'sexual difficulties' appeared to account for some two thirds of the total. Between 1975 and 1982, infidelity as a presenting problem increased from 16 per cent to 26 per cent.

When considering counselling *outcomes*, Tyndall pointed out that confidentiality issues were less of a barrier to effective research than formerly; but that they had been replaced by methodological doubts and problems of funding research (1985c: 110). He identified two ways of assessing outcomes: counsellors' and clients' perspectives.

In the 1953 study counsellors rated 'no improvement' in 30 per cent of cases, 'outcome unknown' in 37 per cent and 'relationship improved' or 'difficulty overcome' in 33 per cent. In the 1975 survey, the same questions elicited change and improvement in 41 per cent

of cases, 25 per cent no improvement and 34 per cent 'don't knows'.
Similar answers were forthcoming in 1982 . . .

(Tyndall 1985c: 110)

Drawing on the work of Jane Keithley (1982), Julia Brannen and Jean
Collard (1982) and Pat Hunt (1985), all of whom conducted client
follow-up studies, Tyndall suggested that a fairly consistent pattern
emerged in which half the clients were 'well-served'. In the 'easier'
field of sex therapy outcome measurement, 46 per cent of the first
1,000 clients seen were treated to the satisfaction of both clients and
therapists (Tyndall 1985c: 112; Crowhurst 1982).

Clearly these figures and findings raise a number of issues. First,
there is the question of absolute numbers; it is very difficult to estimate
the degree of numerical fit between those who use the services of the
marital agencies, of which NMGC is the largest, and those who might
be experiencing 'marital problems' and/or would wish to make use
of counselling services. Despite the problems of evidence, however,
Marriage Matters was quite clear in its views on this: 'It is evident . . .
that the specific agencies are consulted only by a small proportion of
people with marital problems' (Home Office and DHSS 1979: 24).
Certainly, from the 1950s onwards, the total number of cases seen
in marriage guidance consistently under-performed that for divorce
petitions filed. In 1950 cases seen were less than a quarter of petitions
filed and subsequently the proportion has never risen above one third.
If we assume that the numbers of petitions filed themselves under-
represent 'actual' levels of marital unhappiness, then there appears
to be an even bigger mismatch between the 'at risk' population and
those using the service. Nevertheless the 48,000 cases seen in 1988
represented a 33 per cent increase over a five-year period; likewise
over the same period the number of interviews given rose by 25 per
cent to 265,000.[17]

The social class of clients is also a problematic measure of service
provision. Social class must be measured with considerable accuracy
if it is to be used meaningfully (and this may often not be the case with
regard to counsellors' record-keeping). Also, Tyndall's assertion of the
representativeness of the MG client group missed an important point.
As we have already noted, the social distribution of divorce within our
society is heavily weighted towards the lower end of the social class
spectrum, and for true representativeness this weighting should also
be in evidence among the client group. However, as the 1989 Draft
Strategic Review made clear: 'whereas Relate's clients are skewed in
favour of classes 1 and 2, those who divorce are more likely to come

from social classes 4 and 5 or be unemployed'. The report also noted that whereas 21 per cent of Relate clients belonged to social classes 4 and 5, the proportion within the total population was 35 per cent; likewise 33 per cent of clients were in classes 1 and 2, compared to 9 per cent of the population.[18] This evidence points to clear inequalities in the take up of marital counselling services among the population 'at risk'.

It is also apparent from the material presented by Tyndall that the counselling services of the organisation continued to appeal more to women than to men. As his figures showed, the proportion of women seeking help alone remained fairly constant over thirty years.[19] Hunt's study of client's responses to counselling within MG also found that women were not only more likely than men to make the first contact with the agency, but that they were also more likely to attend the first interview (Hunt 1985: 77); a similar finding is reported in Noel Timms and Annette Blampied's study of marriage guidance clients which noted that 'twice as many women as men made the first suggestion' of seeing a counsellor (Timms and Blampied 1985: 21). Brannen and Collard's (1982) study of help-seeking in couples with marital difficulties bears this out and they concluded that women are much more likely than their husbands to initiate contacts with agencies. Brannen and Collard though are unusual in offering a more sociologically grounded explanation for this willingness, which they see as reflecting women's greater preoccupation with relationship difficulties and their tendency to value disclosure. However, such notions, sometimes used in sexist rhetorics to underline the inherent 'sensitivity' of women and their greater attention to the value of relationships, are for Brannen and Collard a manifestation of women's subordinate position both in marriage and the wider society: 'Such subordinate status may have served to generate, on the part of women, a sensitivity to problems and an ideology which emphasized the value of disclosure' (1982: 201).

This point is rarely taken up in MG discourse, which has preferred instead to problematise men for being 'unusual' in not seeking counselling help with the same degree of enthusiasm as women. As Mike Brearley, writing in *Marriage Guidance*, put it:

Women come into therapy more often than men partly because they are by nature more in touch with their inner life than men. They are more likely to understand the point of emotional contact.

(Brearley 1986: 9)

Tyndall showed, however, that the proportion of lone male clients has been declining, and has been matched by a parallel increase in the proportion of clients who come with their spouse. Nevertheless, by the conclusion of this study, in autumn 1989, slightly over half of all cases seen involved only one half of the marital dyad.

These gender differences have been linked by researchers to questions about counselling technique. Hunt (1985) raised the question of whether some male clients might be more helped by a 'task-focused' approach using an explicit 'contract' and some behavioural techniques, rather than client-centred methods which emphasise working with thoughts and feelings. But Brannen and Collard again would see this kind of assumption as mirroring gender differences which originate in the wider society, arguing that men are more likely to expect a directive, advice-giving approach ('guidance' rather than 'counselling') because of their greater orientation to public arenas which are characterised by measurable goals (1982: 201). The introduction of counselling skills into the basic training programme during the mid 1980s suggests however that a more problem-focused approach is believed by Relate to have greater benefit for both male and female clients. This may reflect continuing assumptions about 'the client', rather than evidence of any serious attempt to address some of the questions about gender which have been explored, for example, by feminist psychotherapists (Eichenbaum and Orbach 1984; Greenspan 1983). It is easy to see, from this discussion, some of the ways in which available gender stereotypes may be integrated uncritically into the forms of help which are offered to men and women in the counselling room.[20]

In addition to gender issues, there were also concerns over the years about the nature of help given to clients coming alone, when compared to couples. The marital therapy literature remains equivocal on this, although in a recent review Adrian James and Kate Wilson (1991) have suggested that conjoint therapy (i.e. with both partners attending) is more likely to be successful than when one partner attends alone. Ian Bennum (1985), however, argues that what he calls 'unilateral marital therapy' can be equally effective, provided that the focus of the work remains on the couple relationship. It is this which may have been the problem in the past within MG practice. Certainly for the most part clients have been seen alone and the writings of Wallis, for example, suggest a greater preoccupation with the inner worlds of the individual client than with the marriage relationship. It was this imbalance in MG thinking and practice which the links with the Institute of Marital Studies in the 1970s did much to redress, providing a theory of marital interaction and a framework for counselling interventions.

Duration of counselling, or 'length of case', has also been a cause for concern. In 1988 some 43 per cent of Relate clients attended for only one or two sessions; 27 per cent had between three and five sessions; 20 per cent six to ten sessions; and just 10 per cent had ten or more sessions.[21] Little is known about the meaning of these distributions, although Hunt's work has suggested that clients feel more helped when they attend for a greater number of sessions (1985: 82). Have the largest single group who attend only once or twice simply come to the wrong agency? This would be despite the widespread procedure of offering clients a reception interview in which the presenting problem is identified and the service provided by the agency is made clear. Or are these brief encounters sufficient to resolve the difficulty? Our interviews suggested concerns about these cases, but also about those of longer duration. One of the beliefs within the organisation appeared to be that counsellors 'enjoy' long-term work most, but that managers sometimes regarded this as self-indulgence, not least when waiting lists were long. Some of these differences may be a reflection of the growing interest, during the 1970s and 1980s, in more overtly psychotherapeutic theories and styles of intervention which we described in earlier sections. It is possible that these interests might clash with those of an organisation increasingly preoccupied – by the late 1980s – with issues of through-put and comprehensive service provision.

For his part, Wallis seems to have been prepared to accept that, when considered from the perspective of individual counselling skills, the service offered would be at best variable:

> There are very wide variations indeed, some of it [the work] little more than a single interview between a client and a kindly, well-intentioned but rather ineffective counsellor and some of it amounting to a therapeutic and extended relationship that is both challenging and reassuring to counsellor and client and which enables the client's marriage to reach a level of stability, adjustment to conflict and fulfilment undreamt of at the outset.
>
> (Wallis 1967: 201–2)

There could be several sources for this variation. At any one time approximately one third to a half of all counsellors might still be in training and no attempts have been made to screen out the more difficult cases from novice counsellors.[22] Also many counsellors lacked opportunities to develop their skills, due to insufficient practice experience. While Tyndall was inclined to see this differently, referring to 'a freshness which derives from low case-loads' (1985c: 113), there remains some doubt about whether the average counsellor's caseload (165 interviews per year in 1988)[23] was sufficient to ensure an adequate standard of professional development.

Conclusion: problems of evaluation

This leaves the question of the *value* of marriage counselling still unaddressed. Does it work? On the available evidence, about one half of clients appeared to be satisfied by the help they received (Tyndall 1985c 110–12; Heisler 1980, 1984; Hunt 1985; Timms and Blampied 1985). Nevertheless, what constitutes a satisfactory outcome remains unclear, and is of course likely to be subject to a variety of perceptions. Hunt pointed out that, at least until 1983 when the organisation changed its aims and objectives (see Appendix 2), 'a good outcome from the work of marriage guidance is the preservation of a marriage' (1985: 12). But, as we have seen, a great deal of marital counselling was also about helping couples to part in a less conflictual manner.

The measurement of outcomes in counselling is of course subject to a wide range of technical, methodological difficulties which are further complicated by the numerous presenting problems brought to the counselling room. Research in this field may take a number of approaches: epidemiological survey, record analysis, qualitative case study. To a limited extent these have all been attempted within marriage guidance, though in general the later work, using qualitative methods, seems to have yielded most insights. There is a lack of useful quantitative work focusing on outcomes. But the major barrier to useful research within marriage guidance probably relates more to a lack of clarity about the organisation's agreed goals for intervention in marriage. Without clearly defined goals, worthwhile evaluation remains almost impossible. Reconciliation of the couple; conciliation through the divorce process; divorce counselling, these are all possible goals. Reconciliation has undoubtedly been the organisation's major focus historically, and this remains a popular perception of its work. Conciliation services have not in the main been developed within marriage guidance, though many of them use marriage guidance personnel (Clark and Haldane 1990). Divorce counselling is probably an important part of many counsellors' caseloads and Hunt's research suggested that some 50 per cent of clients may go on to separate or divorce (1985: 16); but against this should be set findings such of those of Mervyn Murch (1980), who among a random sample of 102 divorce petitioners found that only 13 per cent had contacted a marriage guidance counsellor, and that these had not found the counsellor particularly helpful. These complexities surrounding the goals of intervention may explain in part why research into counselling outcomes has remained so underdeveloped within marriage guidance. By contrast a good deal of effort in the early 1980s was put into research on aspects of service provision (rather than the technical issues of intervention in marriage) and these questions continued to preoccupy management after the Relate relaunch.

From the earliest days there was concern about how marriage guidance should best organise its counselling services. The issues reverberated over several decades: appointment systems, waiting lists, payment for counselling, the provision of counselling in various settings. Many of these factors related to the critical mass of individuals and expertise which any one local marriage guidance council could muster, and this has remained a problem since the 1950s. There was also the unremitting difficulty of counsellor 'wastage', with each year roughly as many lost to the system as gained.

By the 1970s some of these issues were exposed to limited research scrutiny, in a variety of small, sometimes local, projects. Heisler conducted work on intake interviews (1975); and on counsellors leaving the organisation (1974, 1987). Indeed this kind of work seems to have proliferated to a far greater extent than studies of counselling process and outcome.

In the early 1980s in particular, several interesting studies were produced which were then published in a series of NMGC research reports. These included an enquiry into salaried counselling (Heisler and Applegarth 1985); studies of the first interview and of reception interviews (Gaunt 1985, 1987); and a project on counsellors in medical settings (de Groot 1985). But efforts to disseminate the findings of these studies may have suffered from an organisational culture which still tended to marginalise academic preoccupations, placing a higher priority on experiential than cognitive learning.

Following the Coopers and Lybrand report, a great deal of this research activity was curtailed, along with the outlets for it; the Rugby seminars ceased and the journal *Marriage Guidance* no longer appeared. There was however a growing interest in management information. An outside consulting company, with expertise in working with charities in corporate planning, was engaged and went on to generate data for use in the formulation of the 1989 strategic plan, providing information on Relate's share of the counselling and training 'markets'. This concern about accurate information was also reflected in the services division's priorities for 1990/91,[24] one of which was stated as research and evaluation. Interestingly, the establishment of a research and evaluation programme was also linked to Relate's plans for a more active voice in public policy debates about family life.

There might be seen in all of this an avoidance of some of the fundamental issues raised by the small amount of research which has been carried out on marriage counselling and its effects. The evidence from such work is at best of limited encouragement and at worst revealing of major unresolved issues on the question of the goals of intervention as well as the comprehensiveness and quality of the service. From the evidence presented in earlier sections of this chapter, it would appear that the considerable efforts which have gone into thinking about the conceptual and theoretical aspects of marital work have not been matched by attention to evaluation. At the same time, it is difficult to see how research and information can easily be harnessed to an intention to speak more publicly on matters of family policy, when no clear value position on such issues has been agreed within the organisation. Research may always have a nebulous role in counselling organisations, being of little concern in periods of buoyancy and expansion, only to be invoked hastily as a problem-solving device when times become difficult. The role of research within NMGC has thus occupied a marginal position, from which it has proved difficult to generate a comprehensive programme of evaluation. Tyndall's foreword to Jill Heisler's first research report, published in 1974, aptly summarises the problem:

> Research is not easy to undertake in a voluntary social service organization. Finance is never adequate, demands are enormous and research tends to slip down the list of priorities in face of the pressure to maintain the service. However, the service can rapidly become sterile unless it is constantly monitored.
>
> (Tyndall 1974b: 5)

Likewise a report produced within Relate in 1989 emphasises a continuing dilemma for the organisation: 'Overall, we do not know the outcomes of the services we provide or the effectiveness of different types of service for different groups of people'.[25]

Such fundamental issues will no doubt continue to exercise the organisation in the foreseeable future, though it is not possible to predict the extent to which they will be addressed through the medium of carefully designed and executed evaluation research programmes. However, research by itself is unlikely to provide simple answers to the more complex question of what Relate is seeking to achieve in its marital counselling service. This is a question about the organisation's fundamental goals and values. In this discussion of the development of the technical aspects of marital work in the organisation, the question of such values has mainly been kept at arm's length. This is legitimate for heuristic purposes, but it is not a useful guide to action. The organisation is concerned to offer help to those experiencing difficulties within the intimate domain of marital relationships. In doing this it cannot ignore the many public ways in which these relationships are constructed and disputed. Marriage, as relationship or institution, is conflicted territory. Intervention in marriage cannot therefore be regarded as a neutral activity, merely constrained by limitations in the technical aspects of counselling and therapy. It remains an open question whether Relate, in its future thinking and development, will be prepared to grasp this nettle.

NOTES

1 Correspondence in *Marriage Guidance* November 1953, pp. 8–10; December 1953, p. 9; February 1954, p. 10.
2 The issue of directive versus non-directive counselling was *still* being discussed in a 1978 *Marriage Guidance* article (Parry-Jones 1978).
3 Interview.
4 NMGC: *A Review of Training in Marital Counselling*, January 1983.
5 Interview.
6 *Ibid.*
7 *IMS/NMGC/PACS Workshops 1972–85.*
8 NMGC: *A Review of Training in Marital Counselling*, January 1983.
9 Interview.
10 *Ibid.*
11 *Ibid.*
12 P. T. Brown *Report to the Counselling Advisory Board of the NMGC of the Research Work of the Marital Sexual Dysfunction Project, October 1973–August 1976*, para. 1.2.
13 *Ibid.*
14 NMGC: *A Review of Training in Marital Counselling*, January 1983.
15 *Ibid.*
16 Interview.
17 Relate: *Draft Strategic Review*, 17 March 1989 ('The Compass Report') p. 9.
18 *Ibid.*

19 But the proportion of couples had been going up and by 1988 had increased to 44 per cent (*Draft Strategic Review*, p. 9).
20 For a more general discussion of men in therapy, see O'Brien (1988).
21 Relate: *Draft Strategic Review*, 17 March 1989, p. 9.
22 Interview.
23 Relate: *Draft Strategic Review*, 17 March 1989, p. 9.
24 Relate: *Services Division Plan 1990–91*, November 1989.
25 Relate: *Draft Strategic Review*, 17 March 1989, p. 10.

Postscript
By no means asunder

Douglas Hooper

The reader who has reached this point in the book will have absorbed a fascinating array of action and opinion, largely about Relate National Marriage Guidance, from which the authors have drawn certain conclusions. This postscript is a brief response to their analysis and their conclusions by someone who has been involved with the organisation – or is it an agency? – for a good deal of the time period covered by the authors.

It will not surprise the reader (whether initiated or not) to find that this writer has found some of the material painful, both because it reflects an unpalatable truth, but also because in places the account has become unnecessarily and negatively critical. Indeed it appears in part to be too gloomy by far. This, the reader may say, is exactly how a respondent who is strongly identified with the organisation would be expected to react. Of course there must be some truth in that assertion, but it *still* may be true that the account in the book is, in fact, not as cool and independent as it might have been.

First we should recognise that in practice the book is an historical account of only one of the marital agencies and therefore cannot inform us about the general state of the marital counselling and therapy scene. Nevertheless, because Relate is by far the biggest and most dispersed agency for marital problems, there is considerable importance in seeing how the broader problems of marital distress have become refracted through the agency prism. This should be helpful more generally because the actions of the principal actors in the history must, in good part, reflect a more general view about working with marital difficulties as they have unfolded and changed through the five decades.

Perhaps the most important point to make is that, despite many difficulties documented here, Relate National Marriage Guidance has survived and is currently flourishing quite well. Any organisation which can take its external fundraising from £290,000 to nearly £700,000 in the last two years must, at the very least, have considerable appeal in its work and objectives. Indeed, had the authors followed their study through for another year, they would have seen the emergence from the period of turmoil and rapid change (which they describe) of a vigorous sense of purpose and competence. This is widespread through the agency in a way that has not been apparent for at least a decade and possibly longer. In addition, the demand for services by clients has also continued both to grow and to be met. In the last year there were 321,000 units of work, the bulk of which were counselling sessions (305,000 interviews) and, despite the figures which are provided for the Westminster Pastoral Foundation, there is no hard evidence that the call on Relate's services is relatively diminishing. This *may* be the case, but there are actually no data to enable such comparisons to be made.

If it is accepted that Relate continues to succeed in its main aim of offering a service to almost all areas of the country, then the shifts and moves over the five decades become in some ways more interesting. And the interest derives as much from the fascinating social history of marital (and perhaps especially sexual) issues as it does from the internal history of the agency. But there are gaps in the present account. The authors seem largely to have ignored the fact that Relate has its own milieu of agencies with which it has had to deal over the years. These range from the full-time, largely statutorily funded services, such as the Tavistock Institute of Marital Studies and the Maudsley Hospital marital and family unit, to analogous organisations in the voluntary sector such as Samaritans.

As an agency Relate has had to maintain the struggle not just for resources but also for recognition and prestige. For example, many of the early disputes between John Wallis and others were, I believe, attributable to the positioning problem. The early hopes of the pioneer marriage guidance workers which were largely pinned on the 'marriage maintenance' banner were clearly doomed to failure after the reforming divorce laws of the 1960s, if only because in practice successive governments were unwilling to make available funds to meet the client need. The National Marriage Guidance Council was actually in the classical cleft stick. Without seed-corn monies it was not possible to train more workers and to publicise the service to meet the demand. Yet without the flow of clients, government was clearly not willing to advance more cash because it was not apparently part of successive policies to do so.

In the early years, too, the agency had to contend with a covert rivalry with the local probation services. Until the 1970s most probation services tried to offer a casework service to failing marriages and the local relationships between the services and local marriage guidance councils were often cooperative and not rivalrous. But the issue of competition was ultimately located in the Home Office which not only partially funded both activities but also may have maintained the funding for NMGC at a comparatively low level in order to protect funding for the statutory service.

If we now consider the main thrust of the critique, it is the authors' contention that after a series of power struggles NMGC lost its purpose and replaced it with an increasing preoccupation with 'technical' issues to the exclusion of much else. Further, that despite the focus on technical matters – moving from 'counsel' to 'counselling' as it is vividly described – the organisation has never demonstrated the efficacy of what the counsellors undertake. In addition, that only latterly has the organisation begun to come to terms with the social thrust of the late twentieth century which one of the authors describes as 'post-modernist' – whatever that may mean. One strand of that, presumably, is the equal opportunity issue with particular reference to gender, and especially female gender. Finally, the authors assert that Relate has been very tardy in devoting resources to demonstrating that it is actually effective in doing the counselling task it says it can do.

It is important to deal with these issues in turn. Certainly, the early thrust of the movement was modified by the post-war experience and in particular by the impact of affluence engendered by control of conception and education amongst other things. David Morgan discusses the emergence of 'permissiveness' and also looks at the concept critically, but does not emphasise how an organisation like NMGC would clearly reflect the interpersonal shift which accompanied the cultural change from marriage as institution to marriage as relationship – a process which is still actively discussed by counsellors, clients and academics.

It is not unreasonable to say that, had NMGC retained its early mission to emphasise the institutional aspects, it would have been by-passed as being out of step with the times. David Morgan makes the point that, indeed, the organisation may have contributed to the shifting of values. But that cannot be determined from the material presented here. A larger portion of resources could have been devoted to educational programmes, and it is clear that in the *internal* battle for resources the counselling group won out over the education group. Yet there were never any signs that substantial *external* resources were available for education and training if the organisation had been willing to develop these.

When the struggle was over and decided in favour of counselling as the prime and core activity, then personnel changes were surely inevitable. This would be no less true of any organisation in which the culture was changing, whether voluntary, statutory or commercial. The question of whether the changes could have been managed more competently or humanely is, of course, quite a different issue.

The authors document that, during these middle decades, the organisation in general, and the National Executive Committee in particular, set up a series of working parties to look at the appropriate organisation and structural issues resulting from the cultural shift, but that there appeared to be little or no will to change matters. They lay the blame for this on the ideological basis of counselling, particularly of the non-directive kind, whose ethos is the extended person-centred consultation process, rather than the decision taking and structuring of a managerial approach. This must certainly be a contributory factor, but may well not be the only explanation of events. Of equal importance may have been the continuing power of local Marriage Guidance Councils to manage their own affairs, and also to resist (through their regional representatives) change which they did not want. This situation changed dramatically, of course, in 1985 by which time an active group of local chairmen pressed for the external inquiry subsequently carried out by Coopers and Lybrand. In the earlier years, however, this was certainly *not* the case.

Next is the issue of a 'modern' approach to the power within the organisation. The authors describe organisations as being positively 'gendered' and posit that Relate is female, presumably by reason of the predominance of women in the counselling activity as well as the predominance of women clients. This incidentally is changing, still, so that the latest figures show that just on 60 per cent of clients are either couples or men alone as compared with 40 per cent women alone. Unfortunately, the authors don't really tease out what this gender effect has been except to point to the anomaly of a largely male management group. Since all the authors come from higher education it would be a better-received comment if that particular very unequal 'house' had also been put into order! Part of the point remains. This must engender some degree of tension both in recruitment of clients – do men get a fair deal over their problems? – and in service and management.

Next there is a need to reply to the critique about research, both big and small. One most important point here is to say that the demonstrations of competence by any of the so-called marital agencies have been very poor as I testified in 1985 (Hooper 1985), although in the sphere of marital sexual intervention other agencies (especially in the health service) *and* National Marriage Guidance Council have collected and published data. In particular NMGC contributed materially to the debate about the need for two therapists. Nevertheless, of course, more could be done – and should be done. It is no excuse to say that agencies offering counselling do not take easily to appraisal of that work, but until the last few years this was certainly true. The authors do give, I feel, grudging approval to the fact that National Marriage Guidance Council did pioneer a series of annual research conferences. These have ceased at the present time, but their revival is imminent, and other structures have also arisen. I am not convinced that, comparatively, Relate has a worse record than similar agencies.

Turning now to the critique of practice, the question of 'eclectism' is discussed again with a degree of negative criticism. I am sure, however, that David Clark knows quite well that there is virtually no evidence from the counselling and psychotherapy literature that any particular method is more efficacious that any other. In some rather narrow circumstances behavioural approaches appear to have the lead, but as between say 'skills' or 'psychodynamics' there is no compelling evidence. Nevertheless, it is fair that the authors should say that the emphasis on experiential *learning* was clearly overstated at the cost of a better, even if simple, theoretical base line. If anything, the base should be an understanding of the concept of marital or couple problems, and appropriate analysis and action to enable these problems to be tackled; and my own contribution to this debate is cited by the authors as going largely unregarded by the agency. I do not think that is the case because the training programme is significantly more problem-focused than before. It seems to me, at least, that it is quite misleading to describe the training as a 'fragile eclectic combination' without asking current counsellors themselves for their opinion. My own observation is that counsellors being trained by Relate in 1990 are emerging with as firm a set of counselling tools as any newly graduated caring professional.

The final point which this postscript needs to make is that, sadly, the book ends in mid-sentence. After such a remarkable exposure to both records and people it is reasonable to expect the authors to speculate about the future for Relate. They have placed the agency in a developing context and pointed up the false starts and wrong avenues. This analysis should have enabled them to help chart the direction which, in their view, Relate should take in order to deliver a more useful service to the community. But on those matters they are largely silent, despite the existence and their knowledge of a widely agreed strategic plan adopted by the organisation in 1989.

Relate will continue to struggle with the conflicts between voluntarism and professionalism, regionalism and centrism, and counselling techniques and management control. None of the studies of voluntary organisations cited by the authors seems to be of great help in these matters. Perhaps the 'encounter between sociology and history' which the authors said in the introduction they wished to undertake will help others as a case history, even though Relate itself may not greatly benefit. They think, I fear, that their purpose has been served but, as this short postscript testifies, I beg to disagree.

Appendix 1
Respondents interviewed and meetings attended

INTERVIEWS

Interviews were tape-recorded and loosely structured, using an *aide memoire*; tapes were partially transcribed and/or detailed notes taken for later analysis. Interview material has not been quoted in detail in the above analysis, but it did serve as an important source in the process of developing our argument.

Geoffrey Applegarth, former NMGC regional officer.
Lady Avebury, former NMGC chair of Council.
David Barkla, Relate research officer.
Jean Barrett and John Schlapobersky, Relate tutor consultants.
Elizabeth Bishop, Relate tutor consultant.
Jeffrey Blumenfeld, director, Jewish Marriage Council.
Sarah Bowler, Relate regional manager.
A.J. Brayshaw, former NMGC general secretary.
Peter Dawson, Relate regional manager.
Colin Fishwick, former NMGC National Executive Committee member.
Moira Fryer, Relate counselling officer.
Sarah Gammage, Relate education officer.
Christopher Gonin, Relate regional manager.
E.J. Griew, former NMGC National Executive Committee member.
Rose Hacker, former NMGC National Executive Committee member.
Bridget Hester, Relate tutor consultant.
Derek Hill, chair STAR.

Douglas Hooper, chair, Relate Services Committee, former chair NMGC Counselling Advisory Board.

Pat Hunt, Relate tutor consultant.

Sarah Hyland, Relate regional manager.

Arthur Jackson, Relate tutor consultant.

Terry John, former NMGC deputy education secretary.

Jean Judge, director, Catholic Marriage Advisory Council.

Adah Kay, director, Family Services Unit.

Ann Leck, Relate National Executive Committee member.

Anthony Mann, former NMGC regional officer.

Doreen E. Massey, director, Family Planning Association.

John Morrison, Relate tutor consultant.

Renate Olins, director, London Marriage Guidance Council.

Sir Paul Osmond, former chairman of Council NMGC/Relate.

Bryan Owen, Relate assistant director, Finance.

Wayne Samuel, Relate regional manager.

Gerald Sanctuary, former NMGC national secretary.

Roger Smith, consultant to Relate.

Erika Stapleton, former NMGC tutor consultant.

Ed Straw, Coopers and Lybrand Associates.

Joan Sullivan, former NMGC head of counselling.

Nicholas Tyndall, former NMGC chief officer.

John Wallis, former NMGC training officer.

Zelda West-Meads, Relate press officer.

Liz Williamson, manager, Manchester Relate.

Mary Wilson, former chair NMGC National Executive Committee.

Ashley Wyatt, Relate regional manager.

MEETINGS

With David French, director Relate, 13/5/88, 24/8/88, 11/11/88, 5/10/89, 17/9/90.

Relate annual general meetings, 18/10/88, 23/9/89.

Relate Managers' Conference 24/4/89.

North West Region tutors' meeting, 8/6/89.

West Region tutors' meeting, 9/5/89.

STAR Executive Committee meeting, 13/5/89.

Appendix 2
Organisational principles, aims and objectives (1943–)

GENERAL PRINCIPLES OF MARRIAGE GUIDANCE COUNCILS (ADOPTED 1943)

That the safeguarding of the family unit as the basis of our community life is of vital importance to the future welfare of the nation.

That the right foundation for this unit is permanent monogamous marriage, which alone provides satisfactory conditions for the birth and upbringing of children, for the expression of the function of sex, and for a secure relationship between man and woman.

That it should be plainly acknowledged that the achievement of successful marriage is no easy task, but that sustained and disciplined effort is required to build up that physical, mental and spiritual harmony which alone can bring the relationship to its full maturity.

That the right approach to marriage, and the choice of a partner, are matters of such paramount importance that it is the clear duty to the rising generation to provide its members with such instruction and guidance as may safeguard them from wrong attitudes and false judgements.

That in addition an adequate course of more detailed preparation should be available to all who are about to marry.

That the right basis for personal and social life is that sexual intercourse should not take place outside marriage.

That it is a public duty to do everything possible to prevent the tragedy of the broken home, and the train of evils which it initiates, by the provision of sympathetic and expert treatment for the prevention and cure of marital disharmony.

That parenthood normally brings to marriage, not only the fulfilment of its racial end, but also the achievement of one of its deepest satisfactions; and that everything possible should therefore be done to promote fertile unions.

That scientific contraception, while serving a purpose in assisting married couples to regulate the spacing of their children, becomes a danger when misused to enable selfish and irresponsible people to escape the duties and disciplines of marriage and parenthood.

That it is essential to bring about a state of society in which the welfare of the family shall receive primary consideration, and where parenthood shall no longer labour under social and economic disabilities.

GENERAL PRINCIPLES AND AIMS OF THE NATIONAL MARRIAGE GUIDANCE COUNCIL (ADOPTED 1952)

Principles

1 Successful marriage, the foundation of happy family life, is vital to the well-being of society.
2 Marriage should be entered upon as a partnership for life, with reverence and a sense of responsibility.
3 Spiritual, emotional and physical harmony in marriage is only achieved by unselfish love and self-discipline.
4 Children are the natural fulfilment of marriage and enrich the relationship between husband and wife; nevertheless, scientific contraception, when used according to conscience within marriage, can contribute to the health and happiness of the whole family.
5 The right basis for personal and social life is that sexual intercourse should take place only within marriage.

Aims

6 To enlist, through a national system of selection and training, the services of men and women qualified for the work of reconciliation and education in marriage and family life.
7 To help parents and others to give children an appreciation of

family life: and to make available to young men and women before marriage such guidance as may promote right relationships in friendship, courtship, marriage and parenthood.

8 To assist those who are about to marry to understand the nature, responsibilities and rewards of the married state.

9 To offer counsel to those who encounter difficulties in the way of married happiness, if possible before these difficulties become serious.

10 To work towards a state of society in which the welfare of the family shall receive primary consideration, and parenthood shall nowhere involve unreasonable social and economic disabilities.

OBJECTIVES (ADOPTED 1968)

The National Marriage Guidance Council is concerned primarily with marriage and family relationships, and believes that the well-being of society is dependent on the stability of marriage. Its objectives are:

1 To provide a confidential counselling service for people who have difficulties or anxieties in their marriages or in other personal relationships.

2 To provide an education service in personal relationships for young people, engaged and newly married couples and parents.

3 To equip men and women to do this work by means of a national system of selection, training, tutorial support and supervision.

4 To publish and distribute literature on a wide variety of topics relating to marriage and family life.

5 To provide courses and conferences for teachers, ministers of religion, youth leaders and others, and to cooperate with workers in related fields.

OBJECTIVES (ADOPTED 1983)

The National Marriage Guidance Council is concerned with marriage and with family and personal relationships and believes that the quality of these relationships is fundamental to the well-being of society. The Council's objectives are:

1 To provide a confidential counselling service for people who have difficulties or anxieties in their marriages or in other personal relationships.

2 To promote and provide education services in personal and family relationships for people of all ages.

3   To provide in some centres a service of sex therapy.
4   To equip men and women to do this work by means of a national system of selection, training, tutorial support and supervision.
5   To promote research and to publish and distribute literature on a wide variety of topics relating to human relationships and in particular to marriage and family life.
6   To provide courses and conferences for, and to cooperate with, workers in related fields.

COMMON PURPOSE STATEMENT (ADOPTED IN 1987)

NB This does not replace the 1983 objectives.

The National Marriage Guidance Council believes that its services must be devoted primarily to helping couples and individuals in the context of their marriages, thus also helping the surrounding family.
MG accepts that in our diverse society its concept of marriage must encompass differing cultural understandings of marriage and other committed adult relationships.
MG's focus on marriage, understood in this way, is its distinctive contribution to strengthening families and thus the concerns of children are significant to the Council's work, as are the relationships between adult partners and their own parents.
MG is therefore concerned with a variety of services, both remedial and preventative:

1   Counselling for specific problems and conflicts in marriage;
2   Counselling to help clients deal constructively with the end of marriage by death, divorce or separation;
3   Counselling and other therapies to enhance marital relationships;
4   To offer education for marriage and family life;
5   To offer training in counselling skills to individuals and other interested agencies and professional groups.

These services are not dependent on any one theoretical or professional view of marriage, family or sexual relationships.
MG's work is for the benefit of the whole community and therefore cannot be committed to any one sectional, social, political, cultural or religious view of marriage.

Bibliography

All places of publication London unless otherwise stated.

Adams, Esther (1958) 'What is it that does them good?' *Marriage Guidance.* October, pp. 355–6.

Adams, Norah (1973) 'Second thoughts about reception counselling'. *Marriage Guidance.* July, pp. 314–8.

Alfred, J. B. (1953) 'Non directive counselling'. *Marriage Guidance.* Sept., pp. 4–5.

Allen, M. E. (1973) Report. *Newsletter* No. 3. November, p. 4.

Ambrose, P., Harper, J. and Pemberton, R. (1983) *Surviving Divorce: Men After Marriage.* Brighton: Wheatsheaf.

Applegarth, G. and Hunt, P. (1986) Letter. *Newsletter* No. 96. July, p. 4.

Archbishop of Canterbury's Group on the Divorce Law (1966) *Putting Asunder. A Divorce Law for Contemporary Society.* SPCK.

Argyle, M. and Henderson, M. (1985) *The Anatomy of Relationships.* Harmondsworth: Penguin.

Armstrong, D. (1983) *Political Anatomy of the Body: Medical Knowledge in Britain in the Twentieth Century.* Cambridge: Cambridge University Press.

Askham, J. (1984) *Identity and Stability in Marriage.* Cambridge: Cambridge University Press.

Aves, Geraldine M. (1969) *The Voluntary Worker in the Social Services.* Bedford Square Press of the NCSS and Allen and Unwin.

Bailey, Derrick Sherwin (1952) *The Mystery of Love and Marriage. a Study in the Theology of Sexual Relations.* SCM Press.

Bailey, Derrick Sherwin (1957) 'Marriage and the family: some theological considerations' in C. H. Rolph (ed.) *The Human Sum.* Heinemann.

Baker, J. (1978) 'Is counselling value-free?' *Marriage Guidance*, Sept., pp. 91–5.

Ball, Kenneth (1948) *The Spiritual Approach to Marriage Preparation.* NMGC.

Bancroft, J. (1984) 'Interaction of psychosocial and biological factors in marital sexuality – differences between men and women'. *British Journal of Guidance and Counselling* 12 (1), pp. 62–71.

Bannister, K. *et. al.* (1955) *Social Casework in Marital Problems. The Development of the Psychodynamic Approach.* Tavistock.

Bannister, K. (1955b) 'A professional casework approach to marriage counselling'. *Marriage Guidance*. June, pp. 7–8.

Barker, D. L. (1978) 'The regulation of marriage: repressive benevolence'. In G. Littlejohn, B. Smart, J. Wakefield and N. Yuval-Davis (eds) *Power and the State*. Croom Helm, pp. 239–66.

Bellah, Robert et. al. (1985) *Habits of the Heart: Individual Commitment in American Life*. Berkeley: University of California Press.

Bennum, I. (1985) 'Unilateral marital therapy'. In W. Dryden (ed.) *Marital Therapy in Britain*, Vol I. Harper & Row.

Berger, P. L. and Kellner, H. (1964) 'Marriage and the construction of reality'. *Diogenes*, pp. 1–23.

Bernard, J. (1976) *The Future of Marriage*. Harmondsworth: Penguin. First edition 1972.

Beveridge, Sir William and others (1932) *Changes in Family Life*. Allen & Unwin.

Billis, David (1984) 'Voluntary Sector Management: Research and Practice'. Working paper No. 1, Centre for Voluntary Organization, LSE.

Billis, David and Harris, M. (1986) 'An Extended Role for the Voluntary Sector: the Challenge of Implementation'. Working paper No. 3, Centre for Voluntary Organization, LSE.

Blood, R. O. (Jnr) and Wolfe, H. J. (1960) *Husbands and Wives*. New York: Free Press.

Bott, E. (1957) *Family and Social Network*. Tavistock.

Boucher, F. (1984) 'Family and personal problems – the CAB approach'. *Marriage Guidance*. Autumn, pp. 17–20.

Bowlby, J. (1946) *Forty Four Juvenile Thieves: their characters and home life*. Balliere Tindall and Cox.

Bowlby, J. (1951) *Maternal Care and Mental Health*. Geneva: World Health Organization.

Brannen, Julia and Collard, Jean (1982) *Marriages in Trouble. The Process of Seeking Help*. Tavistock.

Brayshaw, A. J. (1951) 'Principles of counselling'. *Marriage Guidance*. Oct., pp. 3–5.

Brayshaw, A. J. (1952a) *The Stability of Marriage*. NMGC.

Brayshaw, A. J. (1952b) 'Taking stock of counselling'. *Marriage Guidance*. May 1952, pp. 6–7.

Brayshaw, A. J. (1957) 'Righteous indignation'. *Marriage Guidance*. Oct., pp. 153–5.

Brayshaw, A. J. (1963) *Thou Shalt not Commit Adultery*. NMGC.

Brayshaw, A. J. (1980) *Public Policy and Family Life*. Policy Studies Institute Discussion Paper No. 3.

Brearley, M. (1986) 'Counsellors and clients: men or women?' *Marriage Guidance*. Summer, pp. 2–9.

Brenton, Maria (1985) *The Voluntary Sector in British Social Services*. Longmans.

British Social Hygiene Council (1932) *Preparation for Marriage*. Jonathan Cape.

Brittain, Vera (1933) *Testament of Youth. An Autobiographical Study of the Years 1900–1925*. Gollancz.

Brown, J. (1967) Letter. *Marriage Guidance*, p. 370.

Brown, P. T. (1979) 'Practical modifications of Masters' and Johnson's approach to the treatment of sexual dysfunction'. PhD thesis, University of Leicester.

Brown, R. G. S. (1979) *Reorganizing the NHS*. Oxford: Martin Robertson.

Buber, Martin (1958) *I and Thou*. Edinburgh: T. and J. Clark.

Burgess, E. W. and Locke, H. J. (1945) *The Family: From Institution to Companionship*. New York: American Book Company.

Burgoyne, J. and Clark, D. (1984) *Making A Go of It*. Routledge.

Burgoyne, J., Ormrod, R. and Richards, M. P. M. (1987) *Divorce Matters*. Harmondsworth: Penguin.

Burns, T. and Stalker, G. M. (1961) *The Management of Innovation*. Tavistock.

Butler, R. J. and Wilson, D. C. (1989) *Managing Voluntary and Non-profit Organisations*. London: Routledge.

Carkhuff, R. R. (1969) *Helping and Human Relations*, Vols I and II. New York: Holt, Rinehart & Winston.

Carstairs, G. M. (1962) *This Island Now*. BBC Reith Lectures. Hogarth Press.

Chance, Janet (1930) 'A marriage education centre in London'. In World League for Sexual Reform, *Proceedings of the Third Congress*, edited by Norman Haire. Kegan Paul Trench and Trubner. pp. 37–9.

Chance, Janet (1935a) 'Four years at a sex education centre'. In J. H. Badley et. al. (eds) *Experiments in Sex Education*. Federation of Progressive Societies and Individuals. pp. 45–7.

Chance, Janet (1935b) 'Six years in a sex education centre'. *Marriage Hygiene* Vol. 1, May 1935, pp. 412–14.

Chesser, Eustace (1952) *Marriage and Freedom*. Rich & Cowan. First edition 1946.

Chesser, Eustace (1960) *Is Chastity Outmoded?* Heinemann

Chesser, Eustace (1964) *Love Without Fear. A Plain Guide to Sex Technique for every Married Adult*. Arrow Books. First edition 1941.

Chester, Robert (1973) 'Family and marriage in the post-parental years'. *Marriage Guidance*. Sept. pp. 338–48.

Chester, Robert (1985) 'Shaping the future: from marriage movement to service agency'. *Marriage Guidance*. Autumn, pp. 5–15.

Church of England General Synod (1978) *Marriage and the Church's Task*. Church of England.

Church of England Moral Welfare Council (1954) *The Church and Marriage*. Evidence to the Royal Commission on Marriage and Divorce presented by the Archbishop of Canterbury. Church of England Moral Welfare Council.

Church of England Moral Welfare Council (1956) *Marriage, Divorce and the Royal Commission. A Study Outline of the Report of the Royal Commission on Marriage and Divorce, 1951–5*. Church of England Moral Welfare Council.

Church of England Moral Welfare Council (1958) *The Family in Contemporary Society*. SPCK.

Clark, David and Haldane, Douglas (1990) *Wedlocked?* Cambridge: Polity Press.

Clark, M. (1966) 'Marriage counselling professional or amateur?' *Marriage*

Guidance. July, pp. 106–9.

Clulow, C. (1985) *Marital Therapy*. Aberdeen: Aberdeen University Press.

Clulow, C. and Mattinson, J. (1989) *Marriage Inside Out: Understanding Problems of Intimacy*. Harmondsworth: Penguin.

Conference on Christian Politics, Economics and Citizenship (1924) *The Relation of the Sexes*. Longmans.

Conrad, P. and Schneider, J. W. (eds) (1980) *Deviance and Medicalization: From Badness to Sickness*. New York: C. V. Mosby Co.

Cooper, David (1972) *The Death of the Family*. Harmondsworth: Penguin.

Costello, J. (1985) *Love, Sex and War: Changing Values 1939–45*. Collins.

Crew, F. A. E. (1949) 'Sexuality in relation to self, society and the species'. In S. Neville Rolfe (ed.) *Sex in Social Life*. Allen & Unwin.

Crichton-Miller, H. (1921) *The New Psychology and the Teacher*. Jarrolds.

Crick, Hilary (1974) 'The battered baby syndrome: can the MGC help?' *Marriage Guidance*. Jan/Feb., pp. 8–11.

Crowhurst, H. M. (1982) *The NMGC Client in Sexual Dysfunction Clinics, 1976–80*. Rugby: National Marriage Guidance Council.

Crowlesmith, J. (1951) 'Spiritual values in marriage guidance'. *Marriage Guidance*. June.

Crowlesmith, J. (1957) 'Marriage and the unconscious'. *Marriage Guidance*. June, np.

Daniell, Diana (1985) 'Marital therapy: the psychodynamic approach'. In Windy Dryden (ed.) *Marital Therapy in Britain*, Vol. I. Harper & Row.

Davidoff, L. and Hall, C. (1986) *Family Fortunes*. Hutchinson.

Davies, M. Llewellyn (1915) *Maternity. Letters from Working Women*. G. Bell.

Davy, Charles F. (1964) 'A Reply to Dr. Ronald Fletcher'. *Marriage Guidance*. Jan., pp. 5–8.

Dearlove, John. (1979) *The Reorganisation of British Local Government. Old Orthodoxies and a Political Perspective*. Cambridge: Cambridge University Press.

Demos, J. and Boocock, S. S. (eds) (1978) *Turning Points: Historical and Sociological Essays on the Family*. Chicago: University of Chicago Press.

DHSS (1974) Report of the Committee of Inquiry into the Care and Supervision provided in relation to Maria Colwell. HMSO.

Dick, Barbara (1963) 'Case discussion or what goes on (ii)'. *Marriage Guidance*. March/April, pp. 219–20.

Dicks, H. V. (1967) *Marital Tensions*. Routledge & Kegan Paul.

Dicks, H. V. (1970) *Fifty Years of the Tavistock Clinic*. Routledge & Kegan Paul.

Dodd, Ian (1978) 'Reactions'. *Marriage Guidance*. June, pp. 56–8.

Doherty, Winnifred (1956) 'Some psychodynamic aspects of marriage'. *Marriage Guidance*. Feb., pp. 13–16.

Dominian, Jack (1967) 'The training of counsellors'. *CMAC Bulletin 7*, No. 4, pp. 15–19.

Dominian, Jack (1985) 'Values in marriage: change and continuity'. In W. Dryden (ed.) *Marital Therapy in Britain* Vol. I. Harper & Row, pp. 34–50.

Dryden, Windy and Brown, Paul (1985) 'Issues in the training of marital therapists'. In Windy Dryden (ed.) *Marital Therapy in Britain*, Vol II. Harper & Row.

Dryden, Windy and Hunt, P. (1985) 'Therapeutic alliances in marital therapy'. In W. Dryden (ed.) *Marital Therapy in Britain* Vol 1. Harper & Row, pp. 121–66.

Dukes, Ethel and Hay, Margaret (1949) *Children of Today and Tomorrow*. Allen and Unwin for the British Social Hygiene Council.

Economist (1988) 'Managing consultants'.

Editorial (1979) *Marriage Guidance*. March, p. 147.

Editorial (1982) *Marriage Guidance*. October, p. 103.

Egan, Gerald (1975) *The Skilled Helper*. Monterey, California: Brooks/Cole.

Eichenbaum, L. and Orbach, S (1984) *What Do Women Want?* New York: Berkeley.

Emery, R. E. and Trist, E. L. (1972) *Towards a Social Ecology*. Plenum Press.

Epstein Nord, Deborah (1985) *The Apprenticeship of Beatrice Webb*. Macmillan.

Eversley, David and Bonnerjea, Lucy (1982) 'Social change and indicators of diversity'. In R. N. Rapoport *et. al.* (eds) *Families in Britain*. Routledge & Kegan Paul, pp. 75–94.

Fairbairn, W. R. D. (1952) *Psychoanalytic Studies of the Personality*. Tavistock/Routledge & Kegan Paul.

Family Welfare Association (1946) *Annual Report, 1945–6*. FWA.

Family Welfare Association (1949) *Annual Report, 1948–9*. FWA.

Featherstone, Mike (1988) 'In pursuit of postmodernism. An Introduction'. *Theory Culture and Society* 5, Nos 2–3, pp. 195–215.

Finch, Janet (1989) 'Social policy, social engineering and the family in the 1990s'. In M. Bulmer, J. Lewis and D. Piachaud (eds) *The Goals of Social Policy*. Unwin Hyman.

Fletcher, Peter (1938) *In Search of Personality*. Rich & Cowan.

Fletcher, Ronald (1963) 'Herbert Gray Lecture'. *Marriage Guidance*. Nov., pp. 167–75.

Fletcher, Ronald (1972) 'Marriage today and tomorrow: the marriage of good friends'. *Marriage Guidance*. November, pp. 167–84.

Foucault, M. (1973) *The Birth of the Clinic: An Archaeology of Medical Perception*. Tavistock.

Foucault, M. (1979) *History of Sexuality* Vol 1. Allen Lane.

Four Chaplains to the Forces (1919) A *Cornerstone of Reconstruction. A Book on Working for Social Purity among Men*. SPCK.

Friedan, Betty (1963) *The Feminine Mystique*. Gollancz.

Fryer, Moira (1985) 'Inside marital therapy'. *Marriage Guidance*. Winter, pp. 13–14.

Gaunt, S. (1983) 'Reasons for Resigning'. *Marriage Guidance*. Autumn, pp. 8–15.

Gaunt, S. (1985) *The First Interview in Marriage Guidance*. NMGC Research Paper No. 2. Rugby: National Marriage Guidance Council.

Gaunt, S. (1987) *Reception Interviews in Marriage Guidance*. NMGC Research Report No. 6. Rugby: National Marriage Guidance Council.

Gerard, David (1983) *Charities in Britain: Conservation or Change?* Bedford Square Press.

Giddens, A. (1990) *The Consequences of Modernity*. Cambridge: Polity.

Gillis, John R. (1985) *For Better, For Worse. British Marriages 1600 to the Present*. Oxford: Oxford University Press.

Gladstone, F. J. (1979) *Voluntary Action in a Changing World*. National Council of Social Service Planning Unit. Bedford Square Press.

Goode, W. J. (1970) *World Revolution in Family Patterns*. New York: Free Press.

Gordon, Linda (1989) *Heroes of their Own Lives*. New York: Viking.

Gorer, G. (1950) *Exploring the English Character*. Cresset Press.

Gorer, G. (1971) *Sex and Marriage in England Today*. Nelson.

Gorrell Barnes, Barbara (1960) 'Looking ahead – the training officer'. *Marriage Guidance*. June, pp. 264–6.

Graham-Green, G. J. (1967) 'The CMAC comes of age'. *CMAC Bulletin* 7, No. 4, pp. 11–15.

Gray, A. Herbert (1923) *Men, Women and God. A Discussion of Sex Questions from the Christian Point of View*. Student Christian Movement.

Gray, A. Herbert (1938) *Love: the One Solution*. Rich and Cowan.

Gray, A. Herbert (1941) *Successful Marriage*. Rich and Cowan.

Gray, A. Herbert (1945) *Are Sex Relations without Marriage wrong*? Alliance of Honour.

Gray, A. Herbert (1949) 'Preparation for marriage'. In S. Neville Rolfe (ed.) *Sex in Social Life*. Allen and Unwin.

Gray, A. Herbert (1949b) 'Looking Backwards'. *Marriage Guidance*, Dec., p. 2.

Gray, Kenneth (1976) 'A personal definition for counselling'. *Marriage Guidance*. Nov./Dec., pp. 228–33.

Greenspan, M. (1983) *A New Approach to Women and Therapy*. New York: McGraw-Hill.

Greer, Germaine (1971) *The Female Eunuch*. Paladin.

Griew, E. J. (1972) 'Marital reconciliation: contexts and meanings'. *Cambridge Law Journal* 30. November, pp. 394–415.

Griffith, E. F. (1941) *Sex and Citizenship*. Gollancz.

Griffith, E. F. (1944) 'Marriage Guidance'. *Spectator* 2/3, pp. 9–10.

Griffith, E. F. (ed.) (1947a) *The Road to Maturity*. Methuen. First edition 1944.

Griffith, E. F. (1947b) 'The medical aspects of marriage guidance'. *The Lancet* 1/2. Reprint for the Marriage Guidance Council.

Griffith, E. F. (1948) *Morals in the Melting Pot*. Methuen.

Griffith, E. F. (1949) 'Family planning'. In S. Neville Rolfe (ed.) *Sex in Social Life*. Allen and Unwin.

Griffith, E. F. (1981) *The Pioneer Spirit*. Upton Grey, Hampshire: Green Leaves Press.

de Groot, Marianne (1985) *Marriage Guidance Counsellors in the Medical Setting*. NMGC Research Report No. 1.

Guiver, Pamela (1973) *The Trouble Sharers*. Rugby: National Marriage Guidance Council.

Gummer, J. Selwyn (1971) *The Permissive Society. Fact or Fantasy*? Cassell.

Hakim, C. (1979) *Occupational Segregation*. Research Paper No. 9. Department of Employment.

Hall, Stuart (1989) *The Voluntary Sector under Attack*. . . ? IVAC.

Halmos, Paul (1965) *The Faith of the Counsellors*. Constable.
Halmos, Paul (1966) 'Counselling morality'. *Marriage Guidance*. July, pp. 116–18.
Handy, Charles (1981) *Working Party on Improving Effectiveness in Voluntary Organisations*. National Council of Voluntary Organizations.
Handy, Charles (1982) Report of speech to AGM. *Newsletter* No. 73, Nov.
Handy, Charles (1985) *Understanding Voluntary Organizations*. Harmondsworth: Penguin.
Hareven, T. K. (ed.) (1978) *Transitions: The Family Life Course in Historical Perspective*. New York: Academic Press.
Harman, John D. (ed.) (1982) *Volunteerism in the Eighties. Fundamental Issues in Voluntary Action*. New York: University Press of America.
Harris, J. and Usborne, H. (1972) 'Sexual dysfunction'. *Newsletter* No. 58, p. 2.
Harris, M. (1987) 'Management Committees: Roles and Tasks'. Working Paper No. 4, Centre for Voluntary Organization, LSE.
Harris, M. (1989) 'Problems of Welfare Expansion for Voluntary Organizations'. Unpub. paper, Centre for Voluntary Organization, LSE.
Harris, T. A. (1973) *I'm OK You're OK*. Cape.
Hart, Nicky (1976) *When Marriage Ends*. Tavistock.
Hatch, Stephen (1980) *Outside the State. Voluntary Organizations in Three English Towns*. Croom Helm.
Haynes, Robert J. (1980) *Organisation Theory and Local Government*. Allen & Unwin.
Hearn, J. and Parkin, W. (1987) *'Sex' at 'Work': The Power and Paradox of Organisation Sexuality*. Brighton: Wheatsheaf.
Hearn, J., Sheppard, D. L., Tancred-Sheriff, P. and Burrell, G. (eds) (1989) *The Sexuality of Organization*. Sage.
Heisler, J. (1974) *Why Counsellors Resign*. Rugby: National Marriage Guidance Council.
Heisler, J. (1975) 'Intake interviewing: a study of practice within MGC'. *Marriage Guidance*. Sept/Oct., pp. 399–403.
Heisler, J. (1977a) 'Aspects of the selection process'. *Marriage Guidance*. November/December, pp. 414–21.
Heisler, J. (1977b) 'Client-counsellor interaction'. *Marriage Guidance*. Jan/Feb., pp. 233–8.
Heisler, J. (1980) 'The client writes'. *Marriage Guidance*. Autumn, pp. 115–25.
Heisler, J. (1983) *Sexual therapy in NMGC*. Rugby: National Marriage Guidance Council.
Heisler, J. (1984) *The NMGC Client in 1982*. Rugby: National Marriage Guidance Council.
Heisler, J. (1987) *Dropping Out*. Rugby: National Marriage Guidance Council.
Heisler, J. and Applegarth, G. (1985) *Salaried Counselling: The Salford Scheme*. Rugby: NMGC Research Report No. 4.
Heisler, J. and Whitehouse, A. (1975) 'The NMGC Client, 1975'. *Marriage Guidance*. November/December, pp. 188–93.

Hemming, J. (1967) 'Is there a future for marriage?' *Marriage Guidance*, Sept., pp. 323–7.

Henriques, B. (1955) *The Home Menders: The Prevention of Unhappiness in Children*. Harrap.

Herbert, A. P. (1934) *Holy Deadlock*. Methuen.

Heron, Alistaire (ed.) (1963) *An Essay by a Group of Friends. Towards a Quaker View of Sex*. Friends Home Service Committee.

Hodgkins, William (1956) 'Marriage counselling'. *Marriage Guidance*. Sept., pp. 3–4.

Holt, Nancy (1958) 'What is it that does them good?' *Marriage Guidance*. April, pp. 249–51.

Holt, Nancy (1971) *Counselling in Marriage Problems: Counselling in Personal Relationships*. Rugby: National Marriage Guidance Council.

Home Office and DHSS (1979) *Marriage Matters*. Consultative Document by the Working Party on Marriage Guidance set up by the Home Office in consultation with the DHSS. HMSO.

Hooper, Douglas (1976) 'Yesterday's counsellors for tomorrow's problems?' *Marriage Guidance*. Sept./Oct., pp. 147–53.

Hooper, Douglas (1978) 'Counselling, the meaning, the message and the market place'. *Marriage Guidance*. March, pp. 4–8.

Hooper, Douglas (1982) 'Counselling: change or decay?' *Marriage Guidance*. March, pp. 27–33.

Hooper, Douglas (1985) 'Marital therapy; an overview of research'. In W. Dryden (ed.) *Marital Therapy in Britain*, Vol. I. Harper & Row, pp. 275–300.

Hubback, J. (1957) *Wives Who Went to College*. Heinemann.

Humble, Stephen (1982) *Voluntary Action in the 1980s. A Summary of the Findings of a National Survey*. Berkhamsted: The Volunteer Centre.

Hunt, Pat (1985) *Clients' Responses to Marriage Counselling*. NMGC.

Ingleby, A. H. B. (1957) 'Old wine in new bottles'. *Marriage Guidance*. Mar., pp. 58–60.

Ingleby, A. H. B. (1961) *Learning to Love*. Robert Hale.

Ingram, K. (1922) *An Outline of Sexual Morality*. Jonathan Cape.

Ingram, K. (1930) *The Modern Attitude to the Sex Problem*. Allen & Unwin.

Ingram, K. (1940) *Sex Morality Tomorrow*. Allen & Unwin.

Ingram, K. (1945) *Guide to the New Age*. Allen & Unwin.

Jackson, Janet D. (1961) 'The "ordinary" counsellor'. *Marriage Guidance*. April, pp. 57–8.

James, Adrian and Wilson, Kate (1991) 'Research into therapy with couples: an overview'. In W. Dryden and D. Hooper (eds) *Handbook of Couples Therapy*. Milton Keynes: Open University Press.

Jenkins, Daniel T. (ed.) (1949) *The Doctor's Profession*. SCM Press.

Johnson, Norman (1981) *Voluntary Social Services*. Blackwell.

Kalvemark, Ann-Sofie (1980) *More Children of Better Quality? Aspects on (sic) Swedish Population Policy in the 1930s*. Uppsala: Allmqvist and Wiksell International.

Keays, Sarah (1985) *A Question of Judgement*. Quintessential Press.

Keithley, J. (1977) 'Marriage Guidance Research: A Preview'. University of Durham Working Paper in Social Administration, No. 1.

Keithley, J. (1982) 'Marriage counselling in general practice: an assessment of the work of marriage counsellors in a general medical practice'. Unpublished PhD thesis. University of Durham.

Kent, Susan Kingsley (1990) 'Gender reconstruction after the First World War'. In Harold Smith (ed) *British Feminism in the Twentieth Century*. Aldershot: Edward Elgar.

Kiely, G. M. (1984) 'Social change and marital problems: implications for marriage counselling'. *British Journal of Guidance and Counselling* 12 (1), pp. 92–100.

Klapp, O. E. (1964) *Symbolic Leaders*. Chicago: Aldine Publishing Co.

Klein, Melanie (1932) *The Psychoanalysis of Children*. Hogarth.

Kramer, Ralph M. (1981) *Voluntary Agencies in the Welfare State*. Berkeley: UCLA Press.

Laing, R. D. and Esterson, A. (1970) *Sanity, Madness and the Family*. Harmondsworth: Penguin.

Lambeth Conference (1930) *Report*. SPCK.

Lewis, Jane (1980) *The Politics of Motherhood. Child and Maternal Welfare in England 1900–1939*. Croom Helm.

Lewis, Jane (1986a) *What Price Community Medicine?* Brighton: Wheatsheaf.

Lewis, Jane (1986b) 'Anxieties about the family and the relationships between parents, children and the state in twentieth-century England'. In M. P. M. Richards and Paul Light (eds) *Children of Social Worlds*. Cambridge: Polity Press.

Lewis, Jane (1991) *Women and Social Action in Late Victorian and Edwardian England*. Edward Elgar Publishing.

Lewis, Jane and Brookes, Barbara (1983) 'A reassessment of the work of the Peckham Health Centre, 1926–1951'. *Milbank Memorial Fund Quarterly/Health and Society*, 61, No. 2, pp. 307–50.

Lewis, Jane and Meredith, Barbara (1988) *Daughters who Care*. Routledge.

Lindsey, Judge Ben B. and Evans, Wainright (1928) *The Companionate Marriage*. Brentano's Ltd.

Mace, David R. (1943) *Does Sex Morality Matter?* Rich and Cowan.

Mace, David R. (1945a) 'A stranger to his son'. *The Star*. 5/6.

Mace, David R. (1945b) 'Five years apart; the problem of the homecoming husband'. *The Star*. 29/5.

Mace, David R. (1945c) *The Outlook for Marriage*. MGC.

Mace, David R. (1946a) *Coming Home*. Staples Press.

Mace, David R. (1946b) 'Divorce and the child'. *The Star*. 12/2.

Mace, David R. (1947a) 'The battle of the family'. *Marriage Guidance*, July, Editorial.

Mace, David R. (1947b) 'The mediocre marriage'. *Marriage Guidance*, Dec., Editorial.

Mace, David R. (1948a) *Marriage Crisis*. Delisle.

Mace, David R. (1948b) *Marriage Counselling. The First Full Account of the Remedial Work of the MGC*. J and A Churchill.

Mace, David R. (1948c) 'Married – and bored to tears'. *The Star*. 6/4.

Mace, David R. (1951) 'What is counselling?' *Marriage Guidance*. Sept., pp. 1–3.

Mace, David R. (1952) 'Overcoming marital difficulties'. *Marriage Guidance*. July 1952, pp. 7–8.

Mace, David R. (1959) 'Marriage guidance and the mass media'. *Marriage Guidance*. February 1954, pp. 20–2.

Mace, David R. (1966) 'Marriage counselling in the USA'. *Marriage Guidance*. Jan., pp. 7–10.

Mace, David R. (1972) *Sexual Difficulties in Marriage*. NMGC.

MacFarlane, A. (1986) *Marriage and Love in England, 1300–1848*. Oxford: Basil Blackwell.

MacIntyre, A. (1967) *Secularisation and Moral Change*. Oxford: Oxford University Press.

MacLay, David (1955) 'First year impressions'. *Marriage Guidance*. May, pp. 3–4.

MacMillan, H. (1938) *The Middle Way. A Study of the Problem of Economic and Social Progress in a Free and Democratic Society*. Macmillan.

MacMurray, John (1935) *Reason and Emotion*. Faber & Faber.

McWilliams, William (1985) 'The mission transformed. The professionalisation of probation between the wars'. *The Howard Journal* 24 Nov., pp. 257–74.

Mann, Anthony (1974a) Interview. *Newsletter*. No. 12 October, p. 1.

Mann, Anthony (1974b) *The Human Paradox*. Rugby: National Marriage Guidance Council.

Mansfield, P. and Collard, J. (1988) *The Beginning of the Rest of Your Life?* Basingstoke: Macmillan.

Marshall, John (1978) 'CMAC Reorganisation'. *CMAC Bulletin*. 16, No. 61, pp. 2–4.

Masters, W. H. and Johnson, Virginia E. (1970) *Human Sexual Inadequacy*. Churchill.

Mattinson, Janet and Sinclair, Ian (1979) *Mate and Stalemate*. Institute of Marital Studies.

Mellor, Hugh W. (1985) *The Role of Voluntary Organizations in Social Welfare*. Croom Helm.

Merrivale, Rt Hon. Ld (1936) *Marriage and Divorce. The English Point of View*. Allen & Unwin.

Merton, R. K. (1957) *Social Theory and Social Structure*. Glencoe, Ill. The Free Press.

Middleton Murry, J. Adam and Eve (1944) *An Essay towards a New and Better Society*. Andrew Dakers Ltd.

Miller, E. J. and Rice, A. K. (1967) *Systems of Organization. The Control of Task and Sentient Boundaries*. Tavistock.

Miller, Peter and Rose, Nikolas (1988) 'The Tavistock Programme: the government of subjectivity and social life'. *Sociology* 22, No. 2, May, pp. 171–192.

Mills, C. W. (1959) *The Sociological Imagination*. New York: Oxford University Press.

Mitchell, J. (1971) *Women's Estate*. Harmondsworth: Penguin.

Monger, Mark (1973) 'Reception interviewing'. *Marriage Guidance*. May, pp. 273–6.

Morgan, D. H. J. (1985) *The Family, Politics and Social Theory*. Routledge & Kegan Paul.

Morgan, D. H. J. (1990) 'Institution and relationship within marriage'. Paper presented at World Congress of Sociology, Madrid.

Mount, Ferdinand (1983) *The Subversive Family: an alternative history of love and marriage*. George Allen & Unwin. First Edition 1982.

Murch, Mervyn (1980) *Justice and Welfare in Divorce*. Sweet and Maxwell.

Myrdal, A. (1941) *Nation and Family, the Swedish Experiment in Democratic Family and Population Policy*. New York: Harper Bros.

Myrdal, A. and Klein, V. (1952) *Women's Two Roles*. Routledge & Kegan Paul.

National Council for Voluntary Organisations (1988) *The Voluntary Sector in 1988*. NCVO.

National Marriage Guidance Council (NMGC) (1949a) *Memorandum on the Work of the NMGC, 1948–9*. NMGC.

NMGC (1949b) Annual Report. NMGC.

NMGC (1949c) *Marriage Guidance in a Local Community*. NMGC.

NMGC (1951–2) Annual Report. NMGC.

NMGC (1952) *Memoranda of Evidence submitted to the Royal Commission on Marriage and Divorce*.

NMGC (1954–5) Annual Report. NMGC.

NMGC (1964–5) Annual Report. NMGC.

NMGC (1975a) 'Violence in marriage. Evidence of the NMGC to the Select Committee'. *Marriage Guidance*. Nov./Dec., pp. 446–51.

NMGC (1975b) *Annual Report*. NMGC.

NMGC (1979) *Annual Report*. NMGC.

NMGC (1980) 'Response to Marriage Matters'. *Marriage Guidance*. March, pp. 4–14.

NMGC (1981) *Annual Report*. NMGC.

NMGC (1982) *Change in Marriage*. NMGC.

NMGC (1983) *Annual Report*. NMGC.

NMGC (1984) *The NMGC Client, 1982*. NMGC.

NMGC (1987) Counsellor Basic Training Prospectus. NMGC.

NMGC Social Policy Advisory Board (1982) 'Conciliation: an MG response'. *Marriage Guidance*. October, pp. 104–12.

Ness, Mary (1976) 'Co-therapy and psychosexual dysfunction'. *Marriage Guidance*. Nov./Dec., pp. 201–7.

Newton, Barbara (1973) Letter. *Newsletter*. No. 62, July, p. 14.

Nichols, Kevin (1978) 'Some questions about religion and counselling'. *CMAC Bulletin* Vol 18, No. 69, pp. 2–9.

North, M. (1972) *The Secular Priests*. Allen & Unwin.

Nugent, Peter H. (1978) 'Us'. *CMAC Bulletin* 16. January p. 6.

O'Brien, M. (1988) 'Men and fathers in therapy'. *Journal of Family Therapy* 10: 109–23.

O'Callaghan, Denis (1966) 'The evolving theology of marriage'. *CMAC Bulletin* 6, No. 2, pp. 11–19.

O'Leary, Maurice (1969) 'Humanae Vitae and the work of the CMAC'. *CMAC Bulletin* 8, No. 3, pp. 3–5.

Parr, Eric (1962) 'Joining the family'. *Marriage Guidance*. Jan./Feb., pp. 195–6.

Parry-Jones, W. L. (1978) 'Change to survive? Reflections on the future of marriage counselling services.' *Marriage Guidance*. Sept., pp. 75–83.

Parry-Jones, W. L. (1979) 'Manifesto without a message? Further reflections on Marriage Matters.' *Marriage Guidance*. Sept., pp. 219–24.

Parsons, T. (1943) 'The kinship system of the contemporary United States'. *American Anthropologist* 45, pp. 22–38.

Parsons, T. (1951) *The Social System*. Routledge & Kegan Paul.

Pearse, Innes (1979) *The Quality of Life. The Peckham Approach to Human Ethology*. Scottish Academic Press.

Pearse, Innes and Crocker, Lucy H. (1943) *The Peckham Experiment. A Study in the Living Structure of Society*. Allen & Unwin.

Peters, J. and Waterman, Robert H. (1982) *In Search of Excellence*. New York: Harper & Row.

Phillips, R. (1988) *Putting Asunder. A History of Divorce in Western Society*. Cambridge University Press.

Pilkington, Margery (1957) 'Summer school for counsellors'. *Marriage Guidance*. July, p. 108.

Pincus, Lily (ed.) (1960) *Marriage: Studies in Emotional Conflict and Growth*. Family Discussion Bureau. Methuen.

Pincus, Lily (ed.) (1962) *The Marital Relationship as a Focus for Casework*. Institute for Marital Studies.

Pollard, B. E. (1962) *Social Casework for the State*. Pall Mall Press.

Popenhoe, Paul (1935) 'Divorce as a biologist views it'. *Marriage Hygiene* Vol. 1 Aug. 1934, pp. 247–53.

Poulton, G. (1988) *Managing Voluntary Organizations*. Chichester: Wiley.

Powell, Walter W. (ed.) (1987) *The Non-Profit Sector. A Research Handbook*. New Haven: Yale University Press.

PP. (1936) Cmd 5122. *Report* of the Departmental Committee on the Social Services in the Courts of Summary Jurisdiction.

PP. (1942) Cmd 6404. *Report* by Sir William Beveridge on Social Insurance and Allied Services.

PP. (1947) Cmd 7024. *Final Report* of the Committee on Procedure in Matrimonial Causes.

PP. (1948) Cmd 7566. *Report* of the Departmental Committee on Grants for the Development of Marriage Guidance.

PP. (1956) Cmd 9678. *Report* of the Royal Commission on Marriage and Divorce.

PP. (1962) Cmnd 1650. *Report* of the Departmental Committee on the Probation Service.

PP. (1968) Cmnd 3703. *Report* of the Committee on Local Authority and Allied Personal Social Services.

PP. (1974) Cmnd 5629. *Report* of the Committee on One Parent Families.

Ratcliffe, T. A. (1953) Letter. *Marriage Guidance*. Nov., p. 8.

Redmond, Richard. (1987) *Newsletter* No. 104. October, p. 2.

Rice, A. K. (1963) *The Enterprise and its Environment*. Tavistock.

Richards, Peter G. (1975) *The Local Government Act 1972. Problems of Implementation*. PEP New Local Government Services No. 13. Allen & Unwin.

Riley, Denise (1983) *War in the Nursery*. Virago.

Robinson, John A. T. (Bishop of Woolwich) (1963) *Honest to God*. SCM Press.

Rogers, Carl R. (1957) 'Communication between people'. *Marriage Guidance*. Nov., pp. 167–9.

Rolfe, S. Neville (1935) 'Sex Delinquency'. In H. Llewellyn Smith (ed.) *New Survey of London Life and Labour* Vol IX. P. S. King.

Rolfe, S. Neville (1949a). *Social Biology and Welfare*. Allen & Unwin.

Rolfe, S. Neville (ed.) (1949b). *Sex in Social Life*. Allen & Unwin.

Ross, Ellen (1980) '"The love crisis": couples advice books of the late 1970s'. In Catherine R. Stimpson and Ethel Spector Pearson (eds) *Women, Sex and Sexuality*. Chicago: Chicago University Press.

Rowbotham, Sheila (1977) *A New World for Women: Stella Browne, Socialist Feminist*. Pluto Press.

Rowbottom, R. and Billis, D. (1987) *Organisational Design*. Aldershot: Gower, 1987.

Royden, A. Maude (1922) *Sex and Common Sense*. Hurst & Blackett.

Royden, A. Maude (1925) *The Moral Standards of the New Age*. League of the Church Militant.

Rudolph, G. de M. (1955) 'Psychiatry and the marriage guidance counsellor'. *Marriage Guidance*. Sept., pp. 9–12.

Russell, Bertrand (1985) *Marriage and Morals*. Unwin Paperbacks. First edition 1929.

Schwartz, Florence S. (ed.) (1984) *Voluntarism and Social Work Practice. A Growing Collaboration*. New York: University Press of America.

Shapiro, Alza (1982) 'The counsellor and the client'. *Marriage Guidance*. Dec., pp. 161–9.

Sharrock, W. W. (1974) 'On owning knowledge'. In R. Turner (ed.) *Ethnomethodology*. Harmondsworth: Penguin, pp. 45–53.

Sherrington, Christine Anne (1985) 'The NSPCC in Transition, 1884–1983. A Study of Organizational Survival'. Unpub. PhD University of London.

Skynner, Robin (1975) 'Some consequences of work with natural groups'. *Marriage Guidance* May/June, pp. 319–24.

Skynner, Robin (1976) 'Some approaches to marital therapy'. *Marriage Guidance*. Sept./Oct., pp. 156–62.

Smart, Carol (1984) *The Ties that Bind – Law, Marriage and the Reproduction of Patriarchal Relations*. Routledge & Kegan Paul.

Spence, J. C. (1946) *The Purpose of the Family*. Convocation Lecture for the National Children's Home.

Stafford, Aline (1962) 'Case discussion or what goes on'. Marriage Guidance. Jan/Feb., pp. 201–3.

Stapleton, Erika (1964) 'Some thoughts on assessment'. *Marriage Guidance*. April, pp. 55–7.

Stopes, Marie (1918) *Married Love*. New York: The Critic & Guide Co.

Summerfield, Penny (1984) *Women Workers in the Second World War*. Croom Helm.

Summers, Ann (1988) *Angels and Citizens: British Women as Military Nurses*. Routledge.

Sutherland, John (1962) 'Introduction'. In Lily Pincus (ed.) *The Marital Relationship as a Focus for Casework*. Institute of Marital Studies.

Taylor, S. (1938) 'The Suburban Neurosis'. *Lancet* 1: 759.

Terman, L. M. and Cox Miles, Catherine (1936) *Sex and Personality Studies in Masculinity and Femininity*. New York: McGraw-Hill.

Thornborough, Peggy (1975) 'Groups in sensitivity training'. *Marriage Guidance*. Jan./Feb., pp. 261–5.

Timms, Noel and Blampied, Annette (1985) *Intervention in Marriage. The Experience of Counsellors and their Clients*. University of Sheffield. Social Services Monographs: Research in Practice. Jt. Unit for Social Services Research.

Torrie, A. (1953) 'Psychology and marriage counselling'. *Marriage Guidance*. June, pp. 6–8.

Torrie, A. (1958) 'The place of marriage counselling in family practice'. *Marriage Guidance*. Dec., pp. 376–80.

Torrie, M. (1959) 'Counselling for widows'. *Marriage Guidance*. Dec., pp. 213–4.

Townsin, Bob (1970) 'A view of our counselling service'. *CMAC Bulletin* Vol. 10, No. 3, pp. 9–13.

Tyndall, Nicholas (1970a). 'Marriage guidance in the 1970s'. *Marriage Guidance*. March, pp. 419–25.

Tyndall, Nicholas (1970b). 'Looking ahead'. *Marriage Guidance*. July, pp. 504–8.

Tyndall, Nicholas (1971) 'The training of marriage counsellors'. *Marriage Guidance*. September, pp. 711–15.

Tyndall, Nicholas (1972) '"Marriage Today and Tomorrow": the NMGC standpoint'. *Marriage Guidance*. November, pp. 163–6.

Tyndall, Nicholas (1973) 'Roles and relationships in NMGC'. *Marriage Guidance*. March, pp. 240–6.

Tyndall, Nicholas (1974a) Chief officer's column. *Newsletter*. No. 4. Dec., p. 3.

Tyndall, Nicholas (1974b) Foreword. In J. Heilsler. *Why Counsellors Resign*. Rugby: National Marriage Guidance Council.

Tyndall, Nicholas (1975) 'NMGC: future directions'. *Marriage Guidance*. May/June, pp. 330–5.

Tyndall, Nicholas (1976) Chief officer's column. *Newsletter*. May/June, pp. 2–3.

Tyndall, Nicholas (1979a) Speech to the Annual Conference. *Newsletter* No. 51. October, p. 1.

Tyndall, Nicholas (1979b) 'Marriage Matters'. *Marriage Guidance*. June, pp. 183–9.

Tyndall, Nicholas (1980) Chief Officer's column. *Newsletter*. No. 54, April, p. 5.

Tyndall, Nicholas (1983) Chief Officer's column. *Newsletter*. No. 75, March, p. 3.

Tyndall, Nicholas (1985a) Chief Officer's column. *Newsletter*. No. 88, March, p. 2.

Tyndall, Nicholas (1985b) Chief Officer's column. *Newsletter*. No. 92, November, p. 2.

Tyndall, Nicholas (1985c) 'The work and impact of the National Marriage Guidance Council'. In W. Dryden (ed.) *Marital Therapy in Britain*, Vol I. Harper & Row.

Tyndall, Nicholas (1986) 'An open letter to Bob Chester'. *Marriage Guidance*. Spring, pp. 22–5.

Unwin, J. D. (1934) *Sex and Culture*. Oxford: Oxford University Press.

Usher, Pam (1982) Report. *Newsletter*. No. 72, September.

Van de Velde, Th. H. (1928) *Ideal Marriage. Its Physiology and Technique*.

Trans. Stella Browne. William Heinemann Medical Books.

Van de Velde, Th. H. (1935) 'Marriage hygiene'. *Marriage Hygiene* Vol. 1, May 1935, pp. 339–40.

Van Til, Jon (1988) *Mapping the Third Sector. Voluntarism in a changing Social Economy*. NP: The Foundation Centre.

Venables, Lady (1964) 'The real value of marriage guidance'. *Marriage Guidance*. September pp, 139–41.

Walker, Kenneth (1935) *Sex and a Changing Civilization*. The Bodley Head.

Walker, Kenneth (1940) *The Physiology of Sex and its Social Implications*. Harmondsworth: Penguin.

Walker, Kenneth (1957) *Your Marriage. British Social Biology Council*. Transworld Pubs. First edition 1951.

Walker, Kenneth and Fletcher, Peter (1955) *Sex and Society. A Psychological Study of Sexual Behaviour in a Competitive Culture*. Frederick Muller.

Walker, Kenneth and Whitney, Owen (1965) *The Family and Marriage in a Changing World*. Gollancz.

Wallis, J. H. (1955) 'What is Counselling?' *Marriage Guidance*. June pp. 5–6.

Wallis, J. H. (1959) 'A modern approach to marriage counselling', book review. *Marriage Guidance*. Nov., p. 29.

Wallis, J. H. (1960a) *Counselling and Social Welfare*. Routledge & Kegan Paul.

Wallis, J. H. (1960b) 'Prevention and cure'. *Marriage Guidance*. April, pp. 228–9.

Wallis, J. H. (1961) 'Non-Directors' Meeting'. *Marriage Guidance*. March.

Wallis, J. H. (1963a). Letter. *Marriage Guidance*. Nov., p. 180.

Wallis, J. H. (1963b) *Thinking about Marriage*. Harmondsworth: Penguin.

Wallis, J. H. (1964a) *Sexual Harmony in Marriage*. Routledge & Kegan Paul.

Wallis, J. H. (1964b) 'Difficulties in the selection and training of marriage counsellors'. *Marriage Guidance*. May, pp. 67–9.

Wallis, J. H. (1966) 'Marriage counselling and the professions I'. *Marriage Guidance*. June, pp. 163–5.

Wallis, J. H. (1967) 'Marriage counselling and the professions II'. Jan., pp. 199–201.

Wallis, J. H. (1968a) *Marriage Guidance. A New Introduction*. Routledge & Kegan Paul.

Wallis, J. H. (1968b) 'Is the therapist a real person?' *Marriage Guidance*. Nov., pp. 167–70.

Wallis, J. H. (1970) *Marriage Observed*. Routledge & Kegan Paul.

Wallis, J. H. (1973) 'Marital problems and the CAB – reflections on a sample survey'. *Marriage Guidance*. Sept., pp. 331–4.

Wallis, J. H. (1977) 'Anniversary speech'. *Marriage Guidance*. July/Aug., p. 338.

Wallis, J. H. No. 2. *Marriage Counselling*. NMGC.

Wallis, J. H. No. 13. *Further Aspects of Counselling*. NMGC.

Wallis, J. H. and Booker, H. S. (1958) *Marriage Counselling*. Routledge & Kegan Paul.

Wallis, J. H. and Ratcliffe, T. A. No. 10. *A Conversation between J. H. Wallis and T. A. Ratcliffe*. NMGC.

Ward, Mrs Humphrey (1909) *Daphne. Or Marriage à la Mode*. Cassell.

Watts, Eric (1969) 'Payment for counselling – a pilot experiment. I The dilemma'. *Marriage Guidance*. July, pp. 291–4.

Watts, Eric (1980) 'Retrospect'. *Newsletter*. No. 55. May, p. 3.

Wayland Young (1963) *The Profumo Affair. Aspects of Conservatism*. Harmondsworth: Penguin.

Weeks, Jeffrey (1981) *Sex, Politics and Society*. Longmans.

Weeks, J. (1991) 'Pretended family relationships'. In D. Clark (ed.) *Marriage, Domestic Life and Social Change: Writings for Jacqueline Burgoyne 1944–48*. Routledge.

Weick, A. (1983) 'Issues in overturning a medical model of social work practice'. *Social Work* 28 (6), pp. 467–71.

Westminster Pastoral Foundation (1988) *Report and Accounts for the Year Ended 31st. May 1988*. WPF.

Wicks, Malcolm (1983) 'Enter right: the family patrol group'. *New Society*, 24 February.

Williams, Ruth (1975) 'Psychodrama at the Moreno Institute'. *Marriage Guidance*. Mar./April, pp. 283–5.

Winnicott, D. W. (1958) *Collected Papers*. Tavistock Institute.

Woodhouse, Douglas (1990) 'Non-medical marital therapy: the growth of the Tavistock Institute of Marital Studies'. In C. Clulow (ed.) *Marriage: Disillusion and Hope*. Karnac Books.

Wright, Helena (1930) *The Sex Factor in Marriage*. Noel Douglas.

Wright, Helena (1968) *Sex and Society*. Allen & Unwin.

Wright, Patrick (1987) 'Excellence'. *London Review of Books* 21/5, pp. 8–11.

Wootton, B. (1959) *Social Science and Social Pathology*. Allen & Unwin.

Yelloly, M. A. (1980) *Social Work Theory and Psychoanalysis*. New York: Van Nostrand Reinhold.

Young, M. and Willmott, P. (1975) *The Symmetrical Family*. Harmondsworth: Penguin. First edition 1973.

Younghusband, Eileen (1947) *Report on the Employment and Training of Social Workers*. Edinburgh: Constable.

Name index

Subject index